T0330848

'This book is essential reading for all CSR and critical management researchers. Through rich and fine-grained historical, legal and cultural analysis, Nimruji Jammulamadaka demonstrates the patchwork of modern notions and evolving customary practices that differentially constitutes "the messy borderland" of responsible business in post-colonial India. This highly original work sets exciting new co-ordinates for future CSR scholarship.'

– **Gavin Jack**, Professor, Director of Research and
Co-Deputy Head, Department of Management,
Monash Business School, Australia

Indian Business

This book presents a critical understanding of Indian business situated as an encounter between indigeneity and Western modernity by exploring notions and practices of responsibility. It brings the paradoxical nature of Indian businesses to the fore: though they have a rich history of philanthropic contributions to social causes, they have also been known for labour rights and human rights violations, environmental abuses, destruction of habitats, pollution and corruption. The book shows how Indian firms straddle these two starkly contrasting positions and the many blends in between to conform to global developments in the pursuit of corporate social responsibility (CSR). It also looks at the emergent field of critical studies and analysis of CSR, especially from the context of a developing country.

Part of the 'Contemporary Themes in Business and Management' series, this book will interest scholars of international business studies, management studies, economics, post-colonial management, organisational studies and corporate social responsibility, as well as businesses, corporates and practitioners.

Nimruji Jammulamadaka is Associate Professor with the Organization Behaviour group at the Indian Institute of Management Calcutta, Kolkata, India. She obtained her PhD from the Indian Institute of Technology Kanpur. She was also the Division Co-chair of Critical Management Studies of the Academy of Management for 2016–17. The first Indian resident to be elected to a leadership position at the Academy, her research interests include post-colonial management studies, power, organisation design and corporate social responsibility. Her research has been published widely besides being presented and winning several awards and recognitions. Her forthcoming book is *Governance, Resistance and the Post-Colonial State: Implications for Management* (co-edited with Jonathan Murphy). She is also on the editorial boards of *Decision, Journal of Human Values* and *Journal of Management History*.

Contemporary Themes in Business and Management

Series Editor: Anindya Sen
*Professor of Economics, Indian Institute of Management
Calcutta, Kolkata, West Bengal, India*

Business and management are shaped by both external and internal forces. The external forces are driven by the way society at large views the role of business and management in contributing to the social goals. The internal forces are driven by the changing nature of management thinking and research. These forces raise important recurring debates: should private corporates be left to their own devices or should there be monitoring and channelisation of their activities? How intrusive should the state be in this respect? How to communicate more effectively within the organisation and to the outside world? How to create new markets for basic survival as well as for completely new products?

This series will critically examine some of these themes and issues which have acquired urgency in the contemporary world. It will deal with currently relevant topics with the richness that they deserve and simultaneously eschew fashionable jargon to present lucid and rigorous studies with sound theoretical foundations. The individual volumes will be comprehensive and authoritative resources and will explore major debates from fresh perspectives on economics, management, international business, public policy, development studies and finance.

For a full list of titles in this series, please visit www.routledge.com/Contemporary-Themes-in-Business-and-Management/book-series/CTBM

Books in this series:

Indian Business

Notions and Practices of Responsibility

Nimruji Jammulamadaka

LONDON AND NEW YORK

First published 2018 by Routledge

2 Park Square, Milton Park, Abingdon, Oxfordshire OX14 4RN
52 Vanderbilt Avenue, New York, NY 10017

Routledge is an imprint of the Taylor & Francis Group, an informa
business

First issued in paperback 2019

British Library Cataloguing-in-Publication Data
A catalogue record for this book is available from the British Library

Library of Congress Cataloging-in-Publication Data
A catalog record for this book has been requested

ISBN: 978-1-138-29366-3 (hbk)
ISBN: 978-0-367-27769-7 (pbk)

Typeset in Sabon
by Apex CoVantage, LLC

To my father late Sri J. L. Prasad for teaching me to appreciate the predicament of the colonised and the potential for freedom.

Contents

Figures

Tables

Foreword

Nirmuji's book is a pioneering study of corporate social responsibility (CSR). With deep insight and great scholarship, she traces the evolution of the concept from an Indian stand point. Her work is a radical departure from standard works on CSR, as she claims space for ideas and practices honed in a society once colonised. She seeks to break the stranglehold of metropolitan discourses on social responsibility, which deny alternative motivation to the creation of wealth and its application to social purposes.

She argues persuasively that colonialism, in the garb of enlightenment, undermined the traditions of social obligations that defined the ethos of their Indian competitors. Using the example of the textile industry she shows how the colonial state legislation made illegitimate practices that were good for business and for the working class. Indian mills engaged labour even when the production was low as a way to honour their obligation to their workers and families. She also articulates the power, economic and moral, vested with working class to countervail people with wealth if they reneged on their social obligations.

The significance of the book is profound. It excavates and lays the foundations of corporate social responsibility that are not rooted in a paradigm of wealth creation based on maximising profits and promoting managerial efficiency. Modern corporate responsibility and philanthropy, she argues, is in its essence about mitigating the collateral damage due to capitalism and not about transcending its destructive character.

By locating CSR in a tradition of trusteeship of wealth, she gestures to a model of social responsibility that is politically and socially transformative; aware of man's ethical imperative to promote justice and save the planet from self-destruction.

Her chapter on the Voluntary Sector brings out the range of considerations that define the actions of the NGO sector. While for most part she sees them as accomplices to the needs of the corporate sector, she also points to the strand which identifies with interests of marginalised communities and people displaced by development.

Her book is an attempt to give voice to a perspective on business practices and social responsibility that was silenced by colonial power and the post-colonial state. These States, speaking in the name of the poor and labour, regulated business, but in doing so protected the organised working class at the expense of workers in the much larger informal sector. She highlights the positive role of medium and small business enterprises who she says not only create wealth and employment, but also provide space for workers to exercise autonomy and seek dignity in the way they earn their livelihoods. She does not romanticise Indian business, but she does bring out its potential to serve society at large from the standpoint of seeing themselves as trustees of their power and wealth. This sentiment, she argues, is part of their civilisation heritage of a life based on Dharma.

Her book allows for a radically new imagination on the idea of social responsibility. It is a book that takes one back to the perspective of Gandhiji, who sought to build a civilisation based on non-violence and ethics, and not power and physical force that underlies global capitalism.

Neelima Khaitan
Vice President CSR, Hindustan Zinc Limited,
Ex-Director CSR and Sustainability, Coca-Cola,
India (South West Asia)

Preface

About eight years ago I started teaching CSR to a group of MBA students at the Indian Institute of Management Calcutta. At that time, both my students and I were struck by how much the CSR space in India was informed by Western notions and practices of responsibility. Since then I have grappled with what are Indian notions and practices of responsibility. Over the years I realised that understanding Indian notions and practices of CSR cannot be delinked from the historical, political, legal and social context of the country. And most importantly, it cannot be understood without taking into consideration the over 250 years of colonisation by the British. It cannot also be understood without taking into account the historical and contemporary geopolitical and geohistorical experiences of Indian state, business and society.

The enactment of the 2013 CSR legislation in India sharpened the debates in Indian CSR. It also provided the perfect opportunity, to seriously examine the strange animal called Indian CSR. This book is thus an attempt to map and make sense of the trajectory of Indian CSR from a pre-colonial past into the post-colonial present. Just like the liminal space between day and night, which could be either a sunrise or a sunset, a beginning or an end, CSR in India and Indian businesses too exist in the liminal space between native custom and Western modernity. They thus carry not only the fuzziness and messiness of a borderspace but also the possibilities of hope and emancipation of a borderspace – of a new day. This book is a portrayal of this borderspace in all its fuzziness and its hopes.

Acknowledgements

At the outset, I wish to place on record my thanks to Professor Anindya Sen for inviting me to write this book as a part of the 'Contemporary Themes in Business and Management' series. This book would not have been possible without the unstinting support and encouragement of my husband and father. I am highly indebted to the various business managers, activists and academic colleagues who have given me the privilege of participating in dialogues on CSR with them. I am also thankful to them for trusting me and giving me research access to their work. This work has greatly benefitted from the discussions with students of my graduate course 'Designing Corporate Citizenship Initiatives' over the years. I am also thankful to my wing mates at work for suffering me and keeping my enthusiasm in tact in the process of this book's writing. I continue to remain grateful to the Indian Institute of Management Calcutta for supporting the writing of this book. And last but not the least, Shoma and others at Routledge for making this book possible.

Chapter 1

An exploration begins

A mid-third century BCE to late third century CE inscription 'at Junnar records investment of the income of two fields with the guild at Konachika for planting Karanja trees and banyan trees'.
(Majumdar, 1920:33)

A third century CE inscription from Nasik dated to the reign of King Isvarasena records a perpetual endowment with *srenis* (guilds) of potters, hydraulic craftspersons and oil millers with the object of providing medicines for the sick amongst monks dwelling in the monastery nearby.
(Majumdar, 1920:32)

The *Brihaspati Samhita*, a text from around 300–500 CE cataloguing customary practices and traditions suggests that *srenis*, in addition to their purely occupational and professional activities, pursued objects of public utility and concern like 'construction of a house of assembly, of a shed for accommodating travellers with water, a temple, a pool and a garden . . .'.
(Majumdar, 1920:47)

Jamshetji Tata, the pioneer of industrial India, instituted pension funds, housing for workers, accident compensation and several other amenities for workers at his textile factory the Empress Mills as early as 1886.
(Lala, 2004:13)

The account books of a *Marwari*[1] retail cloth concern for the years 1907–1908 had 'three kinds of *dharmada* (philanthropic) *khatas* (accounts) – one for Sri Ganesh, the firm's safe keeper and a family deity, one for Sri Ram, donated to the local Ram temple in the center of the town, run by another prominent *Marwari* family; and another, created in 1907 called the *Sri Congress ka dharmada khata*, the account for the emerging secular deity, the Indian National Congress. In 1907, it showed Rs. 317 and 10 *annas* that was carried forward to the next year. An ongoing collection to which the firm itself contributed. . . .'

(Birla, 2009:89)

Bombay textile mill owners concerned that their mill workers were wasting their wages on drink, neglecting themselves and their families, lamented, '*The average operative is an indebted personage. He has not learnt thrift while he is more or less addicted to the habit of drink which, thanks to the prosperous Excise Department of the Government of Bombay, has brought liquor shops near his home.*'[2]

(BMOA, 1914)

'Employers should consider themselves as trustees of the country and I do feel that they would be taken as trustees by our people if they will practice self-imposed austerity, lead simple lives and invest the balance of their profits in expanding industry, and thus serve the country as trustees,' said Lala Shri Ram, the founder of Shri Ram group . . . speaking in 1954.

(Sundar, 2000:178)

'The average person is so busy waging a struggle for daily living. And I am a person with the power and the means. It behooves upon me to think for these people who are busy struggling. I have to work for ensuring their well-being.' The Managing Director of a highly successful medium sized Indian firm was saying this in 2015. Neither this company, nor this person was even remotely interested in corporate social responsibility, and yet he was convinced that it was his duty to watch out for the well-being of those unable to do so.

The practices and notions described above through the centuries illustrate the general concern that businesses and commerce in India have had with social well-being and public utility. The fifteenth-century *Indian* poet mystic Kabirdas said it very beautifully: *Bada hua to kya hua jaise ped khajur, Panthi ko chaya nahin, phal laage ati door. (Of what use is your greatness, just like the tall date palm; neither shade for the traveller nor fruits that can be reached.)* Kabirdas sang his poetry during Mughal Emperor Akbar's time. Believed to be a Muslim who sang in praise of lord Rama, Kabirdas's couplet quoted above aptly conveys the Indian sensibility of moral and cultural responsibilities that *ability* has to shoulder. If one is a man with means, with wealth, then one should make oneself useful to society by helping his/her fellow beings. And as the quotes show, this sensibility seems to have pervaded Indian commerce through the centuries. From these quotes and a reading of their source material one can see that there are no special references to profit making but only to purposes of social and public character. It appears that profit making while being accepted as a routine and legitimate activity came with the expectation of and duty for providing and taking care of the needs of less fortunate. The practices described above even though spaced apart by centuries seem to carry a common conviction and belief: wealth comes with the responsibility of caring.

An average Indian in contemporary India could then very well imagine that businesses in India would be behaving responsibly and pursuing their social and public obligations with élan. Prima facie, this century's old sensibility appears to resonate with the core message of what is called corporate social responsibility in contemporary times. Contemporary or modern corporate social responsibility (CSR) practices 'frequently take the shape of businesses or employers providing some form of welfare, whether for employees or for social stakeholders outside the organization' (Brejning, 2012:1).[3] Given such possible equivalence between India's age old cultural[4] behaviours and modern CSR practices followed globally, it is rather perplexing that India has legislated a mandatory 2 per cent post-tax spending by businesses on CSR.

In fact, India is the first country to legislate spending on CSR. India, an outsourcing hub, a country otherwise known for exploitation of labour and polluting production practices, announced to the world in August 2013 that it had arrived into a world of business responsibility by passing the Companies Bill 2013 in the upper house of the Parliament *Rajya Sabha.*[5] Speaking about the Bill, the then Minister for Corporate Affairs Sachin Pilot said, 'such activities should bring smiles to people, rather than profits to the company'. He added, 'CSR (corporate social responsibility) should be viewed as something that you are doing – whether through cash or kind, or man-hours, or anything else – *to bring smiles to the people's faces and not for your EBITDA* (Earnings Before Interest, Taxes, Depreciation and Amortisation)' (emphasis added). He opined that the whole purpose of the innovative legislation to involve corporates into society's welfare would be defeated if they viewed CSR spending as 'profit making opportunities'.[6] The President of India gave assent to the bill on 29 August 2013.[7] The political leadership took a lot of flak from domestic and global business leaders, academics, intellectuals and activists for legislatively mandating something which had to be voluntary (Karnani, 2013). The internet was filled with denunciations and criticisms of the legislation. Many were concerned that the legislation would hinder companies from pursuing 'shared value' (Porter and Kramer, 2006), i.e. simultaneously pursuing business and social value. Yet, the political leadership took pride in overtaking several Western nations to proactively legislate for spending on CSR, in effect declaring to the world that it had the gumption to insist that companies – irrespective of whether they were Indian or foreign multinationals – spend 2 per cent of their post-tax profits on CSR. Here is where the puzzle lies!

In the popular imagination of the country, as revealed by the opening quotes, *we* continue to believe that contributing to social and public utility and purpose is part of the *cultural fabric of this nation*. It is then puzzling as to why *we* have legislated for mandatory spending on CSR. Why does one legislate for something which appears to be a deeper cultural practice? What changes to Indian *practices* do *we expect* this legislation will bring? What *anxieties of the nation* is this legislation addressing? Why do *we have such anxieties*? Cracking this puzzle and answering these questions requires us to apprehend the two subjects in our question – *we* and *corporate social responsibility* together. Deciphering the *we* implies focusing on our *geocultural location*. But in the contemporary globalised world, geocultural location is a complex issue. Can we simply limit it to our geographic and political boundaries when we are living in a hyper-connected world? Is it simply our citizenship? Intuitively we know that this predicament does not have a simple yes-no answer. The Argentinian decolonial scholar, Walter Mignolo, who works in the USA, shares a similar predicament and suggests a way out:

> . . . territories and locations are at once fixed and floating, emergent at the crossroads of places, memories, and sensibilities, where people cross borders, change languages, and deal

with both the imprints of their early cultural legacies (e.g., school or family) and whatever options arise later. The transnational does not, of course, erase the national, in the sense of the place where one is born and educated (even if that place is a borderland), but it does imply such erasure. Nor is the transnational necessarily the postnational. It is, rather, *the coexistence of regional languages, smells, tastes, objects, pictures, and so forth, with international communications, interactions, and the activities of daily life.*

(Mignolo, 1995a:174, emphasis added)

Taking a cue from Mignolo we can then expect *our* cultural beliefs of responsibility to coexist with modern meanings of corporate social responsibility. If coexistence is the possibility, it remains a question as to why *we* should seek to fix a specific Indian meaning for corporate social responsibility through legislation. Why did *we* not continue to follow the practice of diffuse and diverse meanings of corporate social responsibility? Once again, Mignolo helps us. Writing about colonisation as the denial of identity and expression for the colonised; Mignolo says that attempts at fixing meaning by the once colonised are attempts at geocultural identification. He points out, 'geocultural identification is a complex issue: it is a struggle between colonial allocation and oppositional (neocolonial or postcolonial) relocations on a number of fronts. It strives for the (auto) identification (relocation) of people in a cultural place allocated by successive imperialisms . . .' (1995a:173). It follows from this that one can possibly read *the Indian legislation as an attempt at self-identification of ourselves as a responsible society* and a *displacement of successive objectifications* of Indian society. So what have been the objectifications? And why do we need self-identification at this time?

History and post-colonial thought tell us that in successive imperialisms the colonisers called *us* barbaric and uncivilised, the winners of the Second World War called *us* backward in the post-independence period of 1950s and 1960s, the super powers of the world called *us* Third World in the 1980s and the transnational corporations (TNCs) of the West have turned *us* into outsourcing hubs *of cheap labour exploitation and growing middle class markets* in the current global era. Post-colonial thought has a simple phrase for these successive imperial author(itie)s – *the West. The West* as an imaginary – a West that is exemplified not just as a geography but as a coherent set of political, economic, social and epistemic worldviews and practices. Logically, the objectifications and descriptors of India constructed by *the West* in encountering Indian self-identifications should lead to an *inevitable clash* before they can settle down to coexistence. However, the discourse on CSR does not provide evidence of such a clash. It is rather silent to the point of appearing as if an Indian self-identification may not exist!

Post-colonial scholars like Mignolo, Spivak and others help us understand this silence when they say that the self-identifications of the colonised have remained silent from centuries of colonial domination and decades of neocolonial control for want of a *locus of enunciation, a* position to speak from. The colonial and neocolonial regimes have constructed the colonised (including Indians) as objects of investigation and as receivers of knowledge, as peoples in need of civilising. Consequently, the colonised would therefore be incapable of creating and producing their own knowledge. Frantz Fanon, one of the leading intellectual lights of the African freedom struggles says, 'to speak is to assume the weight of a civilisation'. Thus *locus of enunciation,* or *speaking from a place as a subject* includes the weight of speaking with and from a civilisational awareness of oneself, i.e. *from a place – the right to speak as an Indian, as an African, as an Argentinian, as a Navajo, with all the implication of what* 'speaking as someone from a place means' (Mignolo, 1995a, 2000). Colonisation has denied this *place to speak from* to the colonised, because the colonised have been denied *a civilisation,* they being objectified as barbaric. Lacking a civilisational awareness the colonised cannot and do not need to speak. In this manner, the colonised have been denied a *locus of enunciation* and the *author*ity of a subject. As colonised we have therefore lacked the 'right to' and a 'recognition of' self-identifications, the right to speak about corporate social responsibility as an Indian.

The epistemological consequence of the denial of a *locus of enunciation* to a *thinking-speaking* subject which all human beings by virtue of being human are, is that, it shifts the epistemic politics from one of descriptions and definitions of identity to the 'process of constructing identification' itself (Mignolo, 1995a:176). 'As a result of this epistemological shift, the [simple] geocultural question "Who are we?"(Chilean, Argentinian, Caribbean, Andean, Latin American, [Indian] etc.) can be broken down into two, more penetrating questions: (1) Who is constructing what image? and (2) How does one construct a self-image in the face of one's definition or identification by others (whether by other people or by institutions)?' (Mignolo, 1995a:176). Given these epistemological consequences, in order to be able to answer our initial question of 'why did *we* (India) legislate', i.e. construct our self-image we will first have to answer these questions: 'what is the image of modern corporate social responsibility? Who is constructing it?' The next section answers these questions.

What is the image? Who is constructing it?

In answering this question, we will briefly review the discourse of modern corporate social responsibility. We will also look at the trajectory of modern corporate social responsibility briefly and try to identify the route by which this discourse has entered colonised societies generally. Henceforth we will use the abbreviation CSR for corporate social responsibility. To understand this discourse, we will review papers on CSR published in leading journals in the domain like *Journal of Business Ethics, Journal of Corporate Citizenship, Corporate Social Responsibility and Environmental Management* along with papers that have appeared in Management and Organization Theory journals like *Academy of Management Review, Organization Studies, Organization*, special issues on CSR in other journals and other handbooks that constitute the corpus of academic writing on CSR. Rather than restrict ourselves to the academic discourse of CSR by focusing only on journal publications and books, we will also look at business practices as revealed through websites, popular press and reports of TNCs, industry associations, and multilateral agencies like United Nations concurrently. This is in keeping with the post-colonial conventions in analysis which understand discourse as 'intellectual, social, cultural, political, economic and other similar processes and structures [which] form an intricately articulated ensemble of great complexity that seeks to reproduce and perpetuate relations of colonialism and neocolonialism' (Prasad, 2003:8). It is this discourse of CSR: its academics, its business practice and their imbrications that we examine to identify *who* is constructing the image of modern CSR. Since we are using the terms locus of enunciation and subject position, the analysis might appear to be Focauldian, however, as Mignolo (1995b:5) points out, Foucault 'did not give attention to the personal history of the understanding subject . . . thus [did not] raise questions about the locus of enunciation in colonial situations'.

In the colonial situations, since the epistemic subject cannot be detached from the non-disciplinary or the personal, the past cannot be detached from the present (Mignolo, 1995b). As such, this post-colonial approach to analysis is informed by my experience of being an Indian in India. As a student and professional who worked in rural development and management, I became sensitive to the realities of this country. As a management teacher in India's premier business school I became sensitive to the domination of Western managerial knowledge. I observed the rapid entry of Western CSR discourse into the country and as a teacher I became privy to the numerous doubts, justifications, confusions and challenges of practising managers, students and activists in their pursuit of responsible and irresponsible practices. It is with this history and from this location that I approach this analysis.

In January 2005, *The Economist* declared that 'Corporate Social Responsibility has won the battle of ideas', that, CSR is the 'tribute that capitalism pays *everywhere* to virtue' (emphasis added). While the war is pretty old, the recent battle of ideas started in the 1990s. In the 1990s, Western corporations were being plagued by many ethical scandals. If the collapse of Enron, and the scandals at Arthur Andersen, Merck and other large firms due to unethical practices on the one hand maligned corporate reputations, on the other, it was the accusations of labour and human rights exploitations in countries in the Third World that pummelled big business in America. Throughout the 1990s and beyond, the supply chains of firms like Nike, GAP and Adidas were constantly being scrutinised and labour exploitation – under age workers, low wages, poor safety and such other practices – was being highlighted by activist groups leading to consumers boycotting these firms. Similarly, pharmaceutical companies were on the receiving end for prioritising profits over the lives of patients. Glaxo Smithkline had sued the South African government for permitting the generic manufacture of AIDS treatment. South Africa was dealing with an AIDS epidemic and could not afford the high-priced drugs supplied by Glaxo. Around the same time, the petroleum company Shell was facing consumer boycotts for its inaction during the execution of the Nigerian indigenous rights activist Ken Saro Wiva. Environmental groups like Greenpeace were successfully campaigning against all those companies whose environmental report cards were suspect.

In the background of these growing challenges to corporate authority and legitimacy, some Western businesses and governments with foresight started initiatives to introduce the vocabulary of responsibility into business practices. The idea of sustainable development was gaining currency among the top CEOs of the world in the 1990s. The World Business Council for Sustainable Development led by Schmidheiny was championing the idea. Several voluntary codes of conduct were initiated during late 1990s and early 2000s such as Clean Clothes Campaign, Fair Trade and Forest Stewardship Council. By December 2000, the Secretary General of United Nations Kofi Annan had successfully put in place the UN Global Compact with ten principles drawn from the Universal Declaration of Human Rights, the International Labour Organisation's Declaration on Fundamental Principles and Rights at Work, the Rio Declaration on Environment and Development and the United Nations Convention Against Corruption. Thus business practice was veering into the world of modern CSR: a world of voluntary codes of conduct for employee well-being, supply chains, environment, and voluntary disclosures, a world of audits, monitoring of compliance to codes and ranking of companies and countries on responsibility practices, a world of partnerships with civil society organisations to provide well-being and development to areas far and near to the business.

Academic writing on CSR followed this business trajectory very closely, sometimes being ahead of the curve and sometimes being close behind. In 2008, the editors of the *Oxford Handbook on Corporate Social Responsibility* (Crane et al., 2008) suggested that 'the area of CSR is mature enough to warrant the effort of a comprehensive overview in the *Oxford Handbook* series . . .' (p. 31). The authors were in effect acknowledging that CSR as a business practice and as an academic pursuit had arrived. This journey, management history suggests had begun in business practice in the USA in the latter half of the nineteenth century and entered academia's corridors several decades ago with Howard Bowen's (1953) book *Social Responsibilities of the Businessman* published in the USA (Carroll, 2008). The first formal definition of CSR in the academic space 'as obligations of businessesmen to pursue objectives desirable to society', is credited to Howard Bowen (1953). An intensely argued public debate involving businessmen, civil society, governments and last but not the least, academicians like Milton Friedman (1962) followed Howard Bowen's book in the United States, leading to a revision of the notion of CSR (Carroll, 2008). Marens (2010) and Carroll (2008) document a longer history of related research among American academics, with an early twentieth-century focus on labour concerns, followed by a post-war exploration of competing economic systems. Several parallel and inter-related developments in American politics and businesses led to a restatement of CSR from *social obligation* into *a voluntary and liberal pursuit by businesses which did not require government enforcement* (Marens, 2004). It is in the late 1970s and early 1980s that CSR took on its *managerialist* mantle, moving directly into an uncritical and collaborative stance with business schools and the Western corporate world (Marens, 2010). In 1979, Carroll tried reconciling the diverse and sometimes contradictory views on CSR and proposed understanding CSR as a hierarchy of four kinds of responsibilities with economic and legal responsibilities at the lower end of the hierarchy and ethical and discretionary responsibilities at the higher end. In spite of Carroll's efforts at reconciliation of views, the debates have continued.

The 1980s represent the beginning of business ethics courses in US business schools and the emergence of American business ethics journals, textbooks and conferences, and shortly thereafter, a parallel pattern of courses and scholarly activity became evident in Europe (Marens, 2010). The decades of 1990s and 2000s saw a veritable explosion of academic work on CSR. Several new journals like *Journal of Corporate Citizenship* (launched in 2001) and *Corporate Social Responsibility and Environmental Management* (launched in 2002) were launched during this period, as also were the several handbooks on CSR (Crane et al., 2008; Haynes et al., 2012; Scherer and Palazzo, 2008; Smith et al., 2010). Academics started participating in many industry and activist associations' activities for promoting responsible practices. Carroll (2008:19–20) commenting on the contemporary discourse of CSR said, 'The concept had changed, grown in terms of its meaning . . . eventually becoming global in scope.' To give a flavor of what CSR currently is, consider this, it:

> include(s) different components of CSR: legal, ethical, economic and discretionary (Carroll, 1979); the disparate drivers of CSR: which include, civil society, local community, managers, government, investors and consumers (Crane et al., 2008); the basic triggers of demands for CSR which include globalization, concerns with regard to human rights, environment, labour and corruption (Scherer and Palazzo, 2008); the use

of competing terminology such as corporate citizenship, corporate social performance, corporate sustainability, corporate accountability and so on (Amaeshi and Adi, 2007); the adaptation of CSR to subject specific requirements for exposition within management studies, marketing, accounting, sociology, political science and more recently law (McBarnet et al., 2007; Zerk, 2006) and the divergent aims and interests of the exponents of CSR such as academia, researchers, managers and so on; seeking to discern practice from theory and empirical from normative or vice-versa.

(Okoye, 2009:616)

In this attempt at analysing the discourse, we do not take into account specific differences in the field of CSR, the vast variety of concepts, constructs and theories and different things that are meant by the word CSR as seen above, even though Okoye (2009) says that CSR is an essentially contested concept. Instead I focus only on painting a broad brush strokes picture which will enable us to identify the *subject* constructing the image of modern CSR. Consequently, the present analysis can be accused of essentialism, i.e. 'the idea that any specific group of objects or people [or practices] (e.g., a race, gender or class) is marked, identified, and defined by pure, immutable, and transhistorical characteristics and essences that inhere in the specific group in question, and that determine the fundamental and unique nature of that group' (Prasad, 2003:25). While it is true that our analysis essentialises and treats CSR as though it has specific constitutive features and essences we take refuge in Spivak for legitimising our pursuit. Spivak, another illustrious writer on the colonial experience (1988:13) says that it is necessary to engage in essentialism in a strategic manner in order to pursue legitimate ethico-political interests of voicing the concerns of the colonised. Thus, in order to decipher 'who' is constructing the image of modern CSR, it is justifiable for us to adopt an essentialising treatment of CSR discourse.

Taking a broad overview of this variegated field of CSR scholarship, we can identify different streams in writing and talking about CSR. Garriga and Mele (2004) in a comprehensive review of literature on CSR identify four different types of CSR theories – instrumental, political, integrative and ethical. Our analysis while sharing superficial resemblances with their classification, for instance identifying TNCs' approach to CSR as instrumental, departs from it. This is because,

whereas for Garriga and Mele the concern was theorising the relationship between business and society in terms of profit orientation, social
concern and responsible use of corporate power, our concern here is
to identify the subject positions and the image or meaning of CSR discourse. Whereas they were examining how CSR theories differ from
each other and their relative emphasis on aspects like stakeholders,
issues etc., I am interested in how the theories are similar to each other
in the subject position they share.

We can identify five different streams of writing on CSR which
I will briefly summarise below. The first stream of writing looks at
CSR from a business strategy perspective. It is focused on business
practices and is among the more popular views, finding resonance
and audience with business managers and executives readily. This
stream is concerned with using CSR to improve business performance of corporations while also addressing the social concerns
generated by business. In this view, CSR becomes one more tool
in the corporate manager's tool kit to address business and social
demands. This is also popularly known as the 'shared value'
approach to CSR (Porter and Kramer, 2006). This view is the mainstay of literature on CSR and Strategy, and is exemplified in the
essays of journals like *Harvard Business Review* or *California Management Review* and in several handbooks published by multilateral agencies and industry associations.

The second stream continues to look at CSR as a tool, but for
the purpose of development and poverty alleviation. This view
derives its theoretical support from public policy, development
studies, strategy and CSR literatures, and sees CSR practice by
TNCs as capable of alleviating poverty in Third World countries.
The articles in the special issues on CSR in the journals *Development and Change* (2008) and *International Affairs* (2005) examine
CSR from a poverty and development perspective. A related view
can be found in the state failure/state deficit thesis and the role that
TNCs therefore assume of governing societies with weak state governance. This view is evident in Scherer and Palazzo (2007, 2008)
who depict corporations as political actors and CSR as the tool
that fills the governance gaps in countries with weak states. Institutional theorists look at CSR as a practice that can address societal
purposes like governance, poverty alleviation or development in
addition to business benefit. While some authors like Logsdon and
Wood (2005) see potential development benefits from CSR, others like Jenkins (2005), Newell (2005) and Lund-thomsen (2005)

are skeptical. The skeptics argue that CSR is implicated in business management and economic logics which prioritise profits for the shareholder over other claims, as such CSR cannot really address concerns of development.

The third stream examines cross-national and cultural variations in the practice of CSR. The articles in the special issues on Asia (2004), Africa, Latin America and Emerging Economies (2006) in the *Journal of Corporate Citizenship* exemplify this approach. Works like those of Chapple and Moon's (2005) seven country study of CSR practices in Asia, Jamali et al.'s (2009) study of CSR in the Middle East, or Lindgreen et al.'s (2009) study in Africa are exemplars of this kind of work. Matten and Moon's (2008) study compares CSR practices in the United States and Europe. They suggest that the national business systems of a country influence CSR practice and that the United States is characterised by explicit CSR which involves voluntary policies, programmes and strategies emanating from perceived incentives and opportunities of meeting stakeholder expectations (p. 410). They argue that Europe, which witnessed implicit CSR, has slowly been adopting explicit CSR due to effects of institutionalisation in the CSR field. Similarly Quazi and O'Brien (2000) suggest a two-dimensional theoretical model for comparative work on CSR.

The fourth stream in CSR literature reflects the broadly critical views on CSR. This literature looks at CSR as a handmaiden of transnational business and stakeholder management as another colonising corporate practice (Banerjee, 2007, 2008). Banerjee points to the deceptions practised by multinational corporations, who claim to be caring and responsible, while they continue to exploit powerless labourers, land and resources that are occupied by indigenous populations, and insist on the legitimacy of markets colonising over sovereign and independent governance (Banerjee, 2007). Mir et al. (2008) describe corporate citizenship as a corporate practice that is incapable of regulating the behaviour of corporations. Hanlon (2008) argues that CSR actually denies effective politics and is in fact guilty of bringing in more aspects of social life into the ambit of the market place. There are others like Blowfield (2005), Jenkins (2005) and Fleming et al. (2013) who take a more nuanced view towards CSR and suggest that rather than accepting or dismissing CSR as a totality, it is best to look at what CSR can actually do and not do. Fleming et al. (2013) suggest that at least CSR has helped in facilitating a dialogue with the corporation.

The corporation would otherwise have remained inaccessible to society.

The fifth stream in the CSR literature is a broadly self-reflexive take on CSR scholarship. Rather than looking at CSR practices of TNCs and businesses, this stream is concerned with looking at the field of academic writings on CSR. The sparseness of this stream is attributed to the young and evolving nature of the discipline. Lockett et al. (2006) describe the field as characterised by a great diversity, being in a continuing state of emergence and lacking a paradigm. De Bakker et al.'s (2005) bibliometric analysis of 500 papers on CSR similarly suggests that the field is developing, and central concepts are not very clear. Oosterhout and Heugens (2008) argue that there is limited clarity on conceptualisation in the field of CSR scholarship even though great amounts of empirical work is being done.

We had said that we would examine both academic writings and business practices, you might be wondering that the foregoing five streams are all about academic writings. It is important to note here that our engagement with practice has occurred indirectly because of imbrication of business practices into academic writings, in the form of vast empirical writings on CSR which extensively document and describe business practices. Second, business practice is the port of entry of modern CSR into the former colonies, especially through the participation of former colonies and their businesses in the global supply chains of TNCs. The entry of modern CSR into countries like India has happened through the codes of conduct to be adopted by supplier firms of TNCs in the global value chain (Jammulamadaka, 2013a) and the need to develop backward regions through TNC interventions.

With regards to the literature on CSR in developing, Third World or emerging economies like India, it can be found in all streams of CSR scholarship. There are several works which continue to debate the service-delivery and governance potential of CSR in developing countries and the potential of such CSR to replace and/or support public provision of welfare. A few studies have attempted to catalogue and describe contemporary CSR practices of businesses within different developing countries. There are others who have looked at CSR in developing countries critically and argue that CSR practice and scholarship have shown Eurocentric preoccupations (De Neve, 2009; Jammulamadaka and Derry, 2013; Jammulamadaka, 2013a; 2015a; Khan et al., 2010). A small group of scholars have written about CSR practices in India (Arora and Puranik, 2004; Kumar, 2004; Mitra, 2007; Sundar, 2000, 2013). In writing about CSR, these writings make a smooth connection between some past practices in India and the contemporary modern CSR. In these writings the modern CSR version is accepted uncritically.

Deciphering the subject and the image

From the review so far it is evident that in talking about CSR, literature talks about *business* and *society*, the responsibility of *business* and *managers*, the impact of *business* and *managerial* actions and so on. It is as if *business* and *managers* are the same everywhere, but intuitively we know that this cannot be the case. What creates this illusion? The illusion is possible because in practising, discussing, talking and writing about CSR, the practitioner/business/speaker/author, i.e. the *subject* appears as a disembodied third person universal. In talking about the geopolitics of knowledge and the domination implicit in the disembodied universal, Mignolo (2000:110) says that a universal subject is one who is stripped of all geohistorical, cultural and political identification. By talking about *business* and *managers* in a universal way stripping away identifiers like American, Indian etc., CSR discourse creates the universal subject and sustains the illusion of universality. Mignolo explains that this disembodied third person universal is an epistemic sleight of hand that silences all locals through an illusion of equality of locals. But locals are not equal in their ability to transform into the universal. Only that which emerges from the metropolitan centre (or West) backed by the power and resources of the centre has been able to transform into the disembodied universal, thereby silencing all other locals including those in the periphery.

Even though literature portrays a universal subject, we can identify the disembodied subject through a careful reading of CSR discourse from *our position* of post-colonial India. Such a reading shows that the subject is the *Western TNC* and the specific meaning of CSR enunciated by this subject is one of a *voluntary activity into which a responsible business* engages operating in a free market with minimal state regulation and intervention. 'Shared value', a staple of the first strand of literature, i.e. strategic CSR explicitly suggests and elaborates why and how TNCs should engage in CSR. Bondy et al.'s recent (2012) study of the meaning of CSR in Britain validates this hitherto implicit subject. The few writings which seek to look at CSR and SMEs in Europe also attest to the fact that CSR is about voluntary responsible activity by large corporations (Jenkins, 2004, 2006, 2009; Moore and Spence, 2006). That the Western TNC is the subject is very evident in CSR for business performance and poverty alleviation perspectives. All the arguments of this strand of literature are about what these corporations can or cannot do for development with and through CSR as a voluntary strategic practice. Critical perspectives too support the Western TNC as the subject. Given that critical perspectives are contending with claims being made by corporate power, they are affirming the Western TNC as the subject along with its CSR image. Whereas the first three streams within CSR discourse directly concern themselves with the Western TNC, the other streams by virtue of epistemic and knowledge-producing practices of the field such as referencing and literature review reinforce the *Western TNC as the subject* and *its practices as the CSR image.*

The empirical cross-country CSR practice literature professes to right the universality of the discourse. They begin by saying that CSR may not mean the same thing in different countries and that different societies have had different practices of responsibility. But they reinforce the Western TNC as the subject because of the categories, definitions and methods used for studying CSR in the other countries. For instance Lindgreen et al.'s (2009) work seeks to uncover practices in Botswana and Malawi and how they differ from that of the United States. But it actually uses definitions of CSR and instruments that were used to study US organisations. Whether these instruments would actually be able to capture differences if responsible business was carried out differently in Botswana or Malawi is a question that is not even seen as a limitation of the study. Or consider for instance, Jamali et al.'s (2009) study of the Middle East countries that uses eurocentric categories coming from Quazi and O'Brien (2000).

In addition to definitions and theoretical categories, the meaning of data and measurement practices also reinforce Western TNC as the subject. Often data like annual reports or website reporting (Chapple and Moon, 2005) is used. Practices of responsibility which might not find their way into an annual report or a website would automatically be omitted from being considered as CSR. These practices reproduce Western categories of what is CSR data and how it is to be studied. These practices itself emerge from an American understanding or as Matten and Moon (2008) suggest, an attempt at explicit CSR. Using such data for investigation implies that only those practices which are done by the metropolitan centre of the West are the ones which count as CSR. Even for authors from the geographic periphery like Russia, China, Hongkong and Africa, the epistemically legitimate practice of literature review ensures that published papers, i.e. 'texts in circulation' (Mignolo, 2000) are referred to and used, thereby leading to redeployment of definitions, categories and methods of the western centre. This in turn reinforces the Western TNC subject position and image. The fifth stream of reflexive field of scholarship perspective also affirms the Western TNC as the subject because of its practice of reviewing writings on TNCs CSR.

Now that we have identified the Western TNC as the subject and voluntary activity as modern CSR, let us turn our attention to the construction of the former colonies in modern CSR. We had earlier said that CSR discourse has used a universal subject, i.e. business and manager; but there is one place where the universal gives way to the specific. In talking about *society*, the discourse distinguishes between developing countries and developed world. Reports of the World Bank, UNDP and the IMF suggest that developing countries will form the new emerging markets and are also sites where the impacts of globalisation and economic growth will be acutely felt. This necessitates a distinctive treatment of CSR in developing countries (Visser, 2008:474). An instance of such distinctiveness being, '. . . particular relevance for developing countries is the fact that CSR is often seen as a way to plug the "governance gaps" left by weak, corrupt, or under-resourced governments that fail to adequately provide various social services (housing, roads, electricity, healthcare, education etc.)' (Visser, 2008:483). We are left to infer that this treatment will be offered to developing countries by Western TNCs, activists and academia. Some of the most explicit articulations establishing the Western TNC and the Western ideologue as the subject in CSR can be found in works analysing and/or advocating for CSR in developing countries. Nielsen (2005) in his detailed analysis of the events and rationale that led up to the signing of the memorandum of understanding between Bangladeshi textile suppliers, nongovernmental agencies and buyers in the West identifies the privileging of Western interests and views of responsibility and practices. The several studies on codes of conduct and their implementation in the Third World are ample witnesses to the Western TNC as subject. Studies like those of Visser actually suggest how CSR needs to be practised in the developing world. Consider the following, for example:

> If we are to work towards an ideal CSR pyramid for CSR in developing countries, I would argue that improved ethical responsibilities, incorporating good governance, should be assigned the highest CSR priority in developing countries. *It is my contention* that governance reform holds the key to improvements in all the other dimensions, including economic development, rule of law and voluntary action. Hence, embracing more transparent, ethical governance practices *should form the foundation of CSR practice in developing countries*, which in turn will provide the enabling environment for more widespread responsible business.
>
> (Visser, 2008:492, emphasis added)

CSR historians like Carroll and Marens say that the subject – the Western transnational corporation and its corollary, the Western ideologue – actually emerged in the American history of CSR. It is this subject and their image that has become the basis for the *global design* (Mignolo, 2000) of CSR. There is no locus of enunciation for the Third World or the colony in this discourse even though these countries are deeply implicated in the discourse. As Blowfield (2005), Nielsen (2005) and Dobers and Halme (2009), Khan et al. (2010) point out the issues most relevant to developing countries – like the right of foreign capital to leave freely, its right to play states against each other and choose freely the best economic location, the repatriation of profits to headquarters by TNCs in order to avoid paying taxes to the governments of those countries, the supply side pressures created by inventory and purchasing practices of TNCs or the desires of workers – *never* enter the CSR discourse. Instead corruption, labour and environmental violations of the Third World and fortune at the bottom of pyramid markets feature most prominently.

It is worth noting that local and indigenous concerns do not appear as significant reasons for engaging with CSR in developing countries. The developing country and its actors are cast as passive recipients. Do we need more to figure out *who is speaking*? It is this cultural framing of underdevelopment, corruption and irresponsibility that has inaugurated the entry of modern CSR discourse into the developing countries. Cast as violators of *known* ethical codes,

aid dependent, and in need of modernising, civilising and respon-
sibilising through CSR, the Third World becomes a site of cultures
of poverty and exploitation and not a site of different knowledges,
cultures and practices of responsible business. *It is the site about
which the West theorises and in which the West can intervene.* It
is exemplified in writings like those of Jones (1999) which hypoth-
esises that the incidence of stakeholder management is positively
related to the level of economic development. Such hypothesis
implicitly assume that developing countries who are not economically developed do not manage their stakeholders and hence could
be irresponsible.

When such hierarchical, binary representation is put to the service of global capitalist pursuits, the colonial stance is rather telling. Developing countries are caught in a double bind of achieving
growth and economic development, and attracting foreign investment on the one hand, and internationalising into other countries
on the other hand in the new global neoliberal order. Both of these
phenomena require the government and the businesses of countries
like India to participate in the ideologies and practices of the West
in order to gain approval and favour with them. Such a colonising CSR discourse silences the local through mild footnotes or
dismissive, summative assessments which refer to vague 'religious
sentiments of the past' (Frynas, 2006). In the process, it denies a
local like India of its own distinct local history and trajectory of
business–society relations and responsibility. It also reduces the
variegated heritage of relationships and interdependencies between
business, state, communities, governance and society in these countries to simple society–business dyadic relations (Jammulamadaka,
2015a,b, 2016a).

As scholars speaking from the Third World, this would not have
bothered us if it had been simply limited to how the metropolitan
discourse viewed the periphery, *as a fancy and fantasy*, that did
not interfere with business and social practices and lives in the
Third World. However, sadly, this is not the case. It is against such
a backdrop of modern CSR discourse – an enmeshing of colonial,
neocolonial and neoliberal pursuits that the 2013 Indian legislation mandating CSR spending by companies can be understood as
an attempt at geocultural identification. The legislation becomes
an attempt at one's self identification in the face of a colonising
CSR discourse. The present book is also an attempt at geocultural
identification, an attempt to surface some of the silences in CSR

discourse from an Indian locus, an attempt to understand business practices and the practices of responsibility and/or their absence from decolonial categories which reflect the Indian concerns more appropriately rather than subsuming them under definitions and methods of modern Western CSR.

On the one hand Indian businesses have had a rich history of philanthropic contributions to social causes. On the other, Indian businesses have also been known for labour rights and human rights violations, environmental abuses, destruction of habitats, pollution and corruption. Straddling these two starkly contrasting positions and the many blends in between are the efforts of businesses in India to confirm to global developments on CSR whether it be through the introduction of codes of conduct or the production of Triple Bottom Line reports. Adding to this heady cocktail of practices in the field of responsibility is the 2013 legislation.

Given the specific colonial history of India, the aspirations of globalising Indian business, and a modern Indian state in a global neoliberal world, the dynamism and pastiche of practices that the Indian CSR scene is experiencing presents quite an interesting case of encounters between indigenity and Western modernity, between social practices and legal statutes and between Indian and Western notions of responsibility. Exploring these encounters and the silences situated in their confluence, through examining notions and practices of responsibility in Indian business, can provide us a way of critically understanding contemporary Indian business and what it means to be a post-colonial[8] business in a neoliberal world.

About the book

Having inaugurated the need to examine meanings of CSR in the post-colonial Indian condition by foregrounding the character of CSR discourse in the first chapter, the book proceeds further and is divided into two sections. The first section picks up the ethico-politcal and epistemic imperative posed by Indian CSR. It provides an evolutionary and historical perspective to CSR in India. Running from the introduction to Chapter 4 this section examines the notions of responsibility as evidenced in cultural practices and regulatory practices. In engaging with developments in more recent decades, it traces Indian notions and practices and the encounters with Western notions and the run up to the section 135 legislation.

The second section of the book continues from Chapter 5 to Chapter 8 and discusses contemporary CSR practices within large and small Indian businesses. It examines these practices in the light of global notions and Indian legislative notions. It also brings in perspectives of nongovernmental organisations (NGOs) that have now emerged as important partners in the pursuit of CSR. Chapter 9 forms the conclusions of the book and speculates about the future trajectories of Indian CSR.

The second chapter examines historical notions and practices of responsibility in India. Beginning with the centuries old pre-colonial past, it identifies the key markers of customary notion of responsibility as a practice embedded in the everyday conduct of a businessman's life. It teases out the conditions that permitted the pursuit of such responsibility and points out that compliance was achieved through reputational mechanisms, which also enabled the operation of countervailing power. The chapter also dwells upon the colonial encounter and role of colonial jurisprudence in illegalising, silencing and reducing customary practice. By closely examining business practices under colonial rule, it highlights the impact of colonial regulation on altering the conditions of responsible business. It briefly touches upon the different routes and practices of industrial management in India and the West and the implications this has for customary notions of responsibility.

The third chapter continues the historical journey of CSR from independence in 1947 to the enactment of section 135 in 2013. It parallellly traces the developments in the West after the Second World War to the formation of UNGC and the entry of these notions into India. It juxtaposes this against India's own experience with responsibility since Independence. The concerns and pursuits of businesses and state are brought forward. These reveal that unlike the West, Indian trajectory of CSR has been informed by a nation-building imaginary, i.e. making a nation out of a colony and quest for a respectable identity. It suggests that contemporary CSR practice in India is located in the messy intersections of custom and modernity.

The fourth chapter builds on the idea of messy intersection and borders of custom and modernity by taking regulations as the border markers. These regulations encompass not just section 135 but also labour, environment and resource use, investor and consumer protection and other laws. It provides an overview of various statutory frameworks for labour and environment that regulate businesses in India. It traces the central concerns of the statutes and the consequences of these regulations in facilitating (ir)responsibility amongst businesses. It also identifies the challenges posed by the current state of regulations. The chapter also examines the monitoring and administrative machinery of these laws. It argues that regulations, which are frequently a colonial hangover, have created the messy borderland of Indian responsibility by illegalising custom and gradually illegitimising it. In this borderland, responsibility and irresponsibility, custom and modern coexist; where compliance to law does not necessarily mean being responsible.

Chapters 5–7 dwell upon current practices of responsibility amongst large businesses, their issues and their challenges. These chapters dwell upon the enactments, following Mignolo (2000) to develop a description of responsibility that is truer to native categories of knowledge and understanding. Chapter 5 specifically reviews the various surveys to obtain a macro-level understanding of current practice. It then identifies the different models of doing CSR and elaborates upon four types of foundation-based approach to CSR – institution builders, network builders, executors and financiers. It also identifies two other types where CSR is practised through internal departments – generalist and strategic. The chapter ends by pointing several issues and challenges posed by these models. It concludes that CSR practices reveal an amalgam of historical tendencies of societal building, modern compulsions and emergent opportunities and defy a neat categorisation.

Chapter 6 elaborates upon partnerships between businesses and NGOs from a business perspective. Reviewing the emergence of these partnerships over the years, it identifies three broad categories – partnerships of shared philosophies, partnerships of mutual interest and commerce and partnerships of exigency. It discusses the features of each of these types, their concerns, priorities and reasons of large businesses in implementing CSR initiatives and the challenges they pose to contemporary pursuit of responsibility. Chapter 7 examines these partnerships from an NGO perspective. After situating NGOs within the Indian context, it examines NGO needs, problems and aspirations in partnering with business. The chapter suggests that businesses need a better appreciation of NGO and development realities.

Chapter 8 shifts attention to the enactments of doubly marginalised medium, small and micro enterprises (MSMEs) of India. After pointing out their disadvantage both within national and global discourse, it identifies five different models of responsibility practices in MSMEs. These are imitation of large business, code approach, cluster approach, social business approach and native approach. The chapter dwells upon the native approach providing voice to MSME owners and workers. It uses this voice to highlight the challenges facing Indian CSR and the post-colonial condition.

The book concludes with Chapter 9. This chapter reflects on the insights about Indian business and CSR based on the previous chapters. It centerstages the key questions driving this book namely, why does one legislate for something which is likely to be a deeper cultural practice? What changes to Indian *practices* do *we expect* this legislation will bring? What *anxieties of the nation* is this legislation addressing? Why do *we have such anxieties?* It then answers these questions by reading together post-colonial scholars Nandy and Mignolo and the Indian borderland of responsibility. It concludes that the pastiche of Indian practices of responsibility are all efforts at self-identification. They are also attempts at changing the disciplinary meanings of CSR through enactment, since this enactive epistemic space is the only space that is available for the subordinated. These practices are all attempts of India and Indian business to *domesticate* modern Western CSR into a *manageable vector (*Nandy, 1983:xiii*)*. It identifies at least five different actors attempting this self-identification – the nation-state, large Indian business, Indian MSMEs, Indian NGOs and this book itself. Each of these has used a different set of strategies based on its specific position within the matrix of power and their experience of subordination.

All these self-identifications are to varying degrees informed by cultural notions of responsibility and native categories of *conducting* business. It identifies three such notions at work in these self-identifications namely, obligation or duty, person-business as an undifferentiated unity and public/society as spatio-temporally located communities.

It suggests that the future trajectory of Indian CSR could continue to be a melange of practices comprising customary and modern elements. This is because, not only is India at the receiving end of modern CSR but Indian business is also instrumentally using CSR discourse and its underlying neoliberal philosophy to expand its global footprint. The melange will help the nation-state in opportunistically using custom and modern notions of CSR for national well-being. It also permits individual businesses to choose their version of CSR in a manner that is more appropriate to their personal and business strategy context. The melange also enables a reconstruction and repair of custom in a manner similar to philosopher Neurath's repairing the boat while sailing in it on the high seas, one step at a time, thereby gradually decolonising colonial institutional apparatus while retaining national control and order in a globalised world. It argues for a greater role for state, better monitoring, undoing some of the violence of colonial institutions by decolonising them; creating a new vocabulary and a discourse of indigenous managerial knowledge to overcome the epistemic violence of 'Western managerialism' and absolve customary practices from the yoke of illegitimacy.

Notes

1 A traditional business community.
2 It is worth seeing the contrast in the temperaments and sensibilities between the Indian owners and British owners with regards to worker addiction. Simeon (1999) says that British Coal-controlling authority proposed making liquor available at the mine gate and expensive to ensure that workers spent their wages completely and were therefore compelled to come back to work.
3 The words contemporary and modern have been used interchangeably in this book. I am aware of the existence of multiple modernities (Kaviraj, 2005; Chatterjee, 2011). However, in the interest of strategic essentialism, I use modernity in the singular sense of Western modernity to centrestage the silences and conflicts in the encounter between native tradition and Western modernity that starts with the colonial encounter.
4 I use the word culture in the sense used by Mignolo (1995a:179), i.e. that 'what guides actions or patterns of behavior, not the accumulated achievements or accomplishments by which "cultures" are often measured and ranked'.
5 www.thehindu.com/business/Industry/companies-bill-passed/article 5003777.ece dated 8 August 2015, Accessed 27 January 2016.
6 Times of India business, PTI, September 1, 2013, http://timesofindia. indiatimes.com/business/india-business/CSR-should-bring-smile-to-people-not-profit-for-companies-Sachin-Pilot/articleshow/22204015. cms, Accessed 28 January 2016.
7 www.mca.gov.in/MinistryV2/companiesact.html, Accessed 27 January 2016.
8 The hyphenated post-colonial is used to indicate the historical fact and post-colonial is used to refer to the theoretical practice.

Chapter 2

From where did we come here?

> Gifts to dharma performed wealth and status, promoted hierarchies both material and ritual, and enacted social welfare. And the renowned asceticism (also known as miserliness) associated with mercantile castes – including practices such as vegetarianism, sobriety, plain dress, and restricted spending on household consumption – enabled lavish spending on traditional forms of social welfare.
>
> (Birla, 2009:88)

The Indian subcontinent has always prided itself on having a long and rich civilisational history. The region's trade and commercial prosperity would have offered ample opportunities for developing and practising indigenous notions of commerce's social responsibility. But the entry of a modern CSR agnostic of India's commercial-cultural-political-social history has contributed to the silencing of customary notions and practices of responsibility. Thanks to these silences, we do not know whether there existed notions and practices of responsibility in the past and if they did what the characteristics and contours of such notions were. The silent chapter of social responsibility practices of India's past forms the purpose of our explorations in the next few pages. In this chapter we journey into the past of Indian commerce and attempt to listen to the silent and absent voice of Indian business community. In the process we uncover notions and meanings of responsibility which informed their practice and juxtapose them with the development of notions of responsibility in Western capitalism.

Business historians have been a rather rare breed in India. 'The past' instead has been an object of interest of many a scholar – historians, sociologists, anthropologists and economic historians. Accordingly in our explorations we will rely on those works instead of business history alone. We will also need to exercise some caution in appropriating the works of these disciplines because of the epistemic burdens they carry. For example, accounts of economic history while providing empirical details of practices often manifest in themselves a peculiar reproduction of a universal logic of Capital. All practice is explained as subjugated to capital and an economic rationality. As Ritu Birla (2009:10) says,

> [A] functionalist logic often undergirds analysis: many histories of indigenous capitalism detail culturally specific idioms of market practice in order to reclaim merchants' economic rationality. In so reifying misperceptions about culture as a burden for economic development, they assume a universal bearer of capital, a rational actor garbed in ethnic wardrobe. Here, *culture* and *economy* are presupposed as distinct systems, shown, via the rational indigenous actor, . . . validating culture on the grounds of its consistency with capitalist economic rationality.
>
> (emphasis original)

Such a privileging of capital which is just one analytical category amongst several possibilities, leads to the wiping out of alternate rationalities and practices and will therefore only help in reinforcing the silence rather than breaking it. The present journey, therefore, professes a view of understanding business practices as ways of life, of cultures. Paraphrasing Ritu Birla (2009:11) we could say, 'the study of business cultures investigates business practices as culture, and "culture" as a way of being, as the shifting meanings attending lived practice, as ethos and as ethics'. We will therefore not subordinate business practices to rational economic calculation but look at the 'textures of meanings' of business community practices in ongoing social life of which commerce too is a part.

Exploring the past in a non-archival society like India is fraught with challenges – on the one hand there exist very limited forms of 'archival data' which meet standards of the 'discipline' of history. On the other, those that exist would themselves be struggles burdened by the colonial imprint – reinforcing categories, perspectives, values and objects valued by modernity (Chakrabarty, 1992). The very act of writing this book and this chapter is one such struggle – a struggle to converse with the modern in an intelligible way from a native sensibility and subjectivity. It is a struggle to read existing accounts of histories of business practice in India against the grain, in a highly sympathetic and idiomatic way to identify particular characteristics and aspects, which, when focused upon, will not only be true to their customary native world, but will also appear as familiar to a modern reader of business responsibility. In this struggle, I am probably reinforcing the modern as a referent for differentiation, but my only solace and defence is that in 'difference' lies identity and it is in acknowledging difference that identity can be respected, not in denying or subordinating differences one to the other. By highlighting aspects of business practice that resonate with the modern reader, I do not imply that those which have not been chosen are secondary or subordinate or irresponsible in any way. It just means that they are different and might not interest the reader. Probably, as a member of this civilisation, which does not have a history of stable all-encompassing hierarchies (Subrahmanyam, 2005; Alam and Subrahmanyan, 2007), my sensibility helps me to look at the difference in a non-hierarchical, non-threatening way. Surfacing my native identity does not prompt me to deny the modern. With this note, proceeding now to the task at hand, let us dive into the deep and ancient past in Indian commerce.

Business practices in ancient and pre-colonial India

Accounts of ancient India focusing exclusively on business practices are relatively scant. Existing accounts have been primarily concerned with understanding governance, social order and corporate life in ancient India. Much of the data for these accounts has come from archaeological sources like rock and stone edicts on the one hand and from literary sources on the other. An array of literary sources like commentaries on social practices written by scholars of ancient times, stories in literature especially Buddhist *Jataka* tales and accounts of foreign travellers all inform such an understanding. The following discussion of ancient India is based on Majumdar (1920), Ghoshal (1930), Coomaraswamy (1909) and Mookerji (1919).

All evidence consistently point to the existence of a highly sophisticated corporate order in the practices of Indian businessmen of yore. Businessmen were often differentiated into people pursuing different livelihoods like trading, smithery, weaving, milling, weaponery, pottery, animal husbandry and so on. They formed their own associations called *srenis*.[1] These *srenis* were sometimes for single occupations and at other times for more than one. Within the *sreni*, members pursued their specific businesses individually, or in partnerships. *Srenis* were highly autonomous entities which governed themselves not just in business functions, but also in matters of dispute and justice. They followed what was called the *srenidharma*, a conduct of the *sreni* that encompassed the multifarious roles and obligations of a businessman in the routine pursuit of not just business but life per se. The *srenidharma* had to be aligned to '*dharma*' or 'righteous living' in general. The code thus covered all aspects of way of life for members of the *sreni*, their practices, ethics and ethos. Within the decentralised governance processes of India, even royalty could intervene only when *srenidharma* was violated. In other circumstances, royal interest would be construed as a matter of interference in the functioning of the *sreni*. *Srenidharma* did not disapprove profit making. The expectations of *srenidharma* were that profits would be pursued in a manner compliant with *dharma*, or righteous conduct. Righteousness was understood as a contingent category rather than a universal moral standard. The basis of governance of both society at large and within the *sreni* was provided by customary and scriptural understanding of *dharma*. The complexity of multidimensional social life and righteous conduct as a contingent category is well recognised in the *dharmashastras*. Texts drawing upon the Vedas laid out that violations of *dharma* would be judged on the principle of local and neighbourhood knowledge. Thus the text *Sukraniti* laid down that 'foresters are to be tried by foresters, merchants by merchants, soldiers by soldiers and in the village by persons who live with both parties' (Mookerji, 1919:126). The various *Samhitas* like *Yagnyavalka Samhita, Brihaspati Samhita* that were codifications and commentaries on *dharma* informed and guided the practices of royalty, *sreni* members and society at large.

These *srenis* created endowments for charitable purposes like temples, water tanks, way houses, treating the sick and destitute and other such activities. Majumdar (1920:31) says 'perhaps the oldest epigraphic reference to guild [*sreni*] is furnished by an inscription of Huvishka at Mathura dated in the year 28 (c. 106 AD). It refers to an *akshya-nivi* [perpetual endowment] of 550 *puranas* each to two guilds, one of which was that of flourmakers'. Both Majumdar and

Mookerji cite several other epigraphic references where perpetual endowments were made to provide for the needs of monks, wells, temple construction and upkeep, lighting of lamp in the temple, rest houses, ferry boats for the village, cisterns etc. As Mookerji explains, such gift making was duly notified and registered in *sreni* proceedings and public memory. Sometimes these *srenis* themselves made the endowments, at other times *srenis* acted as trustees of the endowments and ensured that the necessary service was performed on an ongoing basis. These endowments also were directed at spatio-temporally specific *groups and communities*. The *srenis* were much more than simple occupational associations. They performed municipal governance functions as well.

Righteous conduct was not just a normative scriptural compulsion. Everyday social practice necessitated that people be openly perceived as righteous. Wealth alone did not guarantee reputation and social standing. People needed to forge their reputations of righteousness and good character. This was an end in itself. It was the means for the self's spiritual growth, addressing family and kinship needs, securing memberships into *srenis*, forging business partnerships, maintaining solvency, gaining political status and assuming roles of governance in the *sreni*. Businessmen therefore necessarily had to invest in charitable and honourable practices that visibly impacted their reputations. Their business practices too had to be perceived as just and honourable. Thus notions of justice, nobleness, character, honesty, fairness pervaded everyday conduct of a businessman's life and occupation in ancient India. Responsibility did not exist as something over and above the pursuit of business. It was intimately woven into the conduct of everyday life of a business man. Across centuries *srenis* and individual wealthy *sreni* members continued to perform activities for general well-being. Sometimes *srenis* levied special cesses on membership for this purpose. 'Banias of Surat taxed themselves by common consent in order to support the hospitals for animals which they maintained in the town' (Das Gupta, 2001:331). Writing about later day *srenis*, Coomaraswamy (1909:9) says,

> [T]he funds of the guilds of western India . . . are for the greater part spent on charities, and particularly charitable hospitals for sick and helpless domestic animals: and in part also on the temples . . . and on guild feasts. A favourite device for raising money is for the men of a craft or trade to agree on a certain

day to shut all their shops but one. The right to keep open this one is then put up to auction and the amount bid goes to the guild fund.

Though it might appear that these are acts of public giving (through auctioning a voluntarily created scarce resource/opportunity) independent of business, it is important to recognise that these acts were at once all four: spiritual, indicators of bankability and creditworthiness, political and social status.

This is not to suggest that business in ancient India was a completely honest affair. It is only fair to assume that fraud, deceit and other dishonest, disreputable and irresponsible behaviours would have been there in ancient India too and historical evidence could also be found for the same. The above account only contends that it would have been easy to govern compliance since mere suspicion was enough to ruin reputations. This in itself would have served as a deterrent. Further, justice too could have been locally and communally administered since *srenis* were the primary mechanism of governing businessman's behaviours and they could both identify wrong doing and perform redressal. Das Gupta (2001) cites instances of such governance in Western India.

Some scholars have termed the publicly considerate/oriented behaviour of businessmen in India's past as charity driven by religion and hence religious philanthropy as the key theme of Indian philanthropy. Theocratic conceptions of Indian society have supported such a treatment. Support for this view has also been garnered from the oft repeated preachings encouraging charity within the belief systems of different religions. However, such an explanation assumes two things. First, a society and a worldview, where religion existed as a separate sphere of the social world. Second, businessmen differed in their practices according to their religious affiliation. This might not be a very accurate characterisation of the pursuits of ancient Indian society and India's mercantile community. Religion as a category is itself a consequence of modernity (Kaviraj, 2009). The ways of life which are today known as Hinduism have always been referred to as *sanatana dharma* or *ancient righteous conduct*. This seems to have informed the practices of many communities. Epigraphic evidence and evidence in folk stories point to widely accepted ideas and practices of everyday conduct which went beyond the specific community affiliations of the people. This evidence indicates that community identifications were based on geographies or *desh*, and *jati*. Stone inscriptions often identified the members by their occupation rather than by belief system. For instance, epigraphic evidence from tenth century like Pandyan inscriptions about *Ayyavole 500 sreni* carried references to *sreni* members as *'nanajati'* meaning those belonging to different *jatis* (Majumdar, 1920:82). Post-colonial sociologists and historians like Partha Chatterjee (1998, 2011) and Gupta (2007) have shown that *jati* as a marker of community identity is not co-terminus with religion or caste but far more complex often including kinship, village, occupational and other systems of social stratification. Coomaraswamy (1909:8) says,

> The trade guilds of the great polytechnical cities of India are not, however always exactly coincident with the sectarian or ethnical caste of a particular caste of artisans. Sometimes the same trade is pursued by men of different castes, and its guild generally includes every member of the trade it represents without strict reference to caste.

Reviewing the diversity of the mercantile communities in India during 1700s and 1800s, Ashin Das Gupta (2001:103) asserts that 'a preoccupation with the caste system [religion], while discussing the mercantile attitudes of eighteenth century India, would scarcely be justified'. He lists Banias, Konkani brahmins, Muslims, Jews, Armenians and Arabs among others as dominant mercantile communities along the Western coast of India during the 1700s. Drawing upon letters written by members of the merchant communities during this period, Das Gupta (2001:105) adds:

> . . . there was no difference between a Hindu and a Muslim, a Christian and a Jew in this approach to business. In fact business dealings were generally untouched by religious considerations. This does not of course, mean that they were not regulated by certain principles but these principles were more or less secular in character and were recognized by all merchants as equally valid. *The most important thing for a merchant to have was character. It was a must for him to have a reputation for honest dealings and for people to have confidence in him . . . the second important thing for a merchant was to remember that business deals had to made and kept in a certain socially approved way . . . belonging to business ethics.*
> (emphasis added)

Such mercantile implications of cultural traditions have been amply showcased by other economic historians and anthropologists like Haynes (1987) and Rudner (1994). Further, as Birla (2009:74) contends,

> [I]ndigenous endowments, grand and ascetic, include sites such as temples, *dharamshalas* (rest houses for travellers), step wells and freshwater wells, panjrapols (shelter for animals), *gaushalas* (shelters for cows), and *mathas* (centers of instruction in Hindu philosophy and Sanskrit literature) were important practices for mercantile groups. Making such gifts for *dharma* whether it be a local temple, *dharmshala*, or other form of social welfare, was a way to negotiate . . . [merchants' entry] to a new social world, performing ritual purity and material conquest . . . they mapped the localized market dominance of business families and performed a kind of localized sovereignty.

Within the 'decentralised governance traditions of India' (Mookerji, 1919), these were therefore important political functions. But, reading these acts as culture put to service of capital or politics misrecognises the way of life as Birla suggests, because these social spheres had very porous boundaries, because dharma itself was *jati or sreni* dharma. These acts were at once religious-spiritual, kinship responsive, politically useful and mercantile supportive. It was religious in being sanctioned by faith. It was political in securing patronage and mercantile in building a network.

The businessman's preoccupation with reputation continued into the twentieth century. In this period, before British mercantile law came into vogue, business practices retained some similarity to *sreni* dharma, in not specifically distinguishing between family-business-charity, conduct of life and business practice. Public purpose and private gain were not strictly delineated. Funds from customary endowments made for temples and other charitable purposes were used by families for businesses. For example, in 1926, a Chettiar business family had agreed to establish and support a vernacular school *pathshala* for teaching hymns. The family used rupees 15,000 from the endowment to construct the building, with the presumption that the remaining endowment would be invested in land and the resultant income would be used for the upkeep of the school. The family instead invested the money in their rice mill business and used the income to support the school (cited in Birla,

2009:98). Endowment thus did not imply an earmarking of funds but a commitment to undertake a certain activity. Funds as such flowed freely within family-business-charity. What this implied was an extensive negotiability of reputational and monetary flows between kinship relations, *jati* relations and mercantile relations. This extensive negotiability hinged on the merchant's reputation and character. Public itself was signified through communities located in specific spatio-temporal contexts who were in a mesh of reciprocal relations with the family-firm. These relations were at once symbolic, reputational, material and also business oriented. Thus customary practices of civic life in ancient, pre-colonial, pre-British mercantile law India involved a deeply contextual involvement of businessmen in the daily lives of communities. As Birla says,

> The activities of the family firm defied categorization into public trading affairs and private household concerns in two broad ways: first, there were porous boundaries between kinship as a symbolic logic and commerce as a material one. Resilient webs of credit operated through unwritten notions of trust, a symbolic currency secured by ties of consanguinity, marriage and lineage. . . . Second, the very notion of family extended beyond the household and encompassed a variety of patriarchal relations. . . . *The family firm then was not simply a discrete institution tied to a single or perhaps a few households. Its successful operation depended upon extensive networks that were as much public in their material import as they were private and personal in their selective construction.*
>
> (2009:16, emphasis added)

The economic, social and political were not distinct arenas with impervious boundaries but what was economic was at once social and also political. All these fused, becoming material and visible in the body of the merchant's person, family and their name, reputation and character. In this world, business was woven into an ethical and community code of living. These embodied practices of reputational materiality apparently made business's social responsibility an intrinsic aspect of conduct of businessman's life and business. Thus, in the past, responsibility implied a visible ethical conduct irrespective of the specific faith of the businessman. Such ethical conduct included responsibility towards society within itself. Responsibility was not something extra over and above or outside of the business. Characterising this complex mechanism of conduct as religious philanthropy reduces the substance and pervasiveness of the mechanism. While it is true that certain texts describing conduct like the *Samhitas* have been identified with Hinduism and Vedas, such identification of specific religions and their religious boundaries is itself a later day modernist practice[2].

Business practices during early modern industrial and colonial era

The encounter with Western modernity, rationality and science that British rule implied, impressed upon some wealthy Indians the need to invest in developing Western style institutions. Colonisation had impressed upon several wealthy Indians the country's *'inadequacies'* in such knowledges as Western medicine, health care, education and science. Several institutions were set up across the country to promote Western education, science and medicine by prominent business families. Thus, the period after 1850 saw philanthropic contributions being made to set up Western style schools, colleges and hospitals.

> The indigenous elites were quick to learn from the colonial model, ... Even as they zealously maintained their religion and identity, their homes. . . . Identifying with the British, they also bought into the colonial urban ideal. They contributed handsomely, to various charities and donated funds for several public institutions. The evidence of their philanthropic investment in the city is visible all over Bombay today, . . . – JJ School of Art, JJ Hospital, Petit Library. . . .
>
> (Prakash, 2011:51)

The wealthy industrialist family of Wadias built housing for poor and middle-class Parsis in Bombay. They also set up educational institutions and hospitals in Pune. A neat list of the several institutions set up by philanthropic wealthy businessmen during this period is provided by Pushpa Sundar (2000). The list is excerpted here in Table 2.1.

Another development during this period was the formation of exclusive charitable trusts with endowments of funds to pursue various philanthropic activities. Such trusts supported educational and medical institutions. The emerging legal frameworks

Table 2.1 Some philanthropic trusts set up during 1850–1914

Jamsetji Jejeebhoy	JJ School of Arts, JJ Hospital	Education, Hospitals
Jamsetji Nuwwerwanjee	JN Tata Endowment Scheme, Indian Institute of Science	Education
Jaggannath Shanker	Grant to Grant Medical College, Victoria Museum, Elphinstone College	Education
Premchand Roychand	Bombay University library, Vol. on Indian architecture	Education
Cowasjee Jehangir	Jahangir Ophthalmic Hospital	Hospital
Hemabhai Vakatchand	Hemabhai Institute	Education
Madhavlal Chotalal	KC Technical Institute	Education
Pacchaiyappa	Pacchaiyappa's College	Education
Rani Swarnamayee	Women's education	Education

Source: Sundar (2000:142–3)

on charity, philanthropy, public service and private gain aided and guided the formation and functioning of these trusts and societies. Trusts and societies were also set up as voluntary organisations to support welfare activities for the poor and underprivileged like housing, relief, promoting social reform and action against various social evils plaguing Indian society during that period like child marriages, untouchability, widow burning etc. (Sundar, 2000). Some trusts like Dorabji Trust, Ratan Tata Trust took on the role of grant making institutions and funded activities for general public welfare. Interestingly, these institutions received support first from individuals – Jamsetji Tata, Dorabji Tata, Ratan Tata, David Sassoon and only later did these relationships transfer into the trusts that were established by these businessmen for philanthropic purposes. Sir Ratan Tata supported the Servants of India Society. Dorabji Trust supported TISS, IISc, TIFR and other such organisations. Such secular Western-oriented philanthropic developments by Indian businessmen were being welcomed by British government. They rewarded people pursuing these activities by giving out titles like Dewan Bahadur and Sir. Those businessmen who were in close association with the British through business relations and those who engaged in social reform activities sanctioned by Western modernity sometimes also assumed advisory positions with the British.

However, these developments masked the struggles facing customary business practices and ways of life. Developments in colonial governance and jurisprudence conflicted with customary practices of governance, responsibility and business that continued from earlier eras. By 1870, colonial rule had already put in place an extensive legal system for civil, criminal, personal and mercantile matters. This legal regime was based on British law and principles of contract. This legal regime regulated Indian society and commerce by sharply dividing the customary way of life into distinct commercial-public and private-social-cultural spheres. Whereas the commercial sphere was subject to British law, they had adopted a policy of non-interference in the cultural so as to sustain imperial control. Culture was designated as the personal arena of religion, caste, family and inheritance which was governed by personal law and for this purpose, categories like Hindu Undivided Family were invented through a misrecognition, reification and ossification of (otherwise fluid and flexible) customary practices and traditions commented upon in *dharmashastra* texts (Birla, 2009). Thus a society which did not recognise distinct social, cultural and economic domains was broken into these domains.

> . . . this history of fixing [meanings and practices which were hitherto flexible and negotiated] had potent effects on what was called the indigenous 'lexmercatoria' or mercantile laws, a term that British and roman jurisprudence had defined as the largely autonomous sphere of common law governing trade and finance.
>
> (Birla, 2009:14)

This legal and jurisprudential regime bisected public purpose and private gains with the logic of contracts, abstract publics, and autonomous markets. Contractual logics and economic gains replaced the social mechanism of obligations and negotiated reciprocities anchored and sustained in reputations. Thus the Chettiar family who set up the *pathshala* mentioned earlier was faced with an income tax demand for '*diverting*' the money to the rice mill, and this demand was upheld by the Madras High Court. The family's pleas that the incomes were still used only for the school did not find any acceptance. The Court held that the endowment belonged to the school and could not and should not have been used by the family for other purposes.

> In the 1871 Privy council case Jagat Mohini Dossee v. Sokheemony Dossee, the judgment "enforced the private nature of the [temple] trust managed by the joint family, and at the same time instituted a safeguard to prevent the property from being tied up within the HUF [Hindu Undivided family]: the criterion of valid dedication. If a trust reverted to other uses than that to which it was dedicated, it was not valid and considered revoked. Irrevocable and perpetual religious or charitable gifts were made distinct and separate from invalid trusts for potentially profitable purposes.
>
> (Birla, 2009:93)

The courts now ruled that the endowments were essentially restricted funds which belonged to the trusts and the specified charitable purposes. They were not to be understood as moral commitments and obligations.

Such a regime impacted fund and cash flows of business families making endowments. The restrictions on fungibility of funds also implied that only the rich and wealthy could now afford to make endowments. Only the rich with funds to spare could now pursue charitable activities. It also impacted customary operational autonomy of the businessmen. Earlier, the businessmen achieved de facto sovereignty for the areas where they invested in by gaining responsibility of municipal functions as well. Under British rule, businessmen were relieved of such municipal and governance responsibilities. Its links with the economic and the political being severed, the ethical conduct of a businessman now became a matter of cultural-religious belief alone manifested as doing charity. Nevertheless customary welfare activities continued. Temples, rest houses and palliative activities continued to be promoted, if only for the spiritual well-being of the wealthy. Some businessmen also actively supported and funded nationalist freedom struggles by financing the Indian National Congress. In this scenario, even though *srenis* continued to function as associations of businessmen and fulfil needs of the community, their prominence in public life declined over the decades. In the evolving lexicon of colonial governance *srenis* were understood as caste groupings and caste regulators rather than secular mercantile and/or occupational governance mechanisms.

Factory organisation and workplace responsibility

Even as notions and practices of ethical conduct pursued by Indian business were acquiring new meanings under colonial rule and law, a new form of organisation, the modern factory form also came into vogue during this era. The factory owners' workplace practices therefore offer another window into examining whether and how earlier ways of life emphasising reputation and conduct were reinvented or reinterpreted into this novel context. Examining these workplace practices will help us infer notions and practices of responsibility of the Indian factory owner. The earliest workforce for the factories in India came from villages. In jute mills, coal mines, tea gardens, ship building, railways and other businesses owned and managed by British, managerial practices were imported from Scotland and England. These managerial practices were racially and imperially informed. For instance, during shortages of workers for coal mines in Jharia, the official coal-controlling authority in its meetings in 1917, actually revived its proposals to raise the price of grog. Their argument was that the indigenous labourers working in the mines were satisfied with their wages and did not come back for work regularly. If, however, the workers could be induced to spend all their wages on grog, then they would come back to work for want of money. Accordingly, the British government increased the number of liquor outlets. These outlets were set up right outside the mines often with adverse consequences for the health and well-being of these worker communities (Simeon, 1999). Their managerial practices also viewed workers as ignorant, unreasonable, indisciplined and juvenile, who needed to be dealt with firmly, including resorting to corporeal punishments (Chakrabarty, 1983:130–31; Chandavarkar, 2008 citing Yolland, 1994).

So instead of looking at workplace practices of just any colonial era business or factory, it would serve our present purposes well if we can focus on businesses or factories which were owned and managed by Indians. Such workplaces are likely to be devoid of racial, imperial burden and therefore better reflect native business's workplace and employee management practices. We will therefore turn our attention to Bombay. Colonial subjugation was much lesser in Bombay than Calcutta since colonial control and commercial activity both arrived much later in Bombay compared to Calcutta

(Markowitz, 2008). Compared to Calcutta, there was scope for native capital to manoeuvre in Bombay. Much of Bombay's commercial and industrial activity was in the hands of Indians – Parsis, Gujaratis, Marwaris, Muslims etc.

Bombay's textile mills were the first and most well-developed factory systems in India, they were the *pace setter for industrialization*' (Morris, 1965). Bombay's textile mills were owned and managed by native Indians – Gujaratis, Marwaris, Parsis and Muslims among others. An 1875 report said that textile mills in Bombay *'are almost exclusively owned by natives, and are under native supervision*' (Morris, 1965 citing Martin, 1862).[3] The first textile mill in Bombay was set up by a successful Indian businessman, Cowasji Davar in 1854. The early promoters raised capital by distributing shares between friends, caste bretheren and business associates. During this period setting up a textile mill involved a huge risk since machinery, trained man power and management had to be imported from Britain.

Within a few years, Indians took over as masters and managers; by 1895 Indians formed more than half of the staff (Morris, 1965). In 1880s, Bombay mills in spite of disadvantages were highly prosperous and paid back all subscribed capital in 4 years (Morris, 1965). In spite of early growth in the number of mills the ground reality was one of significant challenges. High capital costs due to imported machinery, high depreciation due to use of untrained workers, difficulties in raising capital due to unfavourable legal frameworks, precarious domestic and export markets, all created an environment of high risk and uncertainty for the mills. Domestic markets were impoverished from agrarian crisis and famines. The colonial government's political and economic regime that favoured imperial interests subordinated local industry (Birla, 2009; Chandavarkar, 1994). Of the 97 mills set up during 1855–1925, only five remained intact, 12 closed down, 16 were transferred and 45 were liquidated or reconstructed under others (Chandavarkar, 1994). Mills also varied widely in machinery, plant lay out, age of machinery and finally the nature of products produced from these machines (Chandavarkar, 1994; Morris, 1965).

Bombay mills present a striking case of native management practices. Even though in theory the organisational structure and workplace hierarchy corresponded with British mills, in practice the authority structure and workplace management were distinctly native. The authority structure of the mills was anchored in dense information flows and reputational networks spanning workplace and neighbourhoods of workers, jobbers and owners. The structure was not a linear hierarchy, instead it was characterised by decentered and diffuse spheres of influence and a quest for building reputations (see Figure 2.1). Networks of patronage and reputation were important not only for jobbers and managers but also for owners in ensuring credit worthiness, attracting capital and talent.

The workforce was singular in that there were fewer women and children even though there were no legislative compulsions. Available data shows that the wage rates for both women and children were lesser compared to adult males, yet, women and child worker proportion in the workforce was quite less (as given in Table 2.2).

Women worked lesser hours and were provided with greater amounts of lee-way in hours of work and coming and going to facilitate their completion of domestic and parenting responsibilities (Jammulamadaka, 2016a). While children could be found in the mill compound, they were often found playing or simply

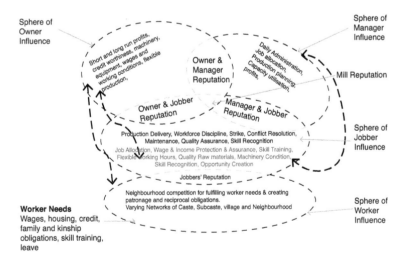

Figure 2.1 Authority relations in Bombay textile mills

Source: Jammulamadaka (2016a)

Table 2.2 Bombay textile mills: number, workforce, wages and performance

Year	No. of mills	No. of workers	Percentage of women workers in total workforce	Gross profit rate on fixed capital	Indexed wages (1882 = 100)*
I	II	III	IV	V	VI
1881	32	31,351			
1887	55	43,270	24.63		105.4
1893	69	67,870	25.87		104.2
1895	69	75,740	24.74		102.9
1899	82	77,169	23.54		100
1901	81	82,162			100
1903	80	86,913			100
1905	81	92,924			100
1907	85	98,101		0.11	118.0
1909	89	105,751	21.36	–	125.6
1911	87	104,500	20.34	0.02	121.9
1913	90	110,033	20.61	0.07	124.6
1915	86	111,924	19.65	–	131.8
1917	87	125,713		0.10	133.6
1919	85	126,368	20.33	–	194.0
1921	83	147,740	20.49	0.13	266.3
1923	81	148,771	20.46	0.02	293.9
1925	82	153,009	22.15	–0.01	
1927	83	154,398	22.10	0.03	
1929	81	106,710	21.42	0.00	
1931	81	136,404	21.96	0.01	
1933	78	129,213		–0.01	
1935	74	136,052		0.01	
1937	69	139,215	15.92	0.02	246.0
1939	68	156,046	14.93		

Columns I, II, III, IV,VI from Morris (1965).
Column V from Wolcott and Clark (1999)
* Morris (1965) computes indexed wage estimates from 1923 onwards from a different
source as against the previous years.

Source: Author

hanging about their older working family members and not necessarily working (Morris, 1965). Morris (1965:65) writes:

> The most striking feature, especially when compared with the
> sectoral and age distributions of textile work forces in other
> countries during the nineteenth and twentieth centuries, is the
> relatively limited use of women and children. Even in the earli-
> est years for which we have evidence adult males never consti-
> tuted less than 69% and women never more than a quarter of
> the total work force. Children, legally defined, never exceeded
> 5.6%.

Wage rates varied extensively even within mills of the same owners.
They were negotiated between the workers-jobbers-managers set
up. The wage structure was an eclectic mix of various aspects:

> If the framework of wage determination was established by the
> subsistence costs of the worker and his family, these did not by
> any means constitute an absolute or objective standard. *Rather,*
> *subsistence was relative category determined by custom, nego-*
> *tiation and struggle. Moral imperatives, not simply principles*
> *of political economy, formed the underpinnings for the percep-*
> *tion of what constituted a living wage.*
> (Chandavarkar, 1994:310, emphasis added)

Primary bread winners of the family were usually discouraged
from taking up the low-paying jobs. Such jobs were usually kept
for older and less able people who fulfilled supplementary income
roles. While an elaborate policy of fines existed, its imposition was
a discretionary affair (Chandavarkar, 1994; Morris, 1965). There
were no mills which were distinctively low paying or high paying
across all the jobs. Information on wages, quantity and quality of
work, jobber reputation, mill reputation, status of mill machinery,
owner/management predispositions and reputations was freely
available to workers in the dense neighbourhood networks of
workers/jobbers. Some mills were specifically known as *khatara*, or
broken down and avoided.

Workers did not unanimously seek higher wages, some wanted
lesser working hours, some wanted certain kinds of machinery, and
some wanted time rates as against piece rates. Better conditions
did not necessarily imply the same thing for everybody but varied

according to personal preferences and circumstances (Morris, 1965; Chandavarkar, 1994). This enabled workers to change jobs and negotiate terms of employment albeit at the cost of a loss of a few days' wages. In spite of severe wage competition mill owners did not resort to concerted action. Such concerted action was not considered proper, in fact it constituted interference into individual mill owner's autonomy. There were no restrictions of labour mobility like blacklisting of employees, or wage control even though Bombay Mill Owners Association (BMOA, various years) was advised concerted action on wages by government.

Strict time discipline was not followed. Work allowed for natural rhythms of the workers. Flexibility was seen in opening and closing time of mill work, shifts, number and duration of breaks, flexible and shorter working hours for women, and flexible periods of employment. In fact these practices were characterised as lax discipline and laziness by British officers and observers. In spite of this, smooth work and continued operation of machines was ensured by hiring excess workers who would share the work load and fill in for those on a break. Seasonal migration was another feature. Workers would leave for their villages to attend to agriculture or other activities and upon returning go back to the same mills. Describing the situation, Fred Stones, an important mill manager, said, '. . . the worker will go away leaving a post card with his address. But when he comes back, he does not go to a jobber or a weaver. He wants a particular loom. He does not roam about for work' (cited in Chandavarkar, 1994:301). It was as if they had a *lien on the loom* (Morris, 1965). Box 2.1 provides some quotes describing the work place and practices.

Box 2.1: Work culture at Bombay Textile Mills

- Perhaps because . . . operatives were typically given some rather vague grace period . . . before they were considered late. Workers were not required to be at their machines when the power was turned on but gradually drifted in to work. . . . Nor did the mills establish regular breaks during which operatives could smoke or relive themselves. They went off as the occasions demanded. The employer was only concerned that when a mill hand took a break his machines were tended by others and did not have to be stopped. In fact, something like an informal shift system was created to provide for meal, rest, and toilet breaks without interrupting work.

(Morris, 1965:112–3)

- In 1894, mill officials estimated that at any one time in individual mills from 7 to 47 % of the workforce was not at its machines.

(Morris, 1965:112–3)

- Ninety percent of the work-people take their meals during working hours, some take from three to five meals per day during working hours, no restriction is put upon them as to the time they take. When they are away from work, at their meals, there is somebody else doing it, and this is the reason why so many people are employed. . . . During this period the operatives are allowed full liberty to go out, to take their meals, to smoke, or do anything they please.

(Morris, 1965:113)

- For example, in 1891 an official spokesman described the situation in the following terms: There are no very strict regulations. The indian operative whose is paid by piece work is allowed to come in half an hour after time of starting work . . . the popular notion of sunrise varying within limits of half an hour. So he keeps a lien on his place by putting in substitutes. He can leave early in the afternoon if necessary and get his half a day's wages . . . so there is no rule or way of seeing him constantly at his post during the working hours of the mill. He is a per- fectly free agent in that regard. He feels himself at liberty to take his meals between the hours of seven and 12, to stretch his legs occasionally, to loiter in the compound or perhaps have his shave and shampoo under little sheds in the mill compound whenever he pleases. The youngsters may be seen having snatches at leap frog even on the mill premises . . . the women have more grace allowed them as to their times of starting work . . . when they have to look after sucklings . . . they have perfect freedom to go to their place and be back at intervals during the day. In fact the Indian operators do not work against their customs or their natural inclinations . . . or their traditional habits . . . walk through a mill at any time of the day and two out of the six operatives told off for sets of machines will not be seen. They are taking it in turns to be out in the compound . . . hardly one percent of the Indian operatives take their meals during their recess hours. Each has his own time and takes it during the working hours. . . .

(Morris, 1965:115)

Source: Morris (1965)

Work sharing was a common practice (Chandavarkar, 1994:123). Said a mill manager, 'the workers in Bombay seem to favour the idea of half work for everybody rather than full work for a few'. Women who were employed as reelers and winders effectively engaged in work-sharing practices to prevent retrenchment (cited in Chandavarkar, 1994:123). Even under conditions when the industry was facing downturn and mills were closing down, there was an increase in overall employment in the mills, likely evidence that more number of people were sharing the same jobs because, they were still better than other opportunities available (Jammulamadaka, 2015b). Such work sharing was customary in other parts of the economy also.

In 1873, for example, a number of the bricklayers in Ahmedabad could not find work. Men of this class sometimes added to their daily wages by rising very early in the morning and working overtime. But when several families complained that they could not get employment, the bricklayers' guild met and decided that as there was not enough work for all, no member should be allowed to work in extra hours . . . the trade guild . . . allows none of its members to starve. It thus acts as a mutual assurance society. . . . The severest social penalty which can be inflicted is to be put out of his caste.

(Coomaraswamy, 1909:9–12)

In these mills driven by custom, conflict sustained cooperation, they were not mutually exclusive. While workers were dependent on owners for wages, labour mobility and freedom for labour to move from mill to mill provided bargaining power and safeguarded workers against vulnerability to unilateral control by mill owners (Jammulamadaka, 2016a). Bombay's textile mills were character-ised by a multitude of strikes. As Chandavarkar (2008) points out, most of the strikes occurred within mills, at the level of depart-ment, jobber or worker gang. They involved temporary stoppages of work. They were often settled at the jobber level or by arbitra-tion of higher authorities. Sometimes there was reshuffling of gangs, sometimes they were fired and at other times, the jobber walked out along with the workers. The hundreds of work stoppages consti-tuted regular and home-grown mechanisms of airing grievances, negotiating settlements and redressal. They were built upon imme-diate, shared perceptions of fairness and solidarities of the shop floor, work place and community. When workers in a shed stopped their work for a few hours, it was because at that moment, a collec-tive albeit small and transient solidarity was forged amongst those workers which prompted the jobber or higher authorities to come to them and settle their grievance. There were also industry-wide general strikes which tackled wider wage and bonus issues.

During the 1910s and 1920s strikes which were hitherto lim-ited to individual department or mill and involved basic workplace grievances tended to become industry wide. The first such large strike that occurred in January 1919 involved 150,000 workers and lasted 12 days. But soon other large-scale strikes broke out (Morris, 1965). Chandavarkar (1994) writes that the 1919 general strike was the first of eight general strikes that occurred over the next 10 years and affected workers in other industries including those outside Bombay. But till about 1928 all these strikes were enabled by neighbourhood solidarities and social control, not by trade unions (Wolcott, 2008). Wage increases agreed by mill own-ers between 1919 and 1923 resulted from a wave of rolling strikes in individual mills – almost 189 between 1917 and 1920 (Chanda-varkar, 2008:155). Such worker protests had a moral force given the high profits the mills were earning during that period.

These strikes were a continuation of customary practices of con-testing and resisting domination in everyday life in the subconti-nent. Boycott, avoidance and flight have all been used to trigger micro-level processes of negotiation and conflict resolution. Guha (1986) and Dharampal (1971) show that villagers aggrieved by royal taxation regimes would boycott payment of tribute, abandon

cultivation and villages. These would trigger a process of fact finding and negotiations by the rulers and lead to reconstructing the
relationship on more acceptable terms. Gyan Prakash (1990) similarly shows how flight formed a means of resistance for the dependent labourers of South Bihar in colonial India.

Another important aspect was mill worker housing. In the mill
districts, '[B]etween 30 and 40 percent of its population lived in single rooms inhabited by six or more people . . . [over years] their proportion rose to 99%' (Chandavarkar, 1994:179). The usual practice
was to build single room tenements or *chawls* for mill workers. By
1926, a percentage of the mill owners had provided housing for
their workers (ranging from about 5–15 per cent of mill work force).
Mill owners faced extensive criticism for providing inadequate and
unhygienic housing to workers who had migrated from the hinter-
land in search of wage employment. The criticism intensified after
the plague attacks. After the bubonic plague of 1896, the colonial
administration formed the Bombay Improvement Trust to improve
housing and sanitary conditions for the poor. The Trust proposed
to supplement accommodation and levied a cess. Nevertheless the
Trust razed more tenements than it built creating a housing deficit
for 17,000 workers (BMOA, 1926). It used only 20 per cent of the
budgeted funds (Arnold, 2012) for worker housing. Under these circumstances, the Trust asked mill owners to build mill worker housing. Mill owners refused, and indicated that the town tax of 1 rupee
per cotton bale had already raised thousands for housing purposes
(BMOA, 1926). Other mill owners argued that the demand be made
applicable to all industries in Bombay and not just textile mills to
avoid free riders. Free riders was a problem since workers from
different industries stayed together and shared accommodation by
drawing upon their kinship and village networks.

The mill owners' stance is understandable (in spite of public
giving being a preferred mode of reputation building in the past)
if we can factor in the implications of mercantile and trust acts.
With restraints on, and illegalisation and consequent illegitimisation of capital fungibility within family-business-charity, it would
have been rather difficult for the average mill owners operating in
adverse business climates to invest in mill worker housing. Only
the very large mill owners could conceivably have had the exclusive
capital to build housing. As Petit, the owner of the largest mills
and the BMOA's head said, 'Bombay mill owners are not in the
same position as Cadburys and Rowtons and their dividends are

precarious, while their industry as a whole is not only at a low ebb but is threatened with unfettered competition in the Far East' (Arnold, 2012). Thus the owners in spite of being concerned about the workers and discussing worker condition in BMOA meetings: 'The average operative is an indebted personage. He has not learnt thrift while he is more or less addicted to the habit of drink which, thanks to the prosperous Excise Department of the Government of Bombay, has brought liquor shops near his home' (BMOA, 1914), could not do much.[4]

It has been argued that flexible mill practices are a consequence of the structural instability of the industry (Chandavarkar, 1994) or labour costs (Morris, 1965). Even lack of worker housing has been linked to strategies of business (Arnold, 2012). Such explanations though, assume an a priori economic rationality, and consequently a singular pursuit of profit or capital logic. Instead looking at them as ways of life, we notice that underlying these flexible, personalised and negotiated practices was a way of life that did not see the factory and the neighbourhood as two distinct spheres. They spilled over and continued into each other.

Reputational pursuit erased the distinction between the owner as an individual and his firm as an economic agent of the market, for these reputations were not limited to firm's ability to earn profits, but extended to political and ethical business conduct, and sensitivity to the social needs of workers. Similarly work roles, kinship, community and family roles got imbricated together. Practices like workers taking breaks or going on leave substituting their positions in factories with someone from their extended network erased distinctions of family and work. All these actors being implicated in unequal status relationships of dependence, reciprocity and reputation provided a material basis, to this way of life (Jammulamadaka, 2015b, 2016a). The customary reputational mechanism of negotiation and discretion also ensured that mill owners were not extracting the maximum out of their workforce and driving down their wage bills. Thus a direct link between mill profit strategy and mill practices seems tenuous.

The managerial practices of these mills were a continuation of the native way of life's intermingling of the economic and social spheres and its socio-ethico-political logic. This logic and conduct compelled the owners to recognise worker autonomy, accommodate workers' needs and interests and limit worker exploitation (evidence for which is found in flexible working hours, improvements in wages and hiring of adult male labour) even as they pursued their own profit motives (Jammulamadaka, 2016a). Thus responsibility was built into the everyday workplace practices. This responsibility was not limited to an economic value, or wage. It was at once political in that it was clearly inscribed in the autonomy of workers, jobbers and owners, it was also socio-ethical in that it recognised and accommodated the essential humanness of the worker. Responsibility was inscribed in and enabled by customary conduct seeking reputation.

From reputational interdependence to autonomy of market

Soon after the emergence of Bombay's mills, British mills found a prima facie threat in Bombay. As early as 1862, when Bombay had just four mills with 94,000 spindles and Britain had 33 million spindles, there was fear that Britain would be outrun by India and duties were levied on Indian imports forcing India to pursue the Chinese markets. R. M. Martin writing in 1862 said, '. . . even the present generation may witness the Lancashire manufacturer beaten by his Hindu competitor' (cited in Morris, 1965). Despite adverse economic policies, Indian mills continued to survive and this attracted continuing imperial-colonial interest. This interest manifested as various laws and policies that disrupted custom and embedded responsibility. It began with the Factories Act, was followed by rationalisation measures, Trade Disputes Act and so on. These acts taken together with the remaining legal-economic infrastructure of the colonial government effectively encouraged an accumulationist amoral market logic over customary conduct and reputation logic. Bayly (1983) calls this customary reputation logic as a non-accumulationist logic.

Responding to mercantile interests in mainland Britain, the crown government advocated a Factories Act in India. Seven different committees were set up between 1875 and 1888 to investigate working conditions and wages. These special committees and commissions set up to investigate factory working conditions in India found that the conditions in Bombay, Surat and Bharuch, the principal factory areas producing cotton in Bombay Presidency were nowhere like those found in Britain (Kydd, 1920). The colonial government also reiterated that there were no exploitative practices and only customary practices were being followed. Yet, the committees found these customary practices as whimsical, cavalier, discriminatory and unjust. The Factories Act was passed in 1881 and amended again in 1891.

As Jammulamadaka (2016a) explains, the act primarily restricted working of women and children. To this extent it should not have inconvenienced the mills since they employed few women and children unlike other parts of the world; however, the act enabled factory inspectors to harass mill owners. BMOA Annual Reports describe mill owners' appeals to courts contesting such harassments and fines. Higher machinery safety requirements like greater distance between machines, operations standards of ventilation which were not followed even in the advanced countries were imposed to disrupt mills. All these were meant to increase the costs of the mills. Such standards gradually were elaborated to include fixed working hours, opening times, break times and so on. The Factory's Act and later a Statistics Act together opened up the mills to the gaze of the British government. The mills which were until then closed networks of natives were now open books: mills were mandated to maintain detailed registers of workers, wages, hours etc. These details enabled the government to intervene even more closely into mill operations. For instance, the insistence on weekly wage payment, which had significant adverse implications for mill cash flow and working capital, even though both mill-workers and mill owners appealed against the new payment system (BMOA, 1924).

A techno-economic logic entered the mills through workforce rationalisation measures. It subordinated man to machine. During the period of 1920s, the Bombay textile industry was under severe strain. They had lost the China market and Bombay's domestic market was being captured by Japanese and Lancashire imports. Describing the conditions, the president of the mill owners association said:

> The year which has ended has unfortunately again proved one of unrelieved depression for the industry . . . several mills were forced into liquidation . . . and most unfortunately for the mill industry and the city of Bombay our competitive ability has been very seriously impaired by two factors both outside the scope of Bombay mill owners . . . and second, the unfair advantage which the Japanese at present enjoy owing to their system of double shift working with a large majority of female

employees, in contravention of the spirit and letter of the Washington conventions.

(BMOA, 1926)

The usual business strategies in response to depressed market conditions, i.e. wage reductions and retrenchment were not available for the mill owners given workers' striking abilities. 'Their attempt to remove the industry-wide bonuses of a month's wages in 1924 resulted in a month-long general strike and a reduction of 11.5% in 1925 led to another general strike from which the mill owners had to withdraw gracefully after three and a half months' (Chandavarkar, 1991:114). Mill owners therefore appealed to the British government for tariff protection against the Japanese. Mill owners argued that unlike Japan they had voluntarily reduced their working hours to 10 from 12, in the spirit of the Washington Convention for worker welfare. The British government also prima facie conceded that the mill owners had a case. 'The government of India in a letter dated 26th march 1926 frankly admitted that the cotton mill industry of the country had a prima facie case for special protection against Japanese competition' (BMOA, 1926). But it was part of the colonial policy to protect imperial interests and keep the markets open for Lancashire. Conceding tariff protection would have adversely impacted not just Japanese but Lancashire as well. As such it set up the tariff board to examine the issue. Tariff board proposed elaborate rationalisation schemes for mill owners.

Thus, the Tariff Board observed in 1927, 'By far the greatest disability from which Bombay suffers is its high costs of labour. . . . So far as costs of production are concerned, it is in labour costs that is to be found the main reason why the depression in the industry has been felt so much more acutely in Bombay than it has elsewhere.' Recommending 'internal economies', the Tariff Board suggested. . . . Since the millowners were 'anxious to avoid another strike', ... 'The only alternative to a reduction in wages is increased efficiency and it is in this direction that, in our view, the true line of advance lies'. Indeed, 'the problem before the Bombay mill industry' was identified as 'the maintenance of its labour efficiency relative to that of other centres'. . . . *Fewer workers would be employed, but their workloads would be increased; they would be paid less*, but they would earn more. The 'true line of advance', therefore, lay in internal reform: especially through the adoption of efficiency measures and rationalization schemes. Tariffs, it was argued, would simply protect the industry at the expense of the consumer and promote and perpetuate inefficiency.

(Chandavarkar, 1994:273 citing Tariff Board's recommendations, emphasis added)

In addition to tariff board, the Fawcett committee[5] formed in 1928 after a general strike to investigate the conditions, suggested standardisation of jobs and wages across the industry to avoid conflict. While minimum wage rates were set pursuant to government instructions, these were often the lowest that was being paid in the industry not the average. And because worker negotiations were now being impeded, such standards led to declining wages. The work became increasingly more standardised, long, less paid, in short, exploitative. As many as nine committees were formed by the British government to look into progress made by mills in standardisation and rationalisation. Any protections were made contingent upon the progress that had been made in rationalisation (Chandavarkar, 1994). However, mill owners and workers resisted. Even as late as 1939, 'less than 10,000 workers were employed in "efficiency schemes"' (Chandavarkar, 1991:113). Gradually, mill owners adopted rationalisation schemes by the later part of 1940s.

The usual strikes in the mills provided another opening for British interventions in the form of the Trade Disputes Act. The Trade Disputes Act which was first introduced into the colonial government's assembly in 1928 was severely criticised as being unfair to workers even by the mill owners themselves. This was however passed eventually in 1934 and as legislated, it moved the grievance redresssal processes of workers outside the mills into hands of the government. Citing the nascency of trade unions, the law introduced the government's labour officer as the most important authority.

This law in effect made it impossible for workers to strike effectively. It drove a powerful wedge into workers' countervailing power. *Badli* workers' were adversely affected due to these interventions. *Badli* worker or 'temporary worker' was an important actor in the mill work place. In the 1880s even though mill owners hardly maintained any written records or formal rosters of permanent and temporary workers, the general relations and employment practice identified a section of the workers as *badli*. While 'temporary' seems to be the translation that has been used in literature, they are more appropriately translated as substitute workers (*badli* from Hindi *badal* meaning change), because these workers got work when there was absenteeism or a sudden increase in workloads which necessitated the hiring of more number of hands. In 1890s *badli* workers formed about a third of the work force (Chandavarkar, 1991:126). They were hired directly by jobbers at the mill gates on a given day after estimating labour force need and accounting for those absent. This was a completely informal system where *badlis* moved from mill to mill to be hired.

The *badli* workers too were embedded in the networks of exchange that characterised the worker/jobber neighbourhoods (Chandavarkar, 1994). There was also a practice of workers giving '*dasturi*' or commission to the jobber for providing work. It was argued by the British that a jobber's self-interest would be to maximise bribes and therefore he would increase the share of temporary workers, which they said was adding to the '*excess supply of labour in the mills*' and leading to 'in-efficiency'. But as Chandavarkar (1994) has shown, the workers including *badli* workers and jobbers were embedded in interdependent relationships of status and reputations and singularly pursuing bribes (as *dasturi* was viewed by British) would have compromised jobber reputation and thus the jobber's occupational well-being.

The Bombay Trade Disputes Act enacted in 1934 by the colonial government created a position of a government labour officer and moved power into the hands of this officer who superseded the mill owners. This officer created a *badli*-control scheme which made attendance mandatory for *badlis* in mills, fixed timings for the *badlis*, and in effect restricted the freedom that *badlis* and jobbers had to negotiate and explore options. It also made it impossible for a *badli* to search for work in two or more mills simultaneously. The *badli*-control scheme was introduced in the name of securing the interests of *badlis* but in effect it created more difficulties for the *badlis* and other workers because it broke their access to social security, i.e. the jobber system.

The jobber's role in the neighbourhood as shown by Chandavarkar (1994, 2008) was not limited to supervision at work. He was the person who provided credit, housing or any other need for the worker. During industry-wide strikes, the jobbers even arranged credit from the grain merchants so that the workers could eat. But under the new scheme, the jobber did not have any say and thus there was no mechanism that created a sustained stake for the jobber to engage with the worker and secure his well-being. The jobbers' role was rendered irrelevant and illegal. The mill owners resisted this intervention with great vigour sometimes arguing about the strength of the jobber system, sometimes pleading that the workers were ignorant and could not navigate the bureaucracy of the new system. But exigencies of colonial rule, imperial interests and the professed value of Taylorian efficiency practices advocated by the coloniser privileged an arbitrary bureaucratic rule over custom.

That existing systems of personalised and negotiated exchanges were quite humane was recognised even by the British. But to suit imperial interests, these differences were reconfigured as 'inefficient', 'native laziness', 'paternalistic', and 'cavalier'; and legal interventions in the form of Factories Act, Trade Disputes Act and rationalisation measures were implemented by British. Kydd (1920) reports that even the British intelligentsia was cognizant of colonial interventions being perceived as aimed at stifling native trade and commerce. While the Factories Act had first introduced fixed working hours in 1891 (some workers[6] are said to have asked for it), the tariff board, and Fawcett committee's recommendations set in motion the process of rationalisation and standardisation. These enactments privileged an abstract bureaucracy, capitalism and techno-economic logic. In this regime what mattered most was compliance to law. This rendered customary work practices of mills illegal. They reduced the scope for micro-level negotiations for all the actors – owners, managers, jobbers and workers. These acts weakened traditional systems of authority by preventing discretion and countervailing power, i.e. the means to develop a reputation. They reduced the significance of a person's reputation, i.e. the scope and compulsion to be responsible to only the spiritual realm. To the extent custom continued, it was as illegal and surreptitious practices. These developments gradually relegated reputational pursuits to the background and seeded the taking over of an amoral market logic.

Trajectory of Western road to modern CSR

Given, illegalisation of embedded responsibility as the characteristic of the trajectory in India's industrial past, it would be interesting to consider the course this journey in the West. We therefore shift our attention to the developments in the history of CSR in the West, primarily the United Kingdom and the United States. However, my effort is imbued with a sense of anxiety. I do not share the same idiomatic understanding of this Western context as I do for India. Nevertheless we proceed with another note of caution. This caution relates to the time periods under consideration. We consider the period of early industrialisation beginning with the eighteenth century and to that extent, the time periods of India and the West are not exactly parallel.

The mills were highly unpopular places because of their dark, dangerous, poorly ventilated workplaces. They were called *dark Satanic places* (Perrow, 1991). The mills were also unpopular because of their highly repetitive tasks. Initially it was very difficult to recruit people to work in these factories and therefore the early factories drew their workforce from displaced farm labour, immigrants, indigents, paupers, convicts and orphans. A strict time discipline was prescribed for the mill workers with strict enforcement and penalties for violations. In the textile mills of the United Kingdom and even the United States, there was a predominance of and preference for women and child workers because of their low wages.

Perrow writes that employers and managers effectively used women workers with lower wages as an antidote to rising male worker wages, he cites a recommendation from a manager to the business owner, 'employing women who would "work for low wages" in the factories would "prevent the rise of wages among the male manufacturers"' (2002:32–3). Employers encouraged the participation of women and children and replaced male workers whose wages were higher. 'In England in cotton factories 74% of the mill operatives consisted of women, young persons and children, and 26% or thereabout are adult males . . .' (Bengallee and Blaney's dissent note in Bombay Factory Commission Report of 1886, cited in Kydd, 1920). In Philadelphia, 'by 1840, two thirds to three quarters of the employees were women and children . . . the working conditions in Philapdelphia were so bad that a state investigation commission in 1837 called for, but did not get, the prohibition of employing children under the age of ten completely, and a ten hour day for those under sixteen' (Perrow, 2002:54).

The working hours were very long and working conditions quite harsh. The inhumanness of these conditions had in fact prompted the enactment of the Factories Act to restrict employment of women and children in the United Kingdom in mid-1880s. Even after implementation of Factory Legislation in Britain, the number of women workers was significantly higher than male workers during 1861–1921 the general reason being low wages of women workers over mens' wages (Kalra, 2000:85; Figure 4.8). Even in conditions of high prosperity, many of the mills (whether textile or steel) were characterised by wage decline and prolonged working hours (Perrow, 1991). Similar wage decline was found in the United Kingdom also. Perrow writes that whereas wage dependency covered about 20 per cent of the US population in 1820, by 1950 it had become 80–90 per cent.

Such increasing wage dependency merely meant that workers could not escape mill work but could only try to change an employer. However, labour mobility was severely restricted since blacklisting of workers who left services with or without cause was a widely prevalent practice among the employers. Such blacklisting prevented workers from easily switching employers. Perrow writes, '[B]lacklisting was extensively used in the first factories, the textile mills of New England where rural recruits from the northeast, then migrants from Ireland and then Canada were virtually indentured servants for their first year' (1991:732). 'The years 1845–46 a period of unprecedented profits, corresponded with a tightening up of regulations, including the one that an operative must serve 12 months at the same factory or not be employed by any factory' (Perrow, 1991:740). In the United Kingdom, workers were forbidden from changing employers. The Master-Servant Act made it a penal offence (Naidu and Yuchtman, 2013). Employers acted as a concerted group and wage decline, working hours and labour discipline were enforced vigorously even in period of high profits (McIvor, 1996). Labour efficiencies were paramount for the employers and Taylorian scientific management practices were widely followed. Workers' human needs mattered less. In the United States in 1880s, 'A Holyoke manager found his hands "langurous" in the early morning because they had breakfasted. He tried working them without breakfast and got 3000 more yards of cloth a week made' (A Massachusetts Senate document report, cited in Perrow, 1991:740).

The mills were highly unsafe places with poor and/or nonexistent protection for workers. Accidents were common place, whether it was textile mills, railways or steel mills. Kydd writing about the history of the Factories Act in the United Kingdom says that it took dedicated efforts and much advocacy and campaigning on behalf of workers by trade unions and sympathisers to introduce the

Factories Act that offered a modicum of protection for workers. In the United States, about a quarter of the iron and steel industry workers were injured during 1910, 'nearly 25% of the recent immigrants employed at the Carneige south works were injured or killed each year between 1907 and 1910' (Perrow, 1991:741 citing Guttman, 1977). The courts however ruled in favour of employers and attributed accidents to workers' carelessness.

Management historians like Wren (2005) and CSR historians like Carroll (2008), Marens (2004) and Perrow (1991, 2002) suggest that the emerging factory system in both the United Kingdom and the United States was facing severe criticism for its employment practices: employment of women and children, long hours, poor wage rates and poor safety. In the United States by late 1800s, there was growing hostility towards big business and their extractive practices. 'The vast increases in production and wealth brought about by industrialisation had neither abolished poverty nor made men more equal' (George, 1879; cited in Hall, 1987:9). Carroll (2008:21) says: '[R]eformers in both countries perceived the factory system to be the source of numerous social problems, including labour unrest, poverty, slums and child and female labour.'

Wren points out that certain employers with their humanitarian beliefs worked during this early industrial period for the welfare of workers leading to an 'uneven mixture of humanitarianism, philanthropy, and business acumen'. Industrialists such as John Patterson of National Cash Register pursued worker welfare and factory town movements and the approach was known as welfare capitalism. These factory towns were characterised by providing living facilities for workers. These facilities had hospital clinics, shops, bathhouses, lunch-rooms and also recreational facilities (Perrow, 2002; Hall, 1987; Carroll, 2008; Wren, 2005). Such 'welfare capitalism embraced a wide variety of possibilities, ranging from the exploitative company towns of the textile and mining regions through more open-ended provisions of health care and insurance, education, pensions, and profit sharing plans for workers...' (Hall, 1987:13). But such welfare practices were contested legally. The emerging legal frameworks specified employer roles and employee rights, private gain and public benefit.

Courts quickly began to privilege shareholder's interest as paramount in business enterprise, relegating welfare of other stakeholders to a peripheral space. An 1883 case in the United Kingdom involved the West Cork Railroad company that wanted to compensate its workers for job losses that were caused by the dissolution of the company. However, Justice Byron presiding over the case ruled that 'charity had no business at the table of the board of directors and that they could spend the company's money only for purposes of carrying on business' (Wren, 2005; cited by Carroll, 2008:21).

At the same time, courts did permit efforts by managements and employers to build churches, schools and libraries for the employees. The argument in favour of these initiatives was that they improved industrial relations and therefore benefitted the company. Records of R. H. Macy of New York show that the company was contributing assistance to social agencies like orphan asylums etc. (Carroll, 22–23). Thus, there were some cases where businesses participated in social causes through philanthropy or even direct worker welfare even though many of these did not have the necessary legal sanction. A research report in 1999 by Sophia Muirhead (cited in Carroll, 2008) concluded that the period from 1870 to 1930 in the United States could be considered as one of a pre-legalisation of corporate participation in welfare and philanthropy. Company benefit was to be paramount in determining engagement with other stakeholders of the corporation. Subordination of all other interests to capital and delineation of charity was very much evident and mediated by jurisprudence.

Developments in trust laws in England differentiated between trusts set up to benefit specific groups and those set up for public at large. The former were considered private trusts and the latter as public charitable trusts. Eventually, it is these public charitable trusts that became the legally accepted forms of public giving. In England, '[R]evisions and new statutes were concentrated first in the 1860s, and again in the period from 1887–1894, and then in 1914 and 1925. The legal definition of charity was descended from an Elizabethan statute of 1601 which had outlined a variety of practices encompassed by charity in its popular sense, as well as a general notion of purposes beneficial to the community' (Birla, 2009:69). They also articulated a change in the object of philanthropy from that of a community located in space and time to an abstract public.

In the United States, legislative and jurisprudential interventions by 1820s were differentiating between private and public purposes and making contractual logics central. In the Dartmouth College case in 1819, the judge ruled against government changing the charter of the college grant. He stated that the college charter was a 'contract' between the donors and the corporation, i.e. the college (Hall, 1987). This led to the emergence of corporate charters as a sphere autonomous from government to be governed only by private contractual considerations. In fact it is these jurisprudential concepts that informed the mercantile laws enforced in India by the British.

In this scenario, trade unions and other associational forms became more important in securing middle class and worker interests. Businessmen increasingly realised that their dominant position in society was being challenged and in order to secure their positions, they would have to accept that 'capitalism along with the large bureaucratic organisation would only aggravate the inequality of condition' and therefore there was a need to create '. . . a rhetoric and a set of institutions that would dramatically equalize (or appear to equalize) opportunity and an ethos of service that would invest social, economic and political hierarchies at all levels with a sense of common purpose' (Hall, 1987:10). In the United States accompanying these jurisprudential developments was the growing importance of the organisational style of the Progressives with their emphasis on expertise derived from education and bureaucratic organisation which had itself been derived from templates provided by Evangelical efforts over the previous century. This organisational style affected all facets of organised activity – government, business and social work (Hall, 1987:11).

The growing inequality and civic frustrations of the period provided the impetus for the large foundations of the twentieth century. While earlier philanthropic trusts and organisations were being set up for specific purposes like houses for orphans, hospitals for the sick and schools and colleges for education, early 1900s saw the emergence of grant making foundations as a new form of business philanthropy. As Hall (1987:11) explains:

> [T]he foundation differed from previous eleemosynary vehicles in three major ways. First, its purpose was open-ended; rather than being devoted to some particular aim like better education or healthcare, the foundation included within its purposes any and all of the charitable uses covered by the Statute of Charitable Uses. Second, it performed its charitable purpose by giving money rather than by operating institutions. Third, although the process of money giving was to be entrusted to a board of self-perpetuating trustees, the identification of worthy aims was to be performed by a staff of expert individuals.

It is in this manner that the foundations such as the Rockefeller foundation and the Carnegie foundation were set up in early 1900s. These foundations believed that philanthropy should not simply be palliative by providing relief, but work with and influence public policy to prevent pauperism and other such social problems. Business philanthropy in effect transformed into think tank–based advocacy and lobbying.

Tales of wanderlust

Our explorations into the messy past tell us tales of struggles – struggles between native custom and modernity; between human ethics and amoral market logic; communitarian governance and colonial might. It becomes apparent that the trajectories and notions of business, responsibility and impetus for business philanthropy have been different in India and the West. Whereas pursuit of reputation, honour, character and the material opportunities thereof seem to have prompted philanthropic and responsible behaviours amongst Indian businessmen, this does not appear to have been a priority in the West. It also becomes apparent that different motives governed workplace and worker management practices of Indian businessman and Western businessman. It draws our attention to the civilisational violence that was perpetrated on Indian culture and society through eurocentric governance and jurisprudential doctrines and practices in order to serve imperial and colonial interests.

Since reputation, honour and character are all contextually configured dimensions, indigenous mercantile practices and policy were characterised by shifting and flexible conventions which were subject to the jurisdiction of practitioners and their specific occupational ethics and *jati* ethics. By incorporating the human, family and community into these ethics, this mechanism reigned in unbridled capital accumulation. The mechanism created a basis for conversation and negotiation amongst unequal actors in society because even though one actor had 'wealth' to offer, the other had 'respect' to offer. It created a mutual interdependence between wealthy business people and the other members of society including workers and communities, providing a material anchor for pursuing ethical and honourable business and engaging in charity and philanthropy. Fungibility of reputational and economic capital because these were porous public-private spaces ensured that intentions became realised behaviours in society. This provided a social control mechanism of business since it was not autonomous from society. In this mechanism, responsibility was not an icing on the business cake but an ingredient in the dough that made the business cake.

> The civilisational mission of British rule as manifest in its legal and jurisprudential doctrines challenged the authority of these conventions in two ways: first, by rendering them directly subject to personal law . . . and second, by imposing contractual models on practices not easily relegated to personal law . . . moreover the public/private divide also established a distinction between legitimate and illegitimate trade . . . vernacular market practices either were tolerated as alternatives to modern market ethics, or were criminalized.
>
> (Birla, 2009:14–15)

By illegitimising and illegalising customary practices of fund movement between business and charitable pursuits, the change dealt a severe blow to the capital management practices of native business communities. The governance and civilisational mission of legal doctrines presented the new regime of contracts as the 'superior and more efficient' mode of market governance which eventually had to replace non-modern reputational mechanisms of the native. This change thus reduced every market participant to a single dimension – his/her capacity for capital and thus put in place a permanent hierarchy. This shift aided by the notion of the 'abstract public' taking over the 'community', rendered all other dimensions of human existence – character, nobility, honesty, family, relationships, obligations, need – insignificant.

This drove deep fractures into the mechanisms of mutual governance and wholistic existence that had been in vogue in India. The insignificance of this wholistic existence in modern life robbed customary performance of local sovereignty, honour and responsible business of its material basis of mutual interdependence, thereby transforming such native custom into an individually pursued spiritual mechanism devoid of any responsibility towards workers and communities. With reputation losing its performativity in the new regime, there was nothing that communities and workers could use as a counter to the might of capital, they became necessarily '*have-nots*' of capital who depended on the '*goodwill*' of wealth for earning incomes. If civilisational mission illegitimised and illegalised native custom and mercantile practice, the imperial interest stifled native business. Thus, we can begin to comprehend the chief transformation in notions and practices of responsibility in Indian business, i.e.

1. Traditional notions and practices of responsibility in Indian business which have been silenced, illegalised and impeded, i.e.

    a. Responsibility as the ethical conduct of business – socio-cultural-economic-political life of the businessman to establish character and reputation – making logic of capital accumulation and profit making subserviant to human and societal concerns in the form of *dharma* or righteous conduct

    b. Spatio-temporally specific communities as the public who had a clear *locusstandi* to make claims on and negotiate with business owners and give respect

    c. Decentralised, embodied, negotiable and flexible systems of management and governance that imbued actors of all levels and spheres with agency and made reputational pursuit possible

    d. Wholistic embodied actor centricity that interpenetrated and interconnected multiple domains of civilised life providing material anchor and countervailing power to stakeholders to negotiate with business.

2. Colonisation and the encounter with Western modernity led to the creation of new practices, notions and institutions of responsibility amongst Indian business:

    a. Abstract public and abstract charity as against righteous conduct, clearly demarcated public and private domains informed by rule compliance as against conduct

    b. Compliance to universal, formal rules against contingent understanding

    c. The privileging of a singular hierarchy of capital and denial of agency to various levels of hierarchy

    d. Modern notions of 'well-being' and 'social development'.

Consequently, by the dawn of independence in India, Indian business had transitioned to the coexistence of centuries side-by-side. Modern, customary and hybrid notions and practices of responsibility became the characteristics of Indian business. It is in the fertile ground of these struggles, some of which have defeated custom, some others the colonial might and yet others which are still being fought that modern CSR takes root in contemporary post-colonial India. We shift our focus to this playing out of 'modern CSR' in post-colonial India in Chapter 3.

Notes

1 Though the term guilds has often been used to designate srenis, there are some essential differences between srenis of ancient India and European guilds. For instance, the leadership of Indian srenis was elected.
2 See D. Lorenzen, 'Who invented Hinduism?', Comaprative Studies in Society and History, 2000 for more on the emergence of the identification of Hinduism as a category.
3 Report on Bombay Mills by Mr John Robertson of Glasgow. Cited in Morris (1965:27).
4 It is worth contrasting this concern with the views of the British coal authority.
5 Both Tariff Board and Fawcett Committee were committees formed by the British to deal with Indian industry.
6 Wider public opinion in India and in Britain looked at the Factories Act being imposed in India as a mechanism to restrict Indian manufacturing and protect Lancashire (see Kydd, 1920) There is a reference to a petition submitted to the Secretary of the Government by about 5,500 workers led by Narayan Lokhande asking for a regulation of working hours. However, it is suspect whether Lokhande carried the backing of workers at large. 'But his influence derived more from the Government of Bomaby's willingness to seek his advice and accredit his status as a spokesman for labour than from the strength of his popular following. Thus in 1892, the Inspector of Factories had observed that although Lokhande rather grandly "describes himself as President of the Bombay Mill-Hands Association, that Association has no existence as an organized body, having no roll of membership, no funds and no rules. I understand that Mr. Lokhanday simply acts as Volunteer Advisor to any mill-hand who may come to him' Chandavarkar,1994:427).

Chapter 3

Where are we going?

Unless globalisation works for all, it will work for nobody'.
– Kofi Annan

On 31 January 1999, Kofi Annan the then Secretary General of the United Nations, addressed business leaders gathered at the Davos World Economic Forum. Laying the foundation for United Nations Global Compact (UNGC) he said:

> I propose that you, the business leaders gathered in Davos, and we, the United Nations, initiate a global compact of shared values and principles, which will give a human face to the global market. . . . The problem is this. The spread of markets outpaces the ability of societies and their political systems to adjust to them . . . such an imbalance between the economic, social and political realms can never be sustained for very long. . . . Finally, I choose these three areas [labour standards, human rights, and environment] because they are ones where I fear that, if we do not act, there may be a threat to the open global market, and especially to the multilateral trade regime. . . . But in the global market, people do not yet have that confidence [that in the end some minimum standards will prevail]. Until they do have it, the global economy will be fragile and vulnerable – vulnerable to backlash from all the 'isms' of our post-cold-war world: protectionism; populism; nationalism; ethnic chauvinism; fanaticism; and terrorism.[1]

This short extract from Annan's speech captures within it a five decade long struggle in the West to govern businesses and thus the trajectory of modern CSR. The UNGC was finally formed in December 2000 with 50 founding members. The UNGC proposed a code of conduct with ten principles drawn from the UN Declaration on Human Rights, International Labour Organisation's Declaration on Fundamental Principles and Rights at Work, Rio Declaration on Environment and Development and UN Convention Against Corruption. Businesses becoming members of UNGC voluntarily followed its code of conduct principles. In the following years, UNGC adopted the Global Reporting Initiative (GRI) as the reporting framework.

Currently, after seven decades since the Second World War, regulating business implies businesses voluntarily following GRI and UNGC's Code of Conduct. These have become a de facto global standard on and the most widely accepted practice of CSR. How did this framework come to be the global standard? Were India's struggles different from the West? Why did *we* (India) become one of the first signatories to UNGC, and, still introduce a mandatory 2 per cent CSR spend? Let us explore these questions in the next few pages. We will probably not have as much difficulty as we had in exploring the past because most of this is recent development. Let us continue to look at the Western route to CSR and then juxtapose the Indian experience against it.

Arriving at CSR: Western route

The formation of UNGC along with GRI framework–based reporting represents a key landmark in Western efforts to regulate businesses for responsibility. How do these international efforts at responsibility connect with the view among scholars and practitioners that CSR emerged in the United States? Well, even though international efforts to govern businesses' international commerce were being made since the Second World War, these efforts were heavily influenced by the American experience of regulating businesses to be responsible. Within the United States, the home of modern CSR, large corporations enjoyed an unparalleled autonomy free from institutional and government controls. Nowhere else in the West, whether the United Kingdom or continental Europe, did such degree of autonomy exist for businesses. Neither state nor unions had effective restraints on corporate action (Marens, 2013; Perrow, 2002; Hall, 1987).

Enjoying this autonomy and free hand implied that American businesses had to voluntarily 'manage their workplace power in the interest of productivity, labour peace and ultimately social legitimacy . . . perceptions of how well firms treated their employees helped shape consumer and political judgments' (Marens, 2013:455–56). Such practices lead to the construction of social responsibility of business, as 'voluntarily pursuing welfare' of workers and others. Voluntarism defined American business-society relations. Such voluntariness has become the substance that has informed all efforts to govern business practices even transnationally.

In broader international commerce we notice that an attempt was made to monitor and regulate international commerce by proposing an organisation similar to the UN. This attempt began with the signing of the Havana charter in 1948 for the establishment of International Trade Organisation. However, the charter was not ratified by American Congress because it permitted the proposed trade organisation to intervene in the domestic economy. Eventually with the absence of the International Trade Organisation as proposed in the charter, the General Agreement on Tariffs and Trade (GATT) became the global mechanism for monitoring and coordinating trade. This eventuality had enormous implications for social regulation of business. Article 7 of the Havana charter had specifically addressed issues of labour standards. It stated: '[T]he members recognise that unfair labour conditions, particularly in production for export, create difficulties in international trade, and accordingly each member shall take whatever action may be appropriate and feasible to eliminate such conditions within its territory.'[2] The charter incorporated references to ILO standards.

But with the coming in of GATT, labour and social issues were firmly placed outside commerce and outside UN involvement (Hamdani and Ruffing, 2015; WCL, 2004). GATT's treatment of social and environmental issues as extra-commercial was in a sense an extension of the American way of regulating business as autonomous actors in the market. Subsequent efforts over the next 50 years by multilateral agencies, nations, NGOs and businesses to regulate corporate activity yielded only voluntary regulation, a tribute to the American version of responsibility as a voluntary pursuit of certain forms of welfare (Marens, 2013).

Politics of extraction and its governance

As early as 1962, developing countries became important sites of multinational activity, especially in the natural resource extraction industry (WCL, 2004). The southern nations desired better consideration of their interests in investments being made by Western TNCs. A UN Resolution (no. 1803) in 1962 included several references to multinational corporations. Following this, with the setting up of United Nations Conference on Trade and Development (UNCTAD) in 1964, another step was taken to reconnect international trade with issues of development and address the concerns of Southern nations for equitable treatment (WCL, 2004). Steps were taken in the direction of multilateral oversight of TNC operations through the setting up of the Economic and Social Council (ECOSOC) in 1974 under UN. ECOSOC provided a special UN interface 'Centre on Transnational Corporations' for interacting with TNCs (Hamdani and Ruffing, 2015:28). In spite of Western skepticism and resistance towards it, the Centre researched into TNC activities in host countries, especially developing countries and found several areas of criticism, some of which were identified for the first time. Tax avoidance, transfer pricing issues, labour abuses, collaborations with apartheid regime, bribery, corruption all came to the fore. But the critical stance of the Centre had led to TNC discontent and impeded subsequent work of the Centre on mandatory principles of TNC conduct (Hamdani and Ruffing, 2015:29). In the face of opposition, the Centre had then recommended that a voluntary Code of Conduct could serve as a useful mechanism to govern the activities of TNCs: 'as an instrument of moral persuasion strengthened by the authority of international organisations and public opinion'. It hoped that the 'code of conduct of the United Nations constituted a unique opportunity that transnational corporations would not let go of' (cited in WCL, 2004). The Centre hoped to develop one such voluntary code by 1978.

While UN was attempting to include developing country interests and socio-political concerns into international trade, the International Chamber of Commerce, which represented corporate interests, published the 'Guide for International Investments' in 1972. It argued that a binding code of conduct would hinder international investments. Organisation for Economic Co-operation and Development (OECD) served as a useful rallying point for the industrialised countries (home to all the TNCs) who were constantly facing developing country opposition in the UN. These industrial countries and their TNCs adopted more convenient and liberal OECD guidelines and policies for their businesses. In a manner that conflated national interest with corporate interest, these countries resisted efforts mandating responsible conduct and in June 1976, adopted in the OECD, the *Guideline principles on international investments and multinational enterprises*. These guidelines effectively limited the control of TNCs (WCL, 2004:11). OECD position impacted ILO resolutions and eventually both OECD and ILO declarations privileged employers' rights over employee rights (WCL, 2004). These declarations along with their background negotiations firmly put in place a preference for voluntary codes over any mandatory responsible conduct for TNCs, whether it was labour issues, human rights or environment that integrated responsibility into pursuit of business.

With advances in communication and transportation technologies, the oligopolistic consolidation of TNCs after 1970s accelerated. Since the late 1970s, global trade and investment came to be increasingly dominated by TNCs. In 1971 there were 333 TNCs and one-third of these had assets over US$1 billion. By 1992, the top 100 TNCs had over US$3.4 trillion in global assets, of which US$1.3 trillion were outside home countries. Between 1988 and 1993 worldwide FDI stock grew from US$1.1 to US$2.1 trillion (Greer and Singh, 2000). In the 1992 restructuring at UN, the Centre for Transnational Corporations lost its independent status. In lieu of the Centre, a new Division on Transnational Corporations and Investment was set up to promote foreign direct investment by TNCs.

Since the 1990s, foreign investment into less developed countries increased steadily, becoming significantly more than multilateral aid. From US$50 billion in 1992, foreign investments jumped to US$71 billion in 1993 and US$80 billion in 1994. During this period, public investments in developing world also declined. According to the World Bank in 1990, in the developing countries, public investment reduced from US$60 billion to US$50 billion and private investment (bulk of it was TNC investments) increased from US$30 billion to US$300 billion (Hu, 2006 citing Wolfensohn). Weakened and driven by structural adjustment programmes, many Third World countries began '*queuing up to attract multinationals*' (The Economist, 1993) after adopting liberal governance regimes.[3]

For TNCs, these countries of the Third World '*offer(ed) not just the potential for market expansion but also lower wages and fewer health and environmental regulations than in the North*' (Greer and Singh, 2000), both of which attracted TNCs to set up manufacturing bases in the developing world.[4] The globalisation of business thrived in a policy regime that promoted international investments and trade flows. In the absence of a global regulation and oversight, policy regime governing international business took the form of over 2,500 bilateral investment treaties, and several more multilateral agreements, all of which expanded the legal rights of TNCs (Ruggie, 2008; Sikka, 2011).

> [W]hile providing legitimate protection to foreign investors, these treaties also permit(ed) those investors to take host States to binding international arbitration, including for alleged damages resulting from implementation of legislation to improve domestic social and environmental standards – even when the legislation . . . [applied] uniformly to all businesses, foreign and domestic.
>
> (Ruggie, 2008:5)

Towards the end of the millennium, 'estimates suggested that the 300 largest TNCs owned or controlled at least one-quarter of the entire world's productive assets, worth about US\$5 trillion' (Greer and Singh, 2000). Though these TNCs were based predominantly in Western Europe, North America, and Japan, their operations spanned the globe. On an average, the largest TNCs operated in over a 100 countries worldwide. Annual sales and budgets of large TNCs exceeded the GDPs of many countries. Thanks to TNC size, many sectors like oil, auto, pharmaceuticals, electronics and chemicals saw oligopolistic consolidation making TNCs among the most powerful actors in global political-economy, more powerful than many sovereign states.

Cross-national variations in laws along with the weak bargaining position of developing countries meant that TNCs were leading the export and import of technologies and substances banned due to their health, safety and environmental hazards. For instance, '25 per cent of total pesticide exports by TNCs from the US in the late 1980s were chemicals that were banned, unregistered, cancelled, or withdrawn in the US itself' (Greer and Singh, 2000). Adding to these business strategies of TNCs were industrial disasters of the 1980s and 1990s. In 1984, methyl isocyanide leaked from the Bhopal plant of Union Carbide. It was the world's worst industrial disaster until then and had killed several thousands immediately and led to several thousands more being permanently disabled. In 1989, Exxon-Valdez's oil tanker hit a reef leading to a spill in

Alaska, one of the largest in North American history. It was the largest ever spill until the 2010 Deepwater Spill off the Gulf coast of the United States. Exxon-Valdez spill even led to the creation of the first credit default swap with JP Morgan agreeing to provide a line of credit for covering Exxon's damage award![5] While a long fought legal battle reduced the punitive damages significantly for Exxon, the spill did much to sensitise public, consumers and managers alike to the cause of environmental consciousness.

In Europe too, the 1980s were years of much protest against the health and safety risks caused by industrial activity. Asbestos became an important rallying symbol. The global asbestos empire was owned by Schmidheinys. Workers and communities across the globe who had created the Schmidheiny wealth were seeking compensation for the failing health conditions caused by asbestos air pollution.[6] Schmidheiny in consequence sold the business along with its liabilities and began advocating against asbestos.

Globalisation, along with neoliberal weakening of the state both in the developed countries and the developing countries consolidated the position of TNCs as the key actors in a global world and made regulating their activities even more important. In the absence of any government oversight over TNCs and the virtual stalemate that had been reached in international negotiations on the issue of a government or a multilateral agency led voluntary code of conduct, research findings of the UN Centre for Transnational Corporations, provided a strong impetus for private action to promote responsible business practices.

Private action and emergence of voluntary codes

In the United States, Joan Bavaria an investment banker realised that some investors were sensitive to social and environmental conduct of corporations and were interested in taking those into account in their investment decisions. To enable such investing, she founded the Trillium Asset Management Company in 1982 in the United States to provide advice on socially responsible investing (SRI).[7] SRI activities received a big fillip from the 1987 Brundtland Commission's report *Our Common Future*. This report became a pivot around which conversations on environment and sustainability got framed. Public awareness of environmentally irresponsible behaviours of oil, pharmaceutical and chemical companies provided the backdrop for investor-led private initiatives for encouraging responsibility such as Trillium. Trillium and Bavaria's efforts to influence capital markets towards building sustainable businesses led to the formation of Ceres, a coalition of business leaders and investors in 1989. Ceres and Trillium championed investment-driven notions of responsibility in North America while partnering with environmental organisations like Forest Stewardship Council, Conservation International, Sierra Club and Greenpeace. Ceres pioneered a business environmental reporting framework in the early 1990s to enable investors to make informed decisions. This framework came to be known as the GRI environmental and social reporting and accountability mechanism for business. Eventually GRI was integrated into the UN's Global Compact as the preferred reporting standard.[8]

Concurrently, the Rio Earth Summit was held in 1992 in view of Brundtland Commission's dire predictions that the world did not have enough resources to sustain its current rate of economic exploitation. The Summit aimed to discuss threats and strategies for action. Being conscious of the growing power of TNCs and the need for TNC participation in this endeavour, the Summit organisers invited Schmidheiny to coordinate business representation at the Summit. Schmidheiny's advocacy against asbestos and his highly influential global business empire gave him the credentials to lead business participation. Unfortunately though, honest discussion and action at the Summit was restricted, TNC power came to the fore and their efforts successfully managed to restrict proposals and discussions at the Rio Earth Summit in 1992 (Greer and Singh, 2000).

Nevertheless the Summit meant a success for Schmidheiny since this was the first time private businesses had participated in such an international forum. Post Summit, Schmidheiny went on to create the Business Council for Sustainable Development (which became WBCSD in 1995) and promoted the idea of *eco-efficiency* and environmental sensitivity inside the firm and provided road maps and advice on transforming business operations for achieving sustainability. Thus, by late 1980s and early 1990s with growing realisation that global resources were limited, environment and sustainability appeared as major issues of responsibility in debates on both sides of the Atlantic. Along with eco-efficiency, notions like *green consumer* (1986) *environmental excellence* (1984) and *triple bottom line* (1994) all of which incidentally were proposed by the British author/activist John Elkington started gaining currency in business conversations on responsibility.

Whereas environment entered responsibility debates through investor, activist and scientific effort, human rights and labour issues entered debates on responsibility with activist efforts and consumer boycotts. The US$176 million law suit against Texaco for racial discrimination, and reports of labour exploitation in the outsourced production factories of Nike located in Vietnam, Indonesia and other Third World countries pulled the lid on labour issues in the 1990s.[9] If the United States was dealing with criticism on these issues, Europe was not far behind. Leading companies like IKEA and retail fashion brands sourcing production from Asian and Latin American countries were becoming alert to poor wages and living conditions of workers just like Nike and GAP.

Fair Trade movement to ensure fair returns to producers had taken root in Europe thanks to Oxfam's efforts. Starting with handicrafts in the 1960s it spread to agricultural commodities like coffee and cocoa by late 1980s and 1990s. Several labelling initiatives were launched to indicate ethical production practices followed by Fair Trade products. Globalisation of production had made the Third World the new shop floor of the world and labour issues generally meant labour in these global supply chains. Persistent global activism that threatened businesses prompted Bill Clinton, the then US President to convene the Apparel Industry Partnership, a voluntary code of conduct–based initiative for large apparel brands in 1996.

While the above efforts centred on labour issues, human rights issues came to the forefront through two shocking cases in the mid-1990s. The first was the execution of indigenous rights activist Ken Saro Wiva in Nigeria in 1995. Shell which drew oil from Nigeria did nothing to prevent the execution even though it had influence with the Nigerian regime. The incident led to widespread boycotts of Shell. Centred on local communities' resistance to state-sponsored violence in support of corporate extraction, this case drew renewed attention after 1970s, to the rights of indigenous and local communities to local resources and the nexus of corrupt governments and large global corporations in resource extraction (Pilkington, 2009). The second was the 1997 court case against the South African government by pharmaceutical giants Glaxo-Smithklime, Bristol-Meyers-Squibb and 37 others charging the government of violating patent rights to promote generic drug making for treating AIDS patients.[10] This case focused on patient rights versus patent rights and put the spotlight on corporations' greed for profits (Hoen et al., 2011). It opened up the debate to intellectual property rights on a range of issues like technology and indigenous knowledge.

Towards the end of the millennium all these diverse concerns around labour rights, human rights and environmental abuse converged. The Seattle demonstrations of 1999 that disrupted the WTO summit marked a watershed in the rising global discontent against Western corporations. Business risks associated with climate change, environmental abuse and human and labour rights violations became significant for corporations. The scene became ripe for adopting codes of responsible business practices. Enlightened self-interest of businesses in the form of 'social license to operate' became the mainstay of the argument. Compliance with voluntary self-regulatory codes of conduct became essential to the process of attesting to a business's responsibility intentions. The UNGC was the outcome of these pressures.

Supplementing these voluntary governance initiatives, were notions of strategic CSR. Strategic CSR sought to provide a managerial logic in support of pursuing responsibility. Ideas like 'shared value' and 'co-creation' (Porter and Kramer, 2006) and 'fortune at the bottom of the pyramid' (Prahalad, 2006) advocated that businesses could develop a strategic approach towards CSR by mitigating negative value chain social and environmental impacts and enhancing positive impacts. CSR was positioned as the new source of competitive advantage.

GRI, Triple Bottom Line and shared value notions fed on each other and took on the status of the norm. Accompanying the logic of codes was an emphasis on disclosures. Disclosures were viewed as means of empowering investors and society at large. Some European governments like France and Britain legally mandated disclosures of social and environmental impacts and processes. Britain even set up a ministry for corporate social responsibility. Disclosures, audits, GRI reporting together with SRI led to the emergence of rankings like Reptrak which ranked businesses on social and environmental performance.

These developments and SRI growth were buttressed by the creation of stock market indices like FTSE4Good, Dow Jones Sustainability Index and Nikko Ecofund. By 2000s, SRI made up about 12 per cent of the US$19.9 trillion global investment assets (Hu, 2006). It grew from US$4 billion in 1995 to US$121.6 billion in 2016 in the United States.[11] In Europe too it grew from just four funds during

1980–84 to 313 funds by 2002 (Hu, 2006). SRI also gave rise to shareholder activism and ethical investors used their stake to introduce discussions on responsibility into the Board.

Being responsible: following voluntary codes of conduct

With UNGC, voluntary code of conduct became the new norm of business responsibility. But UNGC code is not the only voluntary code of conduct. A 2003 World Bank estimate said that there could be over a 1,000 codes of conduct in existence (cited in Hu, 2006). These codes of conduct often referred to as the social contract made by a business are written policies which specify how the business would operate. Codes could also be a statement of principles of intent which were designed to indicate the commitment a corporate was making to society. These codes have covered issues of labour, human rights, environment and governance to varying degrees. Sometimes these codes have specified precise rules of action which are to be made applicable to supplier factories (Hu, 2006).

Having and following codes of conduct has become the most popular means of TNC's responsible behaviour. A 2001 OECD study (cited in Hu, 2006) showed that companies believed that compliance to codes gave them substantial business benefits. Often these codes are developed by the company for itself (48 per cent) or by business associations like Athletic Footwear Association, International Council of Toy Industries (37 per cent). Some codes are developed by multi-stakeholder initiatives involving NGOs like the Tea Sourcing Partnership. World Bank's (2003) analysis of 107 codes finds that ISO 14000 and GRI standards have the highest influence on corporate codes and over 40 per cent of TNCs follow them. This is followed by WBCSD and ILO conventions, i.e. about 40 TNCs follow these (WCL, 2004). Another OECD study of 246 codes shows that 60 per cent refer to labour issues and 59 per cent to environmental issues (cited in WCL, 2004). A 2003 ILO study of 239 codes finds that '*less than 20% of enterprises made reference to*' fundamental ILO standards (WCL, 2004).

Initially, corporations extended the job of monitoring supplier compliance to ethical codes to their statutory auditors, i.e. the accounting firms. The big accounting firms became part of monitoring and auditing. Yet corporations faced continued criticism because the auditing firms were being paid by corporations, creating a conflict of interest. Also these auditors did not have the skills necessary to conduct social and environmental audits. At the same time, stories of business irresponsibility, whether it was the factories producing Apple products or toys for Mattel or coffee for Nestle continued to make headlines. Compliance to codes became the new bone of contention between activists and businesses. Efforts to address continuing criticism led to the increasing importance of multi-stakeholder initiatives (MSIs) and the rise of the third-party auditing industry.

The third party auditing industry is today a US$80 million industry (AFL-CIO, 2015). The monitoring industry essentially has experts located in the West who liaise between Western TNCs and grassroot monitoring agencies located in the Third World who survey production sites. Here the costs of obtaining audit certifications are borne by supplier firms thereby avoiding a conflict of interest. Suppliers bear this cost even when they do not have any assurance of purchase from buyers because such compliance to codes has become a de facto standard for consideration by Western buyers. Activists and worker unions have severely criticised voluntary codes for their inability to protect workers.

> . . . They are generally drawn up in general terms, which leaves moreover room for their stakeholders to interpret them in the way they want. They very often make reference to national laws and rules, which in a lot of cases were reviewed downward under pressure from international financial institutions and/or are inferior to the demands of the law and rules of the countries of origin of multinational companies. Furthermore, concerning freedom of association, (C87) and the right to collective bargaining (C.98), many are the national laws, that limit these rights.
>
> (WCL, 2004)

Critics contend that auditors and monitors only identified the easy problems, rarely spoke to workers. Audits often did not lead to significant improvements on ground since they did not impact TNC purchasing policies. Multi-stakeholder initiatives too remained flawed because, active involvement of unions and NGOs in governance was prevented and disputes were often resolved in favour of TNCs (AFL-CIO, 2015). Since suppliers failing to make the audit were simply removed or blacklisted, audits added a new burden on factories indirectly impacting workers adversely. One of the most glaring examples of such persistent struggles is the response to the Rana Plaza tragedy in Bangladesh in which over a 1,000 people including workers and factory managers lost their lives. Activism after the tragedy led to the formation of a mandatory fire safety accord which made TNCs like Walmart responsible for providing long-term financial support to help supplier firms make transition and Bangladesh government legally responsible for enforcement. Such legally backed enforceable agreements were now gaining more acceptance in the form of Global Framework Agreements that unions negotiate with TNCs.

Charity reinvented

With UNGC and GRI becoming key markers of CSR globally and the global presence of TNCs, pursuit of responsibility also got tied in with the achievement of Millennium Development Goals (MDGs) and human development in the less industrialised countries. It has been argued that TNCs with their resources and market power can positively impact governments and communities and enable them to realise the broader goals of human and social development as specified in the MDGs. Large-scale corporate philanthropy again became attractive. After decades of lull following the Rockefellers and Carnegies, the new generation billionaires like Bill Gates of Microsoft announced the donation of their personal wealth for philanthropic purposes.

New age corporations were setting up departments and foundations to pursue such social support and philanthropic objects as a part of their CSR activities. This was the reworking of the 'charity principle' (Kolk and Tulder, 2002) of early nineteenth-century West. This reworked charity principle is driven by the desire to do good and does not come from any sense of duty or obligation either religious or legal. In the past, charity was anchored in the absence of state social security systems and was 'based on the idea that more fortunate people within society should take care of the less fortunate' (L'Etang, 1995:130 cited in Kolk and Tulder, 2002:9). Early nineteenth century also saw the mention of a trusteeship principle which implied that managers were trustees of general interest. As such current philanthropy and charity has been a little different. Even though trusteeship principle has gained little traction in current times and managers have remained agents and trustees of capital, giving by the wealthy has become the new standard of ethical consciousness and social power of global business leaders and yet another facet of CSR.

Thus modern CSR has been the outcome of a politics of extraction and a resistance to this politics. The trajectory of 'modern CSR' in the West leading to the UNGC and voluntary codes has been formed amidst struggles to govern and make accountable a process of corporate extraction and accumulation, in pursuit of maximum profits. 'Modern CSR' therefore involves a myriad of concepts from sustainability to business ethics to corporate social performance to social accountability to socially responsible investing. In spite of limitations, compliance to voluntary codes and voluntary disclosures has come to be the mainstay of modern CSR. This has limited the trajectory of modern CSR to a governance of the organisation at its boundary in the form of an incentive granting or withdrawing capital and resources. The work organisation itself and internal management and practices of the organisation are left sufficiently decoupled and insulated. Disclosures ostensibly are meant to cover internal processes, but they too privilege markets and activists as the agents of responsibility. Internal stakeholders have limited power and scope to influence the issue and thus business can continue as usual.

Indian trajectory: from nation building to image building

In contrast to the Western trajectory of autonomous businesses pursuing extractive profits and society's attempts to regulate that, Indian business post-independence in 1947 traversed sober terrains. The single biggest challenge facing the country at the dawn of independence was building a nation out of a colony; even political consolidation was not complete let alone economic and social. At the dawn of independence the leadership of the country, in whose hands lay the destiny of the nation, was constituted by two key actors – nationalist leaders, who later became politicians of different parties and businessmen.[12] The general business sentiment combined national quest for well-being and pride, with commerce. Walchand Hirachand, the noted industrialist of the time addressing Dena Bank in Sholapur in 1943 said:

> I long for the day when we shall have India-made motor-cars, locomotives, railway coaches, tramways, buses, aeroplanes, ships, electrical goods, machinery, and the thousand and one

things for which we have to depend on imports. When that consummation is realized, I assure you Gentleman, there will not be a beggar asking for alms. . . .
(Sundar, 2013:120 citing Khanolkar, 1969:xxxvii–xxxviii)

In fact a relationship between nationalist leaders and businessmen had been in existence for several decades and in anticipation of independence, the leading industrialists of the day met in Bombay and came up with the Bombay Plan in 1944. The Plan institutionalised the long-standing relationship between business and nationalist political leadership. Business families

for the first time, unhesitatingly aligned themselves with nationalist aspirations. Underlying the Bombay Plan was the idea of a close partnership between business and the state . . . the central premise of the Bombay Plan was that a national government would undertake the task of economic development in which business would be an equal partner.
(Kudaisya, 2014:97)

The Plan also expressed the intent of business community to share its prosperity and contribute to nation building.[13] The Plan envisaged a 130 per cent increase in per-capita agricultural output, 500 per cent increase in industry and 200 per cent increase in services over a 15-year period (Kudaisya, 2014). The plan envisaged a major role for the state in fostering capital and core goods industries. Paucity of private capital and an economy growth rate of around 3.5 per cent during the 1940s underlined the need for businesses to work with government in building the economic and industrial base of the country. Thus unlike West's autonomous corporations, Indian business was characterised by its openness to a planned and socialistic pattern of state-sponsored industrialisation. Their openness fit in with customary understanding of businessman as a socio-political actor.

Era of optimism: my country, my people

The Industrial Act of 1951 brought in licensing which regulated production capacities and management of industries in India. The government directed the location and pace of industrialisation. Industrial estates were set up to promote industrial development.

The Five Year Plans specified macroeconomic objectives for the country and direction of capital investments. A key feature of the planned socialistic pattern of growth was establishment of Public Sector Enterprises (PSEs).[14] Central PSE investment in 1951 was INR 290 million (Bhattacharya, 2006). The 1956 industrial policy resolution spelt out key objectives and roles that PSEs were expected to play in the socio-economy of the country. It included the following:

- To help in rapid economic growth and industrialisation of the country and create the necessary infrastructure for economic development
- To earn return on investment and thus generate resources for development, to promote redistribution of income and wealth;
- To create employment opportunities
- To promote balanced regional development
- To assist the development of small-scale and ancillary industries
- To promote import substitution, and save and earn foreign exchange for the economy (Bhattacharya, 2006:40)

Thus, PSEs by design had goals other than shareholder value maximisation as their objective functions. The 'social' had been inscribed into their founding logic, whether it was serving as the fulcrum in kick starting development in a remote and infrastructure poor area, or creating employment and tackling poverty or assisting in the attainment of nation's strategic objectives like energy security and financial inclusion. PSEs were a special feature of Indian business landscape (the West had fewer PSEs, the United States hardly had any).

Partnering such government-sponsored industrialisation with a social agenda were businessmen. The nation building sentiment was very much in evidence and anchored in their participation in employment generation and institution building. G. D. Birla, the most prominent of Indian businessmen of the time said, 'I am interested in anything that creates more wealth, more employment. I am a capitalist but I believe in socialism which means equal opportunity, more employment and a fairer standard of living for everyone. Socialism does not mean socializing poverty, but raising the quality of life' (Sundar, 2013:134 citing Ramanujam, 1993:91–2). He adds, in his foreword to *India Progressing*:

It has been the policy of the House of Birlas not to build up businesses just to accumulate capital, but to develop unexplored lines, harness the undeveloped resources of the country, promote know how, create skilled labour and managerial traits, spread education and add to the efforts of the leaders of the country, who throughout this period have been struggling to build a new, independent India, free from want, the scourge of unemployment, ignorance and disease.

(Sundar, 2013:121 citing Ramanujam, 1993:108)

Such aspirational talk was backed up by concrete action. Not only business expansion, but even setting of social and development institutions was actively pursued. Kasturbhai Lalbhai another industrialist who, as a person resisted ostentatious spending, nevertheless contributed his personal wealth liberally to spearhead the setting up of numerous educational, scientific and cultural institutions like Indian Institute of Management Ahmedabad, Physical Research Laboratory, Textile Industry's Research Association, Institute of Indology etc.

During these early years of independence, moral and religious sentiments also fused with commerce in a manner reminiscent of earlier eras. Right from colonial days, M. K. Gandhi had been advocating for the practice of trusteeship amongst businessmen. He spoke about it at every interaction with businessmen whether formal or informal. At a 1931 Federation of Indian Chamber of Commerce and Industry (FICCI) address he said, 'You should regard yourselves as trustees and servants of the poor. Your commerce must be regulated for the benefit of the toiling millions and you must be satisfied with earning an honest penny' (Sundar, 2013:132 citing Joshi, 1975:226).

The Gandhian notion of trusteeship drew its inspirations from customary beliefs of Indian society. It found resonance amongst many devout businessmen and they preferred to deploy their wealth for social benefits. As another Birla family member echoed the sentiment,

Profit cannot be an end in itself. If the river (business) has water (profit), it should be used for watering plants, setting up public water huts, offering it to Mahadeo, as well as for quenching the thirst of the people. It is then alone that profit making has any worth and meaning.

(Sundar, 2013:124 citing Taknet, 1996:52)

Lala Shri Ram of the Shriram group concurred, 'A person having wealth should not, merely because of his wealth, have status and power in life' (Sundar, 2013:124 citing Joshi, 1975:632). He adds in 1954:

> Employers should consider themselves as trustees of the country and I do feel that they would be taken as trustees by our people if they will practice self imposed austerity, lead simple lives, and invest the balance of their profits in expanding industry, and thus serve the country as trustees.
>
> (Sundar, 2013:132; Joshi, 1975:688)

Era of cleavages: discontent, dissent, deviance and development

The optimistic participatory attitude of business in the nation's future in early 1950s soon gave way to much discontent and dissatisfaction. Business optimism died out as 'autarchic features of economic policy became increasingly pronounced in independent India' (Kudaisya, 2014:97). Nehru, the first prime minister of India had remained a staunch critic of Gandhi's trusteeship notion. He believed in tighter control of business. He believed that since businessmen wielded enormous power in society they could not be left to their own will to be responsible (Sundar, 2013:165 citing Upadhyaya, 1976). The government had introduced a policy of very high tax regimes during 1950s. Income tax rates were over 75 per cent.[15] Capacities were limited by policy and the regime of high taxation, going upto 97.5 per cent in the 1970s made securing capital for reinvestment a problem. The government exercised price controls and volume controls. The licensing policy of the government which was meant to be sparingly used had become a tight noose on industrial activity breeding massive corruption. Products were reserved for industries like small and micro enterprises. Products like the Bajaj Scooter had a 10-year waiting period but licences were not granted to increase production capacity (Budhiraja et al., 2002). Business was increasingly under stress due to adverse relationships with the government. Within such unfavourable policy environment, business could be conducted generally through a violation of law.

Conduct and practice of business became tainted with illegality. Reputation, character or conduct of business/man and performance of business itself became divorced from each other. In this environment, which made responsible conduct of business difficult, some opportunist businessmen also sought to profit by hoarding, black marketing and cheating. Poor quality and customer irresponsiveness became new norms. Several investigations by the government through the Wanchoo committee, Mahavir Tyagi committee found that businessmen were evading tax. In this backdrop, one of the earliest conclaves to debate social responsibilities of businessmen was held in 1965 in Delhi. Jointly organised by India International Centre and Institute of Gandhian Studies, notion of trusteeship and its influence on redistribution of business surpluses, as well as the ethical conduct and practice of business were all debated under the guidance of Jayaprakash Narain. Public intellectuals of the time like Acharya Vinobha Bhave and Jaya Prakash Narain were the torch bearers of Gandhian notions of trusteeship during this time.

This was an extremely high-profile conference aimed at addressing important stressors in the business-government-society relationship attracting participation even from the prime minister and representation from policy-makers, business leaders, thinkers and trade union leaders (Mohan, 2001:110). The very fact that this conference was organised indicated the growing need to explicitly spell out social responsibility, thereby drawing it outside the realm of the individual family, business or businessman. Conference debates around the utility and meaning of trusteeship and its relationship with charity reflected the demarcation of charity as a non-economic activity in marked contrast to previous eras and a gradual demarcation of the public and private arenas. No wonder some of the participants strongly argued against seeing responsibility as charity (Sundar, 2013:181). Invoking a citizenship view of the enterprise, where the enterprise too was judged on its actions like other citizens, five days of intense deliberations at this conference led to a Declaration of Social Responsibility of Business. This declaration it was believed would be put up for open debate and discussion across the country. The declaration encapsulated the stakeholder view of business,

> responsibility to itself, to its customers, workers, shareholders and the community . . . every enterprise, no matter how large or small, must if it is to enjoy confidence and respect seek actively to discharge its responsibilities in all directions . . . and not to one or two groups, such as shareholders or workers, at

the expense of community and consumer. Business must be just and humane, as well as efficient and dynamic.

(Mohan, 2001:110)

The obligations were spelt out as

- Justice and fair play in all dealings;
- Making serious attempts at growth and development of all the factors or constituents of business from owners to consumers; utilization of surplus primarily for the above two purposes;
- Utilization of surplus, if at all left over, for any other social purpose deemed fit for assistance such as education, health and research.

(Sundar, 2013:181 citing Upadhyaya, 1976:94–5)

Following up on this conclave, J. R. D. Tata and Ramakrishna Bajaj launched the Fair Trade Practices Association in Bombay in 1966. The Association attempted to put together an ethical practice code and encourage its adoption amongst businesses. In some sense, this wholeness towards stakeholders evident in the declaration reflected custom, but in the emerging differentiation of economic, social and political domains; attempts were made to imbue the new secular logic of capital and enlightened self-interest into traditional understandings of a businessman's power and prestige. J. R. D. Tata speaking in 1969 added:

. . . let us face it, the reputation and image of private enterprise is far from being commensurate . . . hostility which this image of the private sector has generated in the minds of Government. . . . it is being increasingly denied the opportunities to play the full part of which it is capable. . . .

(Tata, 1986:40 cited in Sundar, 2013:182)

Ramakrishna Bajaj argued for enlightened self-interest within the business community and addressing the Maharashtra Chamber of Commerce in 1970 said:

The business community is an essential ingredient of our democratic society and it has a duty not only to create wealth but also to promote the ethical and social goals of the community. *Unless it fulfills both these functions and thereby plays its due*

*role as a responsible section, it will not be able to ensure its
own survival.*

(Bajaj, 1970:52 cited in Sundar, 2013:184,
emphasis added)

The great natural disasters and wars in the country during
1960s–1970s – famines in Bihar, tidal wave in Andhra Pradesh,
provided another opportunity for businessmen to reinvent their
customary understandings and put them in service of the nation and
society. These disasters had renewed interest in voluntary activity in
the country. Just as they had done during the nationalist struggle,
some people now dedicated their lives to social and rural development leading to the genesis of several 'voluntary organisations'
with expertise in working with rural communities to foster development and self-reliance. Organisations like Bhagavatula Charitable Trust, Urmul Trust and Bharatiya Agro Industries Foundation
were formed during this period. These organisations drew funds
from both philanthropists and formal donor agencies coming from
the West like Charities Aid Foundation, GTZ and Oxfam which
entered India with humanitarian and development aid.

Spiritually minded businessmen and those with a social con-
science and concern for society like Tatas, Birlas, Shroffs, Mafatlals
and many others supported these developmental activities. Several new trusts were set up during this period and they engaged in
community development activities (see Table 3.1). The noticeable
increase in quantum of charity by businessmen helped voluntary
organisations pursue their objects. By the end of 1980s, practices of
responsibility in India had experienced important shifts. Rural India
and livelihoods of rural communities had become more important
than building educational institutions and hospitals in cities. Businesses started considering a stakeholder approach for addressing
societal and/or governmental expectations in addition to the social
obligation approach. Businesses now contributed both funds and
managerial skills.

In form, this support to voluntary organisations appeared as a
continuation of pre-independence practice of institution building
and social development through philanthropy but, in essence, it
implied a radical departure. Unlike the past, it was firmly delinked
from everyday conduct of commerce as a way of life. If legalities of
endowments continuing from pre-independence period delinked
conduct and practices of big businesses in monetary flows, the

Table 3.1 Some philanthropic trusts formed during 1960–1980

Tatas	Sir Ratan Tata Trust, Sir Dorabji Tata Trust	Research centres, Schools
Jamnalal Bajaj	Jamnalal Bajaj Seva Trust	Education, community action
Birlas	Birla Education Trust, Hindustan Charitable Trust	Education
Lalbhai	Lalbhai Trust	Schools, research centres
Lala Shri Ram	Commercial Education Trust	Colleges
Singhanias	JK School Building Trust	Schools, colleges
Sir Annamalai	Annamalai University	College, hospital
Muruguppa	AMM Foundation	Hospitals and schools
Aegies Chemical	ANAR De foundation	Rural development
Excel	VRTI	Water harvesting, rural development
Lupin Labs	Foundation	Agriculture development

Source: Sundar (2000:238)

ethical, reputational relationship was severed to an even larger degree under the shadow of autarchic governmental controls and bureaucracy – what has come to be known as the '*licensing raj*' just like the '*British raj*'. Honest reputation or character, and business performance became detached. Corruption, black marketing and tax evasion, large and small, came to define the character of business communities. Notoriety and not honour became the trademark of business. The legal-bureaucratic framework was seeding the demarking of economics, society, religion and politics as rather independent domains and responsibility as something that was not natural to everyday business conduct but, as something extra directed at community, which had to be driven and incentivised by state.

In 1977, there was a 100 per cent tax incentive for contributing to charity for rural development and many businessmen contributed to this cause. While some well-minded businessmen funded NGOs or formed their own trusts and continued such activity even after tax incentive was withdrawn in 1983, others stopped their contributions. Many a businessman was known to have indulged in the formation of fake charitable trusts to avail tax exemptions and route the money back into business. The movement of funds between business and trusts was in a way a continuation of customary financial practices within Indian business communities that was illegalised during British period. The same law continued into post-independence period but it led to a loss of credibility of business community because it was the Indian government and not British that was getting defrauded. In addition, no significant social commitment could be associated with these new practices.

The delinking of reputational stock from the circuit of commerce and differentiation of the social and public life of a businessman had taken its toll and in response to Prime Minister Morarji Desai's call for business participation in rural development in 1978, only 70 business houses came forward (FICCI 1978 report, cited in Sundar, 2013:193). A survey of 39 companies in 1984 showed that 47 per cent spent for social development through company programmes and 30 per cent financed other organisations as aid (cited in Mohan, 2001).

Attenuated Custom – Internal Work Organisation: If the external interface of business with society was thus transformed, the internal organisation of work, i.e. management practices and employee relations were not untouched. But customary practices persisted to a much larger degree within the organisation, constituting the internal work organisation into a kind of borderland between custom and modernity, where custom survived but also got transformed. This borderland impacted workers and the other organisational stakeholders like managers, suppliers and customers differently given that the intensity of modernity's control over these groups varied due to different regulations.

Markowitz (2008) citing other economic historians like Bayly (1983) and Ray (1979) has emphasised the moral and family economy within which Indian business organisations operated. The logic of this moral and family economy prized family prestige over profit maximisation. Customary practices of work organisation centred on individual reputations and sharing continued to be important. '. . . [S]erious doubts are in order regarding a definition of the firm as a profit-maximizing agency in the Indian context' (Markowitz, 2008:154). Maintaining family like relations and flexibly catering to each other's needs was an important feature of such management practice. Whether it was a large business group or much smaller privately owned enterprises, similar personalised family relationship patterns were followed. Previous studies like that of economist Hazari (1966) had already pointed out that unlike the West, big business in India did not mean oligopoly. Bigness was more a function of economies of scale rather than market control.

In their book *World Class in India*, Ghoshal and Ramachandran (2002) profile several Indian businesses like Bajaj Auto, Hero Motors and Reliance. These companies differed on business strategies and product-market spaces, however, they had very similar organisational and managerial practices focused on personalised family-like relationships and trust with employees, suppliers or customers. Rahul Bajaj the head of Bajaj Auto lived in the workers' colony and had developed a reputation for holding the family together, concern for workers and helping his suppliers grow along with him. Several others like Kasturbhai Lalbhai set up businesses with the purpose of helping extended family members find a foothold as the primary motive (Tripathi, 1981). Similarly, Hero Motors too built its journey on strong relationships with suppliers and employees many of whom were known to the owner's family personally. Company management and owners participated in social events of employees and suppliers adding to their prestige and social standing. They worked with suppliers who were in trouble and helped suppliers establish themselves. As a senior manager put it:

> It however is a two way process. I know that if something goes wrong and my family is in trouble, the Ambanis would put the entire RIL corporate muscle behind them to support my family. And this is not restricted to the top. What they do at the top, I do to people down below. Often the issues are not big. For example, if a clerk's child is seriously sick, I send a car for him to use at that time. We practice this with our trade as well. I tell my trade-doing business with us is risk-free. If you lose, come back to us.
>
> (Ghoshal and Ramachandran, 2002:213)

Personal networks and negotiations informed networks, jobs and salaries. Recruitment was usually informal with existing managers and workers bringing in or recommending someone from their kith and kin, usually sons and daughters of employees or friends. Salaries and terms were decided with reference to norms and varied from person to person (Chaudhuri and Barman, 1981). Formal organisational hierarchy had little meaning. Communication frequently bypassed formal channels. Decisions were made informally and written policies were hard to find. Senior managers as well as ordinary clerks were highly proficient in a variety of tasks (Chaudhuri and Barman, 1981). 'The relative roles and status of managers . . . is always in flux . . . relations with family members in the top management often mean a lot more than formal titles or job descriptions . . . authority, responsibility and power have to be taken. They are never given' (Ghoshal and Ramachandran, 2002:213; Akbar, 2008; Chaudhuri and Barman, 1981).

Delegation was the general norm, though there was no formal delegation of authority. 'If there are two people at the same level one could have the authority to sign a cheque for an eight digit figure and the other for trivial amounts. It varies with the role and the confidence the person can evoke' (Ghoshal and Ramachandran, 2002:211 quoting Praful Gupta, a senior manager at Reliance). These organisations were in general non-bureaucratic. The family was the ultimate arbiter of decisions. Trust and asymmetrical relationships of power and obligation anchored these norms and personalised negotiations and enabled them to take up high-risk ventures. Trust was not defined by blood relationship but was anchored in proven ability to deliver (Ghoshal and Ramachandran, 2002; Chaudhuri and Barman, 1981; Kar and Samantarai, 2011; Harriss, 2003). Though the businessman-owner had the final control, suppliers, managers, supervisors and informal labour leaders, workers all had influence and power, negotiated and practised mutually convenient behaviours.

The internal managerial work organisation of family-owned businesses was generally still untouched by modern managerialism and thus customary practices continued. Even though Indian Institutes of Management had been set up in late 1960s to provide trained managers, i.e. those trained in *managerialism* for Indian industry, very few graduates from these institutions joined family-owned businesses (Sancheti, 1986:191).

But modern systems had entered worker management practices. Labour laws such as Factories Act, Industrial Disputes Act and Trade Union Act, which were introduced during colonial period, continued post-independence and further illegalised custom. They delinked individual reputation and worker management practices depriving the workers of an effective countervailing power.

One of the first signs of this delinking was the weakening of the jobber's role across industries. Governmental apparatus regulated the recruitment and management of workers. The system bred massive corruption. Labour officers who were authorised to intervene and decide on grievances failed to account for market and industry conditions. Worker negotiations became increasingly union based, yet failed to account for worker well-being, because unions themselves functioned as extensions of political parties' vote banks. It became very easy for managements to subvert worker power through control of unions and political patronage. Not all managements and business owners cared about reputations with workers.

In time, these fixed inflexible regulations worked towards creating more worker distress and greater extraction and exploitation of workers rather than improving worker bargaining power (De Haan, 1999; Jammulamadaka, 2016a).[16] De Haan (1999:289) reviewing the status of the 'temporary workers' over the decades from pre- to post-independence in the jute industry found that before independence

> both getting and losing a job in the large-scale industries was an uncomplicated affair'. In 1972, according to data from Titagarh Jute Mill no.2, the permanent workers had been temporary for 1.4 years on average; in 1991 this had become 5.6 years. In 1972, 53% of the workers had become permanent in the same year as they joined; in 1991 this figure was 14 %.
>
> (De Haan, 1999:289–90)

And, even though custom was now followed surreptitiously, work sharing itself such as *'bhagavalas'* of jute mills was an illegal practice; workers came in clandestinely and management denied knowledge of and by extension any obligation towards these workers. Custom became toothless as a countervailing power since reputations had been washed free of their performative effects. Society and community well-being was gradually being left outside of the natural conduct of business.

Emergence of Environment as a Stakeholder: Early industrial growth in post-independent India soon alerted the nation to the problem of pollution. While there were concerns about squalor amidst which factory workers were living since the early days of industrialisation, natural environment had not been a significant issue in business practices in pre-independent India. The absence of technology for reducing and preventing pollution too could have been a reason. But by late 1980s environmental abuse from industrial estates and industrial clusters had become apparent. The Central Pollution Control Board (CPCB) had already been set up in mid-1970s after the UN Conference on Human Environment in Stockholm in 1972. In 1989 the CPCB undertook an enumeration of most polluted areas in the country and identified 24 places which needed time-bound plans and mechanisms to address pollution problems. Air, water and soil all three had been impacted in industrial towns like Vapi-Ankaleshwar, Kanpur, Ratlam, Singrauli, Panipat, Thalcher and Tirupur.

Communities suffered from health problems, lack of clean water, air and land. Citizens and affected communities increasingly resorted to courts for redressal. Whether it was the pollution of River Ganga, or air near Taj Mahal or ground water in Patencheru, Hyderabad and Vapi, courts intervened and directed the government to facilitate corrective action by the polluting firms. Common Effluent Treatment Plants (CETPs) were launched as a solution to meet the needs of low-cost technology for industries and safeguarding the environment. Businesses participated to a varying degree in managing CETPs. With these episodes pollution and environmental irresponsibility had firmly rooted itself in Indian debates of business responsibility.

Era of the global, for the global and by the global

In 1991, in the wake of a balance of payments crisis Indian government embarked upon a programme of economic reforms and liberalisation launching the third era in India's economic history after the eras of optimism and discontent. Reforms led to the abolition of '*licensing raj*'. Indian economy was opened to foreign investment and FDI inflow grew from US$16 million in 1991 to US$48,941 million in 2011 (Chopra and Sachdeva, 2014). Inflow of FDIs was accompanied by a growing integration of Indian businesses with global markets. In a sense 1991 marked the beginning of globalisation for Indian business and a transformation in the business landscape.

Transformation in Business Landscape: Export-led economic growth received a big impetus from 1991. Growing at a compounded annual growth rate of 11.5 per cent between 2007 and 2011 MSME sector became a significant feature of India's business landscape.[17] Policy thrust enabled MSMEs to emerge as a large export-oriented sector. From 0.874 million units in 1980–81, the sector grew to 2.8 million by 1995–96.[18] By 2010, there were an estimated 30 million enterprises. Most of these were in the unorganised sector. MSMEs participated extensively in global value chains of TNCs contributing to about 45 per cent of India's manufacturing output and 40 per cent of exports directly or indirectly.[19] The second feature of the landscape was the privatisation of PSEs and entry of private and foreign investments into sectors hitherto reserved for public sector.

Privatisation unleashed the trapped business potential of these PSEs leading to significant business gains. By 2000, investments in PSEs reached INR 2,525 billion (Bhattacharya, 2006). The central government controlled 30 per cent of the 1,700 PSEs in the country. These central PSEs were dominant market players in terms of market size and assets (Jammulamadaka and Jaiswall, 2012). In 2015, six out of ten largest companies as per sales volume were PSEs.[20] The contribution of CPSEs in terms of total turnover as a percentage of GDP had ranged between 20 per cent and 24 per cent, during FY08–FY12 (Bhattacharya, 2006). Adding to these two sectors was the large private sector which included foreign MNCs.

Family-owned and/or managed businesses formed a large part of the private sector, in fact India has the highest percentage of family-owned businesses in Asia. The rise of new economy firms, especially information technology and retail firms like Infosys, Wipro, Satyam (TechMahindra), Future Retail and Pantaloons has greatly expanded private sector and brought in many first-generation businesses. While several new families got added to the ranks of private business as first-generation entrepreneurs, the older groups were seeing a succession by the next generation of sons and daughters – children of an independent India. Several Indian companies expanded operations in various parts of the world becoming MNCs in their own right. Pharmaceutical companies like Cipla and Dr. Reddy's had emerged as global leaders.

This industrial expansion was seen as a sign of a 'Shining India'. With India's entry into the restricted club of nuclear powers, these developments reflected the aspirations of a nation raring to be seen as a super power. The nation-building saga continued to animate business endeavours; however, this time the focus was almost exclusively on economic growth and 'industrial progress'. It became a story of proving to the world that India was no laggard in industrial

capability but could be the best. Politicians, planners and businessmen alike believed that Progress and Growth would 'trickle down'
to the toiling masses. But these aspirations brought in their wake
challenges for business responsibility.

Distressing Images: MSME integration into global value chains
was actively encouraged by government and multilateral agencies
like United Nations Industrial Development Organisation (UNIDO)
through cluster development activities. In the 1990s as a part of
global activism against exploitative practices in global production
networks, MSME clusters and their wage and employment practices
came under intense scrutiny. Garments, carpets, auto components,
sports goods, and in fact many different clusters became notorious
for poor wages, working conditions and child labour. Labour costs
arbitrage and cheap labour was the only comparative advantage of
MSME clusters compared to other production centres across the
world. MSME production practices were criticised for being polluting. Leather exports, one of the top ten export earners for the
country were banned in Europe due to polluting tanning and dyeing practices. Collectively these developments created perceptions
of Indian business practices as irresponsible.

Liberalisation also brought in multinational consulting firms like
McKinsey and BCG into India. These consulting firms examined
management practices within family-owned businesses and suggested that they were not professionally run and often failed to add
value to the shareholder (Pratap, 2016). Such managerial analysis,
akin to the British of the previous era, identified major governance
and transparency deficits in customary personalised informal practices in vogue. Since customary practices were hardly written down
in manuals or company policies, the absence of any clearly written
down standard policy was construed as evidence of deficit, inefficiency and void. Even though a study of organisational practices in
family-owned businesses in India as late as 2008 found that family
owned firms had much more organisational flexibility and less rigid
structures than professional firms, family-owned firms were seen as
less transparent and thus poorly governed (Akbar, 2008).

In these narratives customary practices which actually provided
greater bargaining power, flexibility and higher risk taking ability
were consistently being articulated as constraints for industrial
expansion. Unlike the past, these interpretations resonated with
a generation of business leadership who had been educated in the
West and modern management. This management education and

its vocabulary privileged shareholder value and not conduct with its ethical, social and political (autonomy and bargaining power) content. Such construals along with scams in the stock market and corporate governance fraud at Satyam dented the image of Indian businesses as ethical or professionally managed. Indian businesses and Indian governance was seen to be operating in institutional voids.

Threatened Industrial Progress: A major fall out of rapid industrial expansion was land acquisition. In 2005, the government had enacted the Special Economic Zone (SEZ) Act to promote industrialisation. Four hundred and thirty-six SEZs had received formal approval till March 2015 totalling over 0.2 million hectares (Singala et al., 2011). This massive diversion of agricultural and ecologically sensitive lands for industrial activity met with severe community resistance and impacted the operations of SEZs. Even though, 200,000 hectares had been sanctioned, only about 53,000 hectares of land was acquired by 2015 (Singala et al., 2011).[21] Only 199 SEZs were operational with a total of 3,937 firms working there. In addition to SEZs there were special projects like POSCO and Tata Motors' Singur for which large tracts of land were to be acquired. Affected communities approached Courts with help from national and international activists.

Supreme Court intervened in most cases and protected citizen's rights to the extent possible under prevailing law. In several cases, the law itself was detrimental, given that it was an 1890 Act enacted by British that governed land acquisition in India. Nevertheless such disruptions delayed projects by several years. POSCO is yet to be permitted. Permission for Vedanta has been cancelled by the Ministry of Environment and Forests after protests. A fine of INR 2 billion had been imposed on Adani's Mundra SEZ for environmental violations. These instances of irresponsibility towards environment and communities threatened India's industrial progress.

Massive expansion of industrialisation quickly brought environmental pollution into focus. Unabated pollution and collusion of government machinery in industry's violation of norms became evident in case after case, the granting of environmental clearances for projects like Vedanta Alumina's refinery, Adani's SEZ, or mining industry's rampant abuse of nature as in the iron ore export scam unearthed in Karnataka. Pollution Control Board's inefficacy in monitoring and ensuring compliance to standards was repeatedly borne out in complaints by communities such as those in Vapi. The

Supreme Court had intervened on many occasions and ruled against companies and directed government to take remedial action. Several oil refineries in Mathura, leather processing units in Chennai and chemical industries in Hyderabad had been shut down because of this. However, government's responses were characterised by tardiness. It was caught between the twin objectives of promoting industrial growth and saving the environment. Government's tardiness in equipping monitoring and enforcement departments, and entry of electoral politics into environmental governance mechanisms fostered an era of consistent abuse. A 2004 Supreme Court monitoring committee lamented:

> The committee has found in some of these areas that the indiscriminate dumping of hazardous waste due to nonexistent or negligent [environmental] practices together with lack of enforcement by authorities has affected the ground water and drinking water supply which has been consequently damaged.[22]

The pressure to be globally competitive also had consequences across the shopfloor. For many large businesses which had set their sights on the global field, customary practices and reputations within the domestic community and shopfloor hardly seemed to matter. The new reputations had to be made on the basis of global wealth rankings, social responsibility rankings, investor friendliness rankings, employee friendliness rankings and the like published by magazines and international bodies. Unlike the past, it had now become fashionable to flaunt one's wealth with profligate and conspicuous consumption by business owners even as business was passing through difficult times. Such display was valourised in media. Firms began engaging with new ranking agencies through formal systems, policies and reports instead of engaging with workers, employees and communities through personalised negotiated mechanisms. But formal systems and policies often provided little leverage for workers, employees and other stakeholders, as they were designed to promote shareholder value.

With growing uncertainties in the global market, firms increasingly reported a growing share of non-permanent work force and adverse working conditions. Industrial relations became limited to token compliance with prevailing labour laws (which had already proven to be of limited relevance for workers) making it possible for managements to easily control unions. Incidents like the assassination of a union functionary at Tata Steel (erstwhile TISCO) plant (Sanchez, 2016) become far easier than previous eras. Just as communities had to depend upon spiritual benevolence of the wealthy due to change in trust laws some decades ago, workers now depended on the benevolence of 'owner-management' and were limited in their ability to negotiate. These changes led to worker agitations in many companies just like the one at Maruti's Manesar plant in 2011.

To the extent that businesses continued to follow customary employee and supplier relations (which included most of the MSME and a sizeable portion of large businesses which were not under public glare of globalisation), they became identified with the pejorative term 'lala company', i.e. a family-owned firm which was not run on a professional basis. To the extent, businesses were involved with communities, it was usually around or near areas of their operations to secure the 'social license to operate' especially within manufacturing firms. A 1997 IMRB survey of 650 Indian companies (87 per cent Indian owned) found that most business leaders acknowledged social responsibility,

> . . . in practice this depended on the ability and/or capacity of the company to go beyond minimal legal requirements and whether it helped enhance any business interests. Only 36% reported some sort of policy; of these, only seven had a written policy and a person or department in charge. Indian and foreign companies did not differ on this score. Nearly 81% provided an account of various activities that they supported on an ongoing basis and with long-term commitment.
>
> (Mohan, 2001)

There were some exceptions to this general practice. Some older companies and some new ones like Infosys which had a reputation for their social consciousness carried out community development activities as an obligation. Private initiatives of businessmen motivated by individual spiritual and/or social considerations which had always been there in the past continued into this era too. India presented a great contrast, on the one hand it was a country with some of the fastest growing millionaires; on the other it was a land where millions of people could not afford two square meals a day.

In a manner reminiscent of the nationalism of businessmen during early independence, new age industrialists like Narayana Murthy, the founder of Infosys, known for his compassionate capitalism, argued that wealth had to be redistributed and that this could not be done: 'Unless you create wealth by legal means, you cannot distribute it. And without the two you do not have progress. Putting public good ahead of private good in every decision you make will, in fact result in reaching the private good' (Sundar, 2013:237). However, these were not sufficient to tackle the problem. Businesses had lost credibility as trustees of society due to scams, conspicuous consumption and indiscriminate abuse of nature and people. In this era, delinking not only meant absence of circulation within business-society. It also implied a managerial splitting of the social from responsible business conduct. For instance, Tata group which was facing severe criticism on environmental and employee relations across its flagship industries continued to fund philanthropy through its trusts.

Compromised Credibilities and Salvaging Reputations: It is within these conditions of threatened 'industrial progress' and 'compromised credibilities' of business and government that India's encounter with global CSR trajectory began. India's rise as a growing economic power was being threatened by stories of labour and environmental abuse and irresponsibility whether by MSMEs or big business. The failure of *trickle-down effect* in spreading the benefits of liberalisation and the impoverishment of the poor eroded the credibility of both big business and government. Not only were large Indian businesses facing protest and declining credibility inside the country, they were also at a disadvantage in global expansion because of 'liability of origin'. Many new economy firms were deeply connected into Western TNCs and thus faced a greater need to prove their credibility. They faced legitimation challenges in their host countries stemming from 'institutional voids' in India. These country-of-origin effects led to negative perceptions in Western host countries about company's ability to conduct legitimate business. Attempts to access Western capital and/or consumer markets further exacerbated these perceptions of liability (Marano et al., 2016). Firms with extensive exposure to Western markets and investors in fact were amongst the first to adopt UNGC and GRI standards. Infosys was the first company to do so in 2006. For many other globalising Indian firms,

CSR reporting became a means to legitimise their operations and overcome their 'liability of origin'.[23]

The then Prime Minister Manmohan Singh had urged businesses to pursue social responsibility and reach out to the poor or risk the gains from liberalisation. In 2004 he said, '. . . CSR is not philanthropy. It is not charity. It is an investment in our collective future. In this we are partners . . .' (ASSOCHAM address, cited in Sundar, 2013:224). The government formally recognised businesses' role in social development in the eleventh Five Year Plan. Along with this, the Indian government also enacted a series of empowering legislations and institutions like the Right to Information Act (2005), Forest Rights Act (2006) and Land Acquisition Rehabilitation and Resettlement Act (2013) and National Green Tribunal (2014) to strengthen bargaining power of communities. It had issued a charter for corporate responsibility for environment protection in 2003. These enabling legislations and regulations earned government credibility internally. Parallellly, government embarked upon a brand building initiative through the India Brand Equity Foundation that highlighted India's technical and scientific capabilities among other things (Kaur, 2012). India also became one of the first signatories to the UN Global Compact within the first year of its formation.

Intersecting trajectories: encounters of the Indian and the Western

In these intersecting trajectories, the initial measures such as signing the UNGC showed that India was very much clued into the Western trajectory. The first Indian companies to follow UNGC guidelines were ONGC and NTPC – PSEs in the energy sector. ONGC had been internationalising at a rapid pace and was acquiring gas exploration and extraction rights around the world. Being perceived as responsible was therefore very important. It did not matter that ONGC and NTPC by virtue of their PSE status had the 'social' inscribed into their goal and had had a good track record of working with communities for their rehabilitation. Confederation of Indian Industry (CII), FICCI and other industry bodies consistently carried out awareness programmes on 'modern CSR' and 'Triple Bottom Line'. Nevertheless, the uptake among Indian businesses was less. Globalising Indian firms quickly picked up on these trends. For many others the reasons for CSR were still not clear. To the extent it did, customary philanthropy for social development appeared more appropriate than such modern CSR. In fact some business owners spent much greater amounts on customary philanthropy supporting causes of their choice out of their personal wealth compared to what was officially done through CSR.

Legislation and contemporary practice

The Satyam accounting scandal (which overshadowed the tremendously beneficial EMRI ambulance service introduced by Satyam for Andhra Pradesh), Tata Motors' withdrawal at Singur and delays at POSCO were not helping India's image. As a corrective and supportive endeavour government started actively intervening in CSR through the corporate governance route. It sought to establish India as a strongly governed country. Following Irani Committee's 2005 report on revamping Companies Act and corporate governance, the Voluntary Guidelines on Corporate Governance for Central Public Sector Enterprises (CPSEs) were developed in 2007. Irani committee's recommendations were based on market regulator Securities and Exchange Board of India (SEBI) guidelines for listed companies, which were based on recommendations of Murthy and Birla committees. These recommendations had closely followed the United States and the United Kingdom corporate governance norms (Dewan, 2006b:15; Jammulamadaka and Jaiswall, 2012; Pande, 2011). The 2007 CPSE guidelines were made mandatory the following year.[24]

Towards the end of 2000s the notions of 'shared value' 'sustainable business' and 'bottom of the pyramid' had become fairly familiar and efforts were made to invoke these in promoting CSR. From 2008 onwards, German GIZ initiated a project with the Ministry of Corporate Affairs via the Indian Institute of Corporate Affairs to help stabilise and promote modern CSR in the country. They had aimed at making CSR guidelines resonate with the Western discourse, thus principles of UNGC, WBSCD, Triple Bottom Line all found their way into various versions of government's CSR guidelines (Jammulamadaka, forthcoming). In 2009, the Ministry of Corporate Affairs introduced the Corporate Social Responsibility Voluntary Guidelines (CSRVG). CSRVG provided broad directive principles for businesses to practice responsibility and referred to globally accepted elements of sustainability, environment and labour. However, they also included national development and welfare provision objectives reflecting the Indian situation and the need for philanthropic work for community development. In 2010, CSR was made mandatory for CPSEs and a new set of guidelines that made explicit references to Triple Bottom Line and the UNGC were issued to CPSEs. Here CSR was understood as *a set of activities that* 'extends beyond philanthropic activities and reaches out to the integration of social and business goals' (Department of Public Enterprise, 2010). Several elements were introduced in these guidelines such as, project-based approach for pursuing CSR, a long-term plan for CSR that was in tandem with business plans, geographical focus areas for CSR and implementation partners for CSR. The activities that were suggested under CSR included those indicated by UNGC and sustainable development principles (points vii, viii and ix, pp. 6–7 of the guidelines document). In addition, the list of activities also included those activities related to national development objectives, which had generally not been treated as part of CSR in the West.

Bolstered by the reception of these CSR guidelines, on 8 July 2011, the Union Minister for Corporate Affairs released the National Voluntary Guidelines (NVG) on Social, Environmental and Economic Responsibilities of Business. The idea of value-chain-based sustainability and responsibility was emphasised throughout the NVG, with the guidelines urging businesses to raise the bar in a manner that makes their value-creating *operations sustainable.* The CSR notion adopted in NVGs was from the views of WBCSD. And even though, the ministry used the Western definition, it departed from that definition and NVG guidelines included activities of community development within CSR (Jammulamadaka, 2017).

While the Ministry of Corporate Affairs was debating making CSR spending mandatory, SEBI went ahead and mandated the top 100 listed companies to disclose their environmental and social governance initiatives through the Business Responsibility Reporting (BRR) framework in August 2012. This was an elaboration of its earlier initiative in 2000 specifying corporate governance, social, environmental disclosures as mandatory listing requirement. The BRR framework bore similarities to GRI and Triple Bottom Line and addressed the concern that companies in India were lagging behind in disclosures. The final CSR legislation appeared as Section 135 of Companies Act 2013 with a mandatory 2 per cent spending. Though the guidelines during the course of their entire development drew upon Western trajectory and meaning, the final rules for implementation of the Act, which were released in February 2014 bore little resemblance to Western ideas. The final rules explicitly referred to customary practice of community development as CSR. Global organisations like GIZ which had earlier heaved a sigh of relief that Indian CSR was maturing and becoming in sync with Western CSR (Chahoud, n.d.) now faced frustration at the return of 'philanthropy'. Section 135 also raked up a lot of discontent amongst businesses, who saw this as a new tax, even though the 2 per cent spend of post-tax profits on CSR has a 'comply or explain clause' making it actually 'voluntary'.

Contemporary CSR Practice: Caught in the web of international expectations and domestic pressures, CSR practice in India has now taken on diverse forms. Compliance today has come to mean different things. At the very minimum it implies following the basic laws relating to employment, environment and disclosures. It also means complying with the basic codes of conduct that are advocated globally. One could choose amongst the several available standards – ISO, SA, UNGC and GRI for compliance. A third meaning of compliance involves complying with Section 135, i.e. supporting community development activities through NGOs. And that which businesses do voluntarily, going above and beyond compliance, includes all those practices and activities over and above codes and legislation, as the minimum standard.

Some businesses have followed a generalist approach to activities for social benefit by supporting NGOs or social enterprises. If voluntary organisations had been the mantra in the 1980s, social enterprises promoted by venture capitalists, funding agencies and socially minded individuals have become the mantra of the new millennium to create 'shared value' and help achieve the MDGs. Other businesses have followed strategic initiatives for social benefit. They differ in choice of partners. Some large and small businesses have set up their own foundations and trusts to carry out social activities whereas others operate through internal departments for this purpose. In addition to all these company-driven initiatives, there is a plethora of multi-stakeholder initiatives financed by Western donors and buyers that have been implemented through enterprise associations in the MSME sector to improve labour and environmental practices. Thus CSR practice in India is today a myriad of things and is informed by a wide variety of motives, from custom to coercion to self-interest (see Figures 3.1 and 3.2).

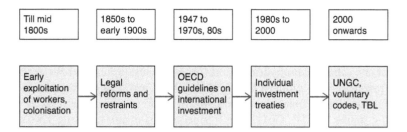

Figure 3.1 Developments in responsibility in the West

Source: Author

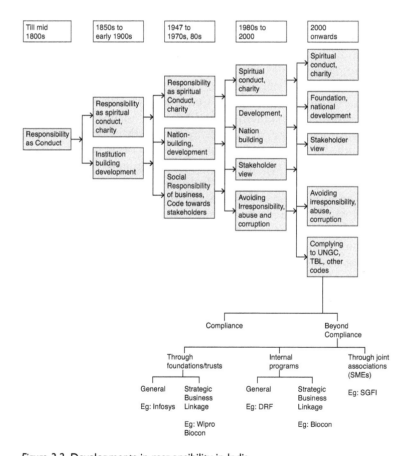

Figure 3.2 Developments in responsibility in India

Source: Author

Silences and amplifications in intersecting trajectories

The foregoing account spanning over six decades provides a glimpse of the different motivations and forces driving Indian and Western trajectories of 'modern CSR'. In the West, governing autonomous functioning of businesses in pursuit of profit has been the underlying theme of CSR. Governing businesses has meant enabling TNCs to voluntarily adopt codes of conduct that comply with global labour, environmental and human rights standards. Such CSR is practised through disclosures which enable outsiders – investors, customers and activists to evaluate a business on its word. Thus CSR in the West has been about attempting to govern an economics of extraction and profit maximisation.

Such modern CSR has shifted the focus away from state-centric negotiations of the earlier decades to govern TNC activity. The demands in 1970s were based on voices of the South calling for greater Northern responsibility. Contemporary calls for voluntary TNC governance standards and CSR, in a manner reminiscent of colonial enterprise, are driven by the North to be imposed on the South. Environmental concern, by virtue of its global nature, and its amenability to a universal singular notion of humanity, has enabled an easy and subtle shift from Southern interests to Northern impositions. The discussions on voluntary codes for environmental well-being and sustainability have effectively marginalised Southern worldviews of human and social relationships as inclusive of nature and firmly hoisted a 'use and replenish' environmental logic for business. It has become one more tool for TNCs for dealing with competition from local businesses.

India's experience too shares this marginalisation and modern CSR here has been about redeeming its image in the global arena. It would be tempting to attribute this marginalisation solely to global neoliberalism. However, marginalisation appears to be much more a consequence of the encounter with Western modernity. It is modernity and its understanding of society as differentiated into economic, social, political and public, private spheres that has ensured that the colonial legal infrastructure has continued almost in toto and at times even expanded post-independence. This illegalised custom, and enabled business performance to be examined independent of the socio-ethico-political. The consequences of this were quite significant as is evident in the notoriety which Indian business earned for itself in the 1960s and 1970s. As for illegitimisation of custom, it appears to be the onslaught of management consulting post-liberalisation which did much in this regard even though managerialism entered the country post-independence.

The intersections of Western modernity and Indian custom have led to silencing customary practices of bargaining and negotiation as a characteristic of being responsible. This silencing is noteworthy because, it is ultimately for this *'ability to negotiate'* that the Western world is fighting for. Commenting on codes of conduct, the American Federation of Labour-Congress of Industrial Organization (AFL-CIO) said: '. . . they are not a perfect solution. . . . Nevertheless, the fact that they are negotiated, instead of unilaterally imposed by companies, . . . means organized labour has been able to use them to deliver international solidarity . . .' (AFL-CIO, 2015:6, emphasis added). Note the emphasis on negotiation. In some parts of Indian businesses, these practices of negotiation and flexible personalised systems have died out but in many other cases they are still surviving as illegal and/or, illegitimate subterranean practices which carry an external mask of formal policies (Jammulamadaka, 2016b; Jammulamadaka and Saha, 2016).

At the same time, the sucking out of the social, economic and political from custom ensured that custom lost most of its tooth, being reduced to an empty carapace of faith. Conduct has no place in this scheme. Ignoring, demonising and misrecognising custom has also ensured that the country appears as an *institutional void* where businesses are driven by whims. The power of communities, employees and workers has been attenuated in this encounter and devoid of customary restraint, both greed and neoliberal pressures have made business exploitation and rapacious extraction frequent. Modern CSR in India has therefore been the antidote to this *institutional void*, a means to redeem some of the tarnished image and ensure a seat at the global neoliberal table. But the void is far from filled.

While the power of external centres of power like global investors, global ranking agencies, Western buyers and multilateral agencies has been amplified, the loss of power of communities and employees has not been redressed. Governance of business is nowhere close to providing the kind of bargaining power that had hitherto been enjoyed by communities, employees and workers nor is the restraint on rapacious profits as effective as in past. The outward orientation of businesses has ensured that even as companies may be rewarded for being good corporate citizens by rankings and agencies in the West, they do not necessarily address the expectations or legitimate demands and concerns of communities where they are operating, whether it be India or in other locations where they have operations. The cases of withdrawal of awards from companies after massive protests prove this.

But Indian CSR has not been only about modern CSR. It has also been animated by a nation-building imaginary, both from business and governmental points of view. Whether it is social development, institution building, poverty alleviation, pursuing economic growth and globalisation for 'India shining', all are part of the same 'nation-building' imaginary. In an ironic kind of way, in spite of silencing and reducing custom to a dubious status, it is the customary notion of wealth's obligation that has animated the nation-building imaginary. So the answer to the question, where are we going?, is *to the borderland between custom and modernity, a borderland of nostalgic longing and pragmatics which is at once responsible and also irresponsible.* Let us continue exploring this *borderland.*

Notes

1 www.un.org/press/en/1999/19990201.sgsm6881.html, Accessed 1 March 2016.
2 www.cabinda.net/havana_e.pdf
3 *The Economist*, Survey of Multinationals, 27 March 1993.
4 www.globalpolicy.org/empire/47068-a-brief-history-of-transnational-corporations.html
5 www.marketwatch.com/story/exxon-valdez-and-the-birth-of-credit-default-swaps-2010-05-03
6 www.ibasecretariat.org/eb-curse-of-asbestos.php
7 www.ceres.org/conferences/joan-bavaria-award/joan-bavaria
8 www.globalreporting.org/information/about-gri/gri-history/Pages/GRI's%20history.aspx
9 www.ipsnews.net/1996/11/united-states-texaco-racial-flap-continues-despite-settlement/
10 www.nytimes.com/2001/04/20/world/drug-makers-drop-south-africa-suit-over-aids-medicine.html?pagewanted=allwww.wsws.org/en/articles/2001/04/aids-a21.html
11 www.ussif.org/sribasics
12 In the early decades after independence it was mostly the menfolk who were engaged in business, hence the use of the word businessmen. Later towards 1990s women, i.e. wives and daughters took over the reins of business, but the word businessmen instead of businesspersons has been used for consistency in the chapter.

pressures including the demands of transnational business. It also mediates between customary forms of life and governance and exigencies of the modern capitalist economy.

(Jammulamadaka and Murphy, forthcoming)

Whereas a border usually belongs to both sides; in post-colonial conditions like India, the legal governance structure is essentially a colonial bequeathment and represents the reification of Western modernity and its associated capitalist values. The regime of rules and regulations this legal system sets up has divided business practice into modernity and its *other* – that which is responsible and that which is not, that which confirms to modernity and that which does not. Thus border here does not belong to both sides, but creates the residual – business custom is modernity's residual and business irresponsibility is compliance's residual. At the same time, the administrative side of the regime carries with it the limitations of the post-colonial such as plural and often contradictory priorities, and scarce resources and capacities. The concurrent pressures of reified law and limited administration have significant implications for the conduct of business and responsibility in contemporary India.

Therefore in clarifying this border which demarcates responsibility, we will shift our attention to the specific regulation of business by government. With all the current talk on CSR and responsibility centred on Section 135, we might be misled into thinking that this is the only statute, the only regulation that has encouraged businesses to be responsible. There are many other regulations and statutes in India, not just Section 135 which impinge upon business practices and define the minimum acceptable standards of business thereby impacting competitiveness and responsibility. One such recent legislation the Mining and Minerals Development (Regulation) Act 2015 compels mining industries to pursue responsible growth. It specifically prescribes the creation of a District Mineral Fund to provide for development and rehabilitation of the area that has borne the brunt of mining.

Some of the important statutes and policies cover employee and labour practices, environment and resource use. In addition there are frameworks that exist for consumer and investor protection. The system of laws and rules in India practically encompasses all the common stakeholders of a business. To this extent, it is a fairly elaborate system of oversight and governance of business practice. I will therefore focus on the frameworks for labour, environment and resource use keeping in line with the general emphasis on 'people' and 'planet' in 'modern CSR' and only briefly touch upon other aspects like consumer and investor protection, suppliers and communities. Depending upon the nature and extent of these regulations and the attendant governance practices, sheer compliance to law of the land can imply ir/responsibility in business practices in the statutory sense. Statutory compliance to responsibility might itself either facilitate and/or constrain responsible practices in the customary ethical-social-political sense. I will therefore examine various dimensions of the regulatory system in India and their role in promoting (ir)responsibilities amongst businesses. The aim here is not to compile a list of various laws and rules impacting businesses but to build an understanding of the regime's key concerns, facilitations and the constraints and challenges it poses. Hence in what follows, I will not exhaustively list laws but reference the breadth and depth of regulation and its enforcement/administration. Let us proceed by taking stock of Section 135, the latest CSR regulation first.

CSR

In 2013, India enacted a first of its kind legislation on mandatory CSR spending. The law specifies that companies having net worth of INR 5 billion or more, or turnover of INR 10 billion or more or a net profit of INR 50 million or more during a financial year would have to spend at least 2 per cent of their average net profit for the immediately preceding three financial years on CSR activities. Activities carried out as part of the normal course of business would not be considered as CSR, even if they might be in the realm of energy efficiency or sustainability etc. The activities would have to be carried out in a project mode with separate reporting of the same. Companies could either do it themselves, or through trusts, foundations, NGOs or even partner with other companies for this purpose. Thus partnership is an important feature of this legislation. It specifies that a Board subcommittee of at least three directors, including an independent director would have to be designated as the CSR committee. This committee would be responsible for setting up the CSR policy and spending plan of the company.

The specific activities that can be considered as admissible under the spending are listed in detail. They are generally of a charitable and philanthropic nature such as eradicating hunger, poverty and malnutrition, promoting preventive health care, promoting education and promoting gender equality, setting up homes for women, orphans and senior citizens, measures for reducing inequalities faced by socially and economically back-ward groups, ensuring environmental sustainability and ecologi-cal balance, animal welfare, protection of national heritage and art and culture, measures for the benefit of armed forces veter-ans, war widows and their dependents etc. The act also specifies that in implementing projects preference should be given to local areas where the company operates.

The Indian Institute of Corporate Affairs under Ministry of Cor-porate Affairs has been tasked with overseeing the implementation of this provision. The act also provides for an explain clause in the eventuality that the company is unable to spend the budgeted 2 per cent. Given that the act is very new, there exists a lot of uncer-tainty regarding the specific treatment of different kinds of spend-ing and the consequences of non-compliance. The administrative machinery that oversees the implementation of the act is currently at a very rudimentary level. The specific impact of this act remains to be seen. However, mandating CSR has been criticised as a bad idea that amounts to a form of tax which would adversely impact the competitiveness of businesses. This is in keeping with the global notion of CSR as voluntary. The act has also been criticised for keeping pursuit of shared value outside CSR spending. The statute's sole focus on philanthropy it has been argued is detrimental to the pursuit of 'shared value' by businesses.

Regulating employee and labour practices

The Constitution of India has placed labour on the concurrent list, as such both central and state governments have the power to leg-islate on issues of labour. Currently, there are more than 47 central and over 100 state legislations aimed at promoting worker wel-fare (Saini, 2014) like the Factories Act, Trade Union Act, Indus-trial Disputes Act, Industrial Employment (Standing Orders) Act, Contract Labour Act, Minimum Wages Act, Prevention of Child Labour Act, Payment of Wages Act, Employees State Insurance Act and so on. These statutes have been designed to be pro-labour, pro-employee and compel employers to behave justly and responsibly towards those whom they hire for work. Most of the labour laws were enacted during British rule. Very few changes have generally been made to the labour laws derived from the colonial period. The few changes that were made in the legal regime after 1947 related to practices derived from ILO, British and American law. Since those legal systems share a common perception of employer–employee relationship as adversarial, this spilled over into Indian laws too (Mitchell et al., 2014; Kennedy, 1958).

Currently what exists is therefore a very elaborate system of labour laws covering all aspects of the employer–worker relationship like wages and benefits, working conditions, health and safety, social security, conflicts, termination, lay-offs, appointments and right to association are in place. All these apply to workers in the formal registered sector, only a few are applicable to the executive or administrative employees or informal sector workers.

The Factories Act was first enacted in 1881 and subsequently revised several times. This act is applicable to every establishment that employs ten people and works with electricity or employs twenty people and does not use electricity. The Factories Act prescribes things like work hours, breaks etc. Another crucial legislation in the labour sphere is the Industrial Disputes Act of 1947. Its statutes are based on Section 81A of the Defence of India Rules that were promulgated by British in 1942 to enable them to control production in India and ensure that the empire was fully enabled to fight the Second World War (Sengupta and Sett, 2000). The act provides for extensive and almost total state intervention in industrial relations and employer–employee disputes. Post-independence the Act has more or less stayed the same. The Act prevents firing of workers, lay-offs, retrenchments or closure of establishments without permission from government. For establishments above a certain size, it also prevents striking without due process. Similarly Contract Labour Act prevents hiring of contractual workers for perennial jobs and necessitates government permission to hire contract workers from licensed labour contractors. These laws also provide that the standing orders in a business need to be vetted and approved by the government.

With regards to the administering of this regime, the entire labour law implementation and monitoring is entrusted to labour departments and labour courts in each state of the country. Every state has a labour department headed by a labour commissioner who is supported by a whole hierarchy of officers and inspectors for monitoring businesses, issuing licences, approvals, intervening and adjudicating in matters of dispute.

Even though in principle labour laws are applicable to all workers in the formal sector, in practice very few workers are under their ambit since the formal sector itself is quite small in India. As Badigannavar and Kelly (2012:449) report:

> There are about 440 million workers in the Indian labour market. Of these, around 93% are employed in the informal or unregistered sector of the economy. Only about 7% are employed in the registered sector enterprises operating in the formal sector. Some estimates suggest that within this regulated sector about 60–70% are contract workers without legal protection.

Papola et al. (2007) estimate that only about 15 per cent of the total workforce are covered under some provisions of the industrial relations and welfare laws in India. In fact, labour laws itself have been blamed for this dismal state of affairs. The most noticeable feature of these laws is the mandate for state control, interference and adjudication in operational matters of worker welfare. This labour regulation regime has constrained business flexibility for employers given the necessity of government permissions for hiring and firing workers. Several commentators have called this regulatory regime a lop-sided regime which suffers from the problems of delay, formalism and inaccessibility (Baxi, 1995; Saini, 1997, 2014).

In any economy and society, businesses operate under uncertainty. In India too, fluctuations have been common, whether it was the 1970s where economic stagnation, famines and wars (Sengupta and Sett, 2000) made business difficult or the economic liberalisation of 1991 which opened up the Indian economy to global markets and competition. Flexibility in labour operations enables businesses to restructure their workforce according to market conditions and constitutes an important survival strategy. This strategy was followed very successfully in the pre-independence period by Bombay's textile mills before labour laws were being put in place. Post-independence such labour flexibility was reduced due to state control. Though in letter, this regime does provide government with the discretion necessary to incorporate responsiveness to industry/business cycle needs, in actual practice; the government has been less than forthcoming in permitting businesses to be flexible in industrial relations or employment. Often driven by vote-bank electoral politics and populism, government refused permissions to hire workers on contract or lay off workers to adjust to market conditions. The processes for securing permissions and necessary licences were itself time-consuming and difficult, mired as they were in complicated procedures (Sengupta and Sett, 2000). With circuitous procedures and lack of transparency in the process, much corruption had taken root. Even basic things like getting a licence were driven by bribes.

This regime on the other hand also facilitated greater violation, corruption and increased casualisation of workers leading to their vulnerability (Badigannavar and Kelly, 2012; Saini, 2014; Fagernäs, 2010). In order to continue being in business, the focus of employers shifted to discovering ways of bypassing the law. One of the most common practices was to stop hiring workers on a 'permanent' basis, since many laws kicked in only for permanent workers. They shifted to hiring workers on contract through contractors. Since law forbids hiring contract workers for jobs of perennial nature, the contracts were often given out in the form of service contracts even for jobs of a regular nature. Job contractor effectively provided workers on a temporary basis to management. From 1971 to 1991, the percentage of casual workforce in organised sector increased from 23 per cent to 35 per cent. Similarly, unorganised sector employment grew at 4.57 per cent whereas organised sector unemployment grew at 1.44 per cent from 1972–73 to 1987–88 (Sengupta and Sett, 2000). Cutting across sectors and industries, all kinds of businesses were shifting towards more casual workers to avoid the ambit of labour laws.

In some cases workers were hired without any written records for either wages or attendance. Employees and workers, especially those working on contracts were sometimes forced to change names, or even sign on incorrect wage receipts. The wage receipts would mention the legally necessary wages but a percentage of the wage would be returned to the contractor or the employer in cash. This practice was not just for blue-collar workers, even professionally qualified people who worked in other executive and administrative positions were subject to similar treatment. This was being done in all kinds of enterprises. Companies also started inventing new designations like 'learner' and 'trainee' to avoid the ambit of the law (Sengupta and Sett, 2000). Employees would be designated as trainees and retained in the same position for several years. For white-collar workers, designations and responsibilities were modified by calling telephone operators as communication officers to avoid legal compliance (Sengupta and Sett, 2000 citing Davala, 1995).

Within the private sector, some employers shifted workers between various group companies so that the required period of continuous work under a single employer would not be achieved and they would be exempt from legal compliance. Employers' inventiveness extended to finding legal and illegal ways of closing factories under adverse circumstances. In order to shut down an operation, employers forced employee transfers and/or defaulted on payment to creditors. Sometimes, they stopped paying electricity bills so that the electricity department would terminate power supply, eventually leading to stopping of operations. Defaulting on payments provided a legitimate route to closing a business through a filing of a civil suit by some of the creditors. Yet another means was to declare lock-outs. Lock-outs are the employer equivalent of a strike. During a lock-out employer was not obligated to pay any wages. Thus all these methods of closing an operation denied any severance pay to workers (Sengupta and Sett, 2000). Corruption in the system facilitated all these practices to continue without much difficulty.

The prevalence of corruption has led to worker distress while swinging the balance in favour of those employers who have the resources to bribe officials to turn a blind eye to violations. The deep embedding of trade unions in electoral party politics has also often constrained unions in their ability to meaningfully respond to worker and organisational issues (Sengupta and Sett, 2000; Kennedy, 1958, 1965). Laws do not facilitate meaningful negotiations with trade unions since the Trade Union Act in India permits unions with just 10 per cent of membership in an industry to form a union. Adding to this, many genuine unions are frequently denied recognition and thus a chance to legally represent worker interests. Further the adversarial tone of the union's engagement aggravates the situation since it contrasts with traditional understanding of employment relationships and cultural attitudes informed by collaboration between workers, employers and state for national progress and deeper beliefs towards work, workers and employers including the just duties of employers towards workers (Mitchell et al., 2014; Kennedy, 1958). Strikes earlier were mechanisms for airing grievances and initiating negotiations. Trends thus report a decline in the ability of workers to strike effectively (Sengupta and Sett, 2000). Decline in effective strikes shows increasing employer power and the growing vulnerability of workers (Sengupta and Sett, 2000).

Formal dispute resolution through the labour courts has also been ineffective. With numerous departments and steps involved in the process, delays and lack of coordination amongst various offices in sharing information and background details adversely affecting industrial relations. The entire referral and adjudication process is rendered extremely slow (Ghose, 2003) and the state machinery has failed to handle a large share of disputes (Sen, 2003). And even within those small number of disputes which enter the state machinery for resolution only a small percentage are resolved in a year, the significant delays leading to detrimental consequences for both workers and owners (Fagernäs, 2010).

From the workers' point of view also, the regime has been inaccessible because often workers do not have either the awareness or the skills necessary to seek formal recourse. This is in addition to the long-winding, cumbersome and labyrinthine processes (highly legalised and expensive process putting it out of reach of the ordinary folk). The processes also lack enforcement capabilities and this makes them ineffective. Not only has this regime left workers in a precarious condition, it has also reduced competitiveness of industry (Maira, 2014).

The single most important problem that has been identified is the cumbersome process of state control of industrial relations and its inflexibility. Two national labour commissions set up in the past have recommended reforming labour laws to improve worker outcomes and industrial competitiveness. However, amendments to labour laws reflected political struggles within the country for votes rather than improvement in conditions for either workers or industry. Instead of formal reforms which has been a political hot potato, what has occurred is *'labour reforms on the sly'* (ShaymSundar, 2014; Bardhan, 2002; ShyamSundar and Ratnam, 2007).

Even though hardly any labour laws have been repealed, post-liberalisation the introduction of Special Economic Zones Act in 2005 has exempted businesses operating in SEZs from complying with labour laws. Similarly policies have exempted new age sectors like organised retail and information technology from complying with labour laws. Similarly procedural changes have also been introduced to improve ease of business including self-certification by employers. States like Maharashtra, Gujarat and Andhra Pradesh competing for investment, have begun relaxing and/or reforming labour laws making them more convenient for employers without any safeguards or measures to restrain exploitation of employees. This is even though worker exploitation has become more frequent in many businesses. From actual practice of the regime and these covert reforms, it becomes evident that the central concerns of formal labour governance system in India appear to be (a) ensuring control of the state, (b) attracting investment and (c) satisfying trade union vote bank constituencies.

The challenge such a regulatory and governance regime poses for CSR is therefore two fold. On the one hand it suggests that formal sector companies need to make serious efforts to get out of the current practices of worker exploitation at the very minimum. They need to put in place far more progressive mechanisms for managing their people. They need to do this voluntarily because the regulatory regime does not compel them to do so. It also needs to be done in the face of adverse statutes which have disrupted the operation of countervailing power within traditional forms of employment relations thereby making workers/employees vulnerable for exploitation. In the absence of countervailing power, this situation places great expectations of responsibility and a moral imperative on employers to pursue responsible practices towards workers.

On the other hand, this system also suggests the need to create effective mechanisms of countervailing power for workers and employees so that workers themselves can ensure and protect their well-being and interests. As Pettit (1996:578) says, for countervailing power to be effective, it needs to be able to prevent the capacity of the powerful actor in this case the employer to interfere with impunity and at will in the employment contract of the worker (Pettit, 1996:578). Drawing from Pettit (1996) we can figure that some measures for establishing countervailing power for workers include improving the day-to-day capacities of workers through skilling and awareness which provides them more employment options, reducing dependence on employer through state provision of some welfare in the form of social security etc. Other measures could also examine the possibility of rejuvenating and/or recasting the informal practices of countervailing power in the form of reputations (which anecdotal evidence suggests are still in vogue in some parts of business) through a degree of formalisation by creating linkages between such reputation and credit or product markets as happens in microfinance sector.

Regulating environment and resource use

Like labour, environment and resource use also has been the subject of many colonial legislations. Legislations during the British period, namely rules on land acquisition, forest, water and river use essentially enforced the concept of 'eminent domain' of the state and declared that all commons belonged to the state and not the communities. The twin ideas of eminent domain and state ownership usurped the customary rights of communities to commons. In usurping these rights, the British statutes were designed to facilitate extraction and exploitation of both resources and communities for revenue maximisation. Damodaran (2006) shows how statutory developments with respect to forests and logging of *sal* trees during British period were responsible for starvation and famines among tribals. In the face of violent rebellions following some such statutes related to use of forest lumber, laws were introduced under colonial rule which restricted the use/possession of forests by non-tribals affording protection to tribals from imperial exploitation. In addition to such resource use laws, there were some laws for air and smoke pollution in Bombay and Calcutta, the major industrial centres in colonial times. For instance, public nuisance laws in Bombay included some aspects of pollution and entailed criminal prosecution and liability (Singh, 2013).

Article 372(1) of the Constitution of India held that all the laws in force before the Constitution was adopted would continue to be in force until they were specifically repealed or amended. As such the statutes on resource use and pollution continued *as is* even in post-independent India. The protection to tribal groups afforded under Schedule V of the Constitution of India continued through the designation of Scheduled Areas. Unlike labour, the legal regime regulating resource use and environment is marked by a greater number of changes. These changes reflect a changing understanding of *environment*. India's signing of the Stockholm Declaration on Environment in 1972 triggered a series of legislations that specifically protected the environment – air, water, wildlife and forests. There are over 500 different statutes that govern environment in India (Singh, 2013). Subjects of environment feature in the state, central and concurrent lists of the Constitution of India as such both central and state governments have enacted legislations in this regard. Following this, specific policies for forests and other aspects of environment were developed.

Hitherto the idea of eminent domain was alien to India; even though the king had royal lands, it was not as if royalty owned and controlled all the land (Ghoshal, 1930). Feudalism in India was not akin to European experience (Mukhia, 1981, 1985), communities' rights were recognised and negotiations were necessary to obtain their permissions. Post-independence legislative changes also reflect efforts to restore rights of communities usurped during colonial rule.

While the environmental sphere had continuing pro-active legislations since the 1970s, statutes on resource use have been revised only recently. The years following 1970s saw increasingly intense protests against industrial activity because of either the pollution, displacement by large dams and factories or denied access to forests and other common resources. The protests against the Sardar Sarovar Project highlighted the challenge of rehabilitation and resettlement. Subsequently, the Special Economic Zones Act 2005 triggered large scale and nation-wide campaigns against land acquisition for business and industrial activity. It was the acquisition of several thousands of hectares of land for industrial activity often involving displacement of thousands accompanied by destruction of critical environments that brought the force of colonial laws on land, forests and mining to bear upon the citizens of post-independent India (see Table 4.1 and Figure 4.1). Massive protests by affected communities and civil society activism finally led to revisions. New laws such as Land Acquisition Rehabilitation and Resettlement Act 2013, Forest Rights Act 2007 and Mines and Minerals Development (Regulation) Act 2015 were enacted to recognise and safeguard the rights of communities over resources (Jammulamadaka and Saha, forthcoming). These revisions have been accompanied by other policy reforms such as mandating environmental impact assessments of industrial activity.

An elaborate administrative apparatus has been set up in the form of Central and State Pollution Control Boards to check pollution in

Table 4.1 Land area to be converted to SEZs

SEZ approval type	Total area covered (sq. km)
Formally approved inclusive of notified SEZ	676
SEZ having inprinciple approvals	1,209

Source: Singala et al. (2011)

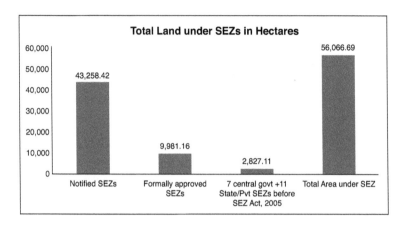

Figure 4.1 Total land under SEZs

Source: https://factly.in/the-special-economic-zones-in-india-fact-sheet/#prettyPhoto/2/

the 1970s. Later the Ministry of Environment and Forests was set up in 1985. Pollution Control Boards and Environment Ministry are responsible for licensing and monitoring environmental use and abuse. Environmental impact assessments have been introduced to gauge the impact of development and industrial activity. An elaborate system of public interest litigation served as another institutional control mechanism for ensuring compliance. Environment Protection Tribunal and more recently the National Green Tribunal (2013) have been set up to deal with disputes and complaints on environmental issues.

However, this elaborate administrative system has limited monitoring capabilities, given insufficient staff in Pollution Control Boards, forest, mining and other related government departments (Trivedi, 2014). Staff limitations made monitoring ineffective. Even though 367 technical staff were sanctioned for Central Pollution Control Board in 2009, they only had 264 staff (see Table 4.2). For a country as large and industrially diverse as India, a strength of 367 staff members provides a very small and inadequate base for effective monitoring of the environment (IIM Lucknow, 2010). About 12 to 24 staff members across the MOEF's six regional offices are responsible for monitoring some 6,000 mines and other projects nationwide (HRW, 2012).

Table 4.2 Sanctioned and filled positions in Pollution Control Board – technical staff

Year	Total sanctioned positions	Total filled positions
1984	100	64
1994	310	180
2004	326	235
2009	364	267

Source: IIM Lucknow (2010)

Inadequate infrastructure has also constrained the timely avail-ability of data to facilitate adequate monitoring. Central Pollution Control Board monitors water quality through 1,700 monitoring stations in India, which is about one station per 1,935 sq. km, whereas in developed countries stations are available for every 356 sq. km (Rajaram and Das, 2008 cited in Murty and Kumar, 2011). '. . .32 percent of the stations have frequency of monitoring on a monthly basis, 28.82 % on a half yearly basis, and 38.64% on a quarterly basis' (Murty and Kumar, 2011).

A second problem is the lack of a consistent approach to monitor-ing. Regional offices of ministry of environment and forests differ in the frequency and extent of monitoring (HRW, 2012). A third prob-lem is the presence of multiple institutions like Ministry of Envi-ronment and Forests, Central and State Pollution Board with no clear demarcations of their authorities. This has severely constrained coordination, exchange of information and working relationships (IIM Lucknow, 2010). A fourth problem relates to limited expertise and skill in monitoring. In many cases staff being generalists are ill equipped to understand and decipher the highly technical nature of problems. A Supreme Court monitoring committee on hazardous waste observed that 77 per cent of the chairpersons and 55 per cent of the member secretaries in different State Pollution Control Boards are not qualified for their positions, that they do not have the neces-sary technical competence (cited in IIM lucknow, 2010). 'There is no doubt that regulatory institutions of the [mining] sector are under-funded, understaffed and overstretched' (HRW, 2012).

Such a regulatory and governance system has promoted blatant dis-regard for environment, violation and corruption. With inad-equate infrastructure the over-burdened departments, rely solely on self-certifications and assessments of companies and thus there is dereliction of governance. There is no independent vetting or ascertainment of the facts and impact. This has led to severely flawed environment impact assessment procedures with companies hiring consultants to prepare favourable reports (Jammulamadaka, 2013b). Take the instance of mining industry. Data from Ministry of Environment and Forests show that during the period 2006–08, out of 587 new mining projects which applied for environmental clearance, only 10 were rejected. Similarly between August 2009 and July 2010, 102 new mining projects were approved and only 3 were rejected. Out of a total of 2,515 projects in mining, power, construction and other industries, the ministry denied permission to only 20 projects suggesting that compliance was being paid lip service (HRW, 2012). Experts say that in some cases, the law is so stringent or poorly designed that it promotes corruption and non-compliance (HRW, 2012). '. . . the conditions laid down in environmental clearances are sometimes so vague or poorly constructed that objective monitoring of compliance was arguably impossible' (HRW, 2012).

Even with regards to pollution control, inadequate monitoring infrastructure, infrequency of monitoring and lack of penal authority have encouraged businesses to indiscriminately dump their pollutants in water, soil or air. Many chemical industries have simply dumped untreated waste water into nearby rivers and streams or even directly pumped it into the soil to avoid costs of treatment. The nexus of corruption has also made it extremely difficult to catch the culprits in the act and satisfy the burden of proof in any penal process. Such contradictions notwithstanding, ineffective implementation of environmental law stemming from developmental pressures and inadequate resources, had led to dangerous levels of pollutions in several industrial areas like Tirupur, Vapi, Kanpur and Kolkata.

As can be inferred from the above, the central concerns in regulating and governing environment and resource use have been (a) state's control over resource use, (b) safeguarding environment, (c) promoting economic and industrial development and (d) respecting community rights over resources. These four concerns set up contradictions and tensions in governance. State control conflicts with community control, safeguarding environment conflicts with promoting industrial growth. This regulatory sphere has therefore been marked by great contestation and activism. The conflict between environmental goals and development goals has also led to frequent amendments in the rules of monitoring. The Coastal

Regulation Zone Act has been amended 31 times in 28 years and environment impact assessment rules have been amended 21 times in 18 years (Jammulamadaka, 2013b). Many a times, these amendments have been made to cater to the needs of specific business interests. For instance, even as the Forest Rights Act continues to hold, changes have been brought about to the definitions of Forest so as to enable certain industries to operate without necessarily getting clearances under Forest Rights Act.

Whereas labour issues were driven by political parties through their trade union partners, issues of environment have been driven by civil society and academia. Even though the environmental discourse and regulatory regime have been driven by civil society interests, they have become highly technicised with scientific measurements of polluting substances (Saha and Jammulamadaka, 2016) thereby constraining easy participation by affected communities and citizens who have neither the resources nor the skills to supply technical data and establish causation for the pollution effects they experience.

The public interest litigation route while effective in many ways, does also contribute to constraining voice of, and control by communities, by 'legalising' the governance of environment. The involvement of judiciary has also prompted more of an obligatory action (March and Olsen, 1989) rather than anticipatory action which ensures inter-generational equity and safe environments. Obligatory action as March and Olsen (1989:23) explain is driven by questions like, 'What kind of a situation is this? Who am I? How appropriate are different actions for me in this situation?' And decisions are driven by doing '*what is most appropriate*' Whereas an anticipatory action is likely to have the most socially beneficial outcomes. As March and Olsen explain anticipatory action on the other hand is driven by questions like, 'What are my alternatives? What are my values? What are the consequences of my alternatives for my values?' Action is geared towards choosing 'the alternative that has the best consequences' (1989:23).

The challenges this regime of environmental irresponsibility and resource exploitation presents for CSR are first, providing mechanisms for consultation and voice and second, balancing the twin objectives of sustainability and development. Recent legislations recognise and restore community rights that were usurped over a century ago. However what is still missing is the availability of meaningful institutional mechanisms where communities and businesses (whether large or small) can converse and consult with each other to arrive at mutually satisfying outcomes. The relationship between communities and businesses is still adversarial and the rights of communities are still subservient to government control. As such it depends on businesses to learn new competencies to reach out and engage with communities to understand and then address their concerns to mutual satisfaction. Businesses need to learn to move away from 'giving doles' or 'purchasing permissions' as a way of working with communities to an engagement approach that provides for flexibility in business planning. The engagement approach of working with communities will enable businesses to pursue more responsible practices vis-à-vis resource use and environment. Governments also need to strengthen the monitoring machinery and make it meaningful so that businesses actually have an incentive to pursue responsible practices.

Regulating interaction with consumers, investors, suppliers and communities

Investors

Any discussion of regulating business practices of responsibility would be incomplete without looking at investors, consumers, suppliers and communities. The Ministry of Corporate Affairs through the Companies Act, and the Securities and Exchange Board of India together have laid out a fairly elaborate system of corporate governance norms, disclosures and reporting standards to facilitate decision making by investors. Regulatory authorities of different industries such as the Insurance Regulatory and Development Authority, Telecom Regulatory Authority of India, Reserve Bank of India also oversee quality of service provision, investor protection and customer protection in different sectors. Investor protection has been an on going effort in India. As has already been discussed, some of the stock market scams and corporate governance frauds have prompted decisive action by the government and led to the creation of stringent rules and monitoring. Many of the resultant statutes have been developed to be in sync with global standards of corporate governance and reporting to enable India's participation in global commerce. Mandatory reporting, audits and investigation of malpractices compel companies to behave responsibly towards investors.

Suppliers

With regards to suppliers and supply chain, current regulations provide for some kind of preferential procurement for small and medium sized businesses and businesses of the underprivileged. The initial policy thrust beginning in 1977 fostering the growth of small and medium scale enterprises by restricting the production of certain goods to small and medium scale businesses led to the emergence of a vibrant sector. The product reservation policy was in vogue until recently. Even in 1996, there were 836 different reserved products. Consequently, the sector has become an important contributor to the country's GDP, exports and fast growth in employment etc., but this has also caused adverse impact on the environment through unsafe disposal of effluents and pollution. The ability of these businesses to work with safe, clean technologies has been limited, as has been their ability to provide better wages etc. Given the small asset and limited resource base of SMEs many were unable to adopt safer and cleaner technologies.

As such government started the policy of common effluent treatment plants. Such common treatment plants were set up with government assistance and the running costs were borne by industries and their associations (Jammulamadaka, 2013a; Saha and Jammulamadaka, 2016). But these effluent treatment plants have been struggling with problems of insufficient capacity and ineffective enforcement of member firm compliance. In addition to these pollution reduction measures, various skill development and technology development programmes have been introduced with assistance from United Nations Industrial Development Organisation, and other international development agencies to reduce the vulnerability of workers and firms in the global value chains.

Consumers

With respect to consumer protection a gamut of legislations like Weights, Standards and Measures Act, Prevention of Food Adulteration Act, Restrictive Trade Practices Act among others have focused on ensuring that consumers get assured quality and a fair price. In 1986, the Consumer Protection Act was also legislated to specifically provide for consumer rights and a forum for redressing consumer grievances. The statutes guarantee consumers the right to safety, right to be informed, right against exploitation, right to protection from unfair practices, right to free choice and right to redressal. The administrative machinery here includes the constitution of a consumer forum at the district, state and national levels. Just as in the case of pollution control, various standards have been prescribed for food safety and companies need to get licences and are monitored for compliance. The Food Safety and Standards Authority of India is responsible for setting these standards and monitoring their implementation. Similarly, weights and measures department also monitors compliance by businesses. While there is some seriousness in the monitoring of various standards of food, weights and the like, the area of consumer redressal is quite weak. Weak redressal is probably linked both to the unorganised nature of business in India and delays in the process of redressal.

Communities

With regards to communities, the Right to Information Act, along with Forest Rights Act, Land Acquisition, Rehabilitation and Resettlement Act and Mines and Minerals Development (Regulation) Act have come a long way in guaranteeing rights to communities. These rights include control over their resources and access to information. Communities can now access information from government departments including about government's tie-ups with business and monitoring of businesses by government. These laws empower communities to raise their voice against injustice including corporate injustice. Section 135 of the Companies Act also encourages companies to approach communities and explore means of partnerships for community development.

Understanding the borderland

From the very brief review above, it is evident that the Government of India has laid out a highly elaborate legislative and regulatory framework for governing businesses and ensuring that they behave responsibly. It has spelt out in great detail the *border*, i.e. the minimum that businesses should comply with to be responsible. However, the administrative and monitoring systems are slow, inaccessible, ineffective and corrupt.

On the one hand, some aspects of this regime have outlawed custom and thus branded customary practice itself as irresponsible in the statutory sense. On the other, this regime has to varying degrees disrupted customary mechanisms of countervailing power. Such disruptions, coupled with limited, inadequate enforcement resulting from a scarcity of resources in a post-colonial developing country breed corruption. This makes it possible for businesses to comply with law and yet be irresponsible in the customary sense. Consequently, the borderland acquires a distinctly messy character where all kinds of responsible and irresponsible practices coexist. And often, workers, communities and environment fall through the cracks of this messy stitching together of custom and regulation.

Thus, in spite of such an elaborate system, India and Indian businesses (big and small) have been in the news from time to time for irresponsible behaviours. Several big businesses like the Tata group, Reliance, Vedanta, Adani, Coco Cola, have been in the news for protests against land acquisition, violation of human rights, destruction of environment and habitats. In fact, Adani's land acquisition in Mundhra was perfectly legal but it was an act of great injustice in the customary sense, since it did not involve any engagement with affected communities. Only after protests did some of the engagement processes start. Big businesses like Maruti Suzuki, Hero Honda, Hyundai and Regency Ceramics have also been in the news for poor treatment of workers, even though they are statutorily on the right side of law. Similar is the case of TCS which recently faced large-scale criticism for poorly managing lay-offs. A lot of small businesses from apparel, leather and automotive industries have also made headlines for statutorily insufficient wages and poor working conditions, even though many of them might be following customary practices of responsibility. At the same time, several businesses have also voluntarily pursued activities beyond statutory requirement contributing to the well-being of this country and its people.

Thus the borderland is constituted by a modernist, globally aware law whose implementation however is constrained by post-colonial priorities and resource constraints. Let us look at what businesses in this borderland are actually doing in the next few chapters.

Chapter 5

Experience of the borderland

Large business practices

This is my home, this thin edge of barbwire. But the skin of the earth is seamless, the sea cannot be fenced.

(Anzaldúa, 1987:3)

The border is a meeting place of conjoinment where persons and ideas come together, where people and places meet, abut, mingle and neighbor.

(Mountz, 2009:200)

In our explorations of silences in the confluence of modern and traditional notions of responsibility, we notice that what exists in contemporary Indian condition is a distinctly messy borderland. Indian businesses inhabit this borderland and cope and contend with not only the global discourse of modern CSR but also the specific boundaries put in place by a modernist legal-regulatory system. How do Indian businesses actually do this? Several observers of Indian CSR scene make a convenient distinction calling charity as a traditional practice and strategic CSR as the modern practice. But as Mignolo says, describing this difference on either side of the border is not the real problem. Identifying this difference is always easy, especially when one uses the dominant or Western categories of understanding. What is really challenging is to do it from the perspective of those who are on the outside of this border, i.e. those who do not have the voice in deciding the border. *'The problem is to do it from its exteriority'* (Mignolo, 2000:18, emphasis added) using categories of the native.

So, how do Indian businesses actually see this *borderland*? Do they see two distinct sides? Or because they are living in the borderland where all influences intermingle (Anzaldúa, 1987; Mountz, 2009) do they see a unity and harmony that merges these sides? Well, once again, we are met with silence since Indian business has hardly had a voice in this discourse. Just like the post-colonial Indian state in the global discourse, Indian business also has mostly been a recipient of these meanings in contemporary discourse. So how do we begin to break this silence, amplify the voice of Indian business and describe the borderland from their perspective? As Mignolo (2000) points out, such silent positions, lacking the authority or opportunity to actually make statements using native categories and meanings about their ideas, i.e. denotative pronouncements; reveal their knowledge through enactments, in their doings and behaviours. An enactment emerges from a view of the world – a way of knowing and making sense of the world. Such making sense of the world is not limited to formal Western knowledge or theory but uses all *means of knowing* that are available to the native. Thus an enactment slips outside the constraints of Western categories of knowledge and formal theory. Enactment thereby provides us a proxy through which we can infer the understanding of those who are silenced by Western categories of knowledge.

Therefore we will seek to uncover businesses' enactment of responsibility in contemporary India and articulate their experience of the borderland. We will do this by examining trends and issues in actual practices of responsibility in contemporary Indian business. A consideration of business size is important at this juncture because of several reasons. First, Indian regulations impacting responsible practices differentiate on the basis of size. Second, large businesses have greater resources and power at their disposal to affect society and thus in turn are subject to greater expectations of responsibility. Third, the terms of engagement of large businesses in the global economy and by extension their enrolment into global CSR discourse are different from those of small businesses. All the three factors imply large businesses will *know* CSR differently from small businesses. Therefore in mapping responsibility practices, this chapter will focus specifically on large businesses.

Given the exploding interest in the field of CSR in India, there is a burgeoning output of surveys, rankings and comparative reports. There are detailed expositions of a company's CSR activity in the form of company hagiographies, sustainability reports, case study documents, websites etc. All these provide us profiles of CSR activities of companies, and comparisons. Such formal sources, as stated earlier are themselves manifestations of a modern version of CSR. They are also more often than not self-congratulatory, generally lacking in critical reflections. Relying solely on these sources will not really help us in surfacing the Indian business perspective. Therefore in seeking to map the landscape, I will not be limited to these kinds of *sources* but draw upon the many conversations I have had a chance to participate in and observe in the past several years as an academic. Some of these conversations are formal, official and bound by rules of the *say-able*. Many other conversations occurred on the side-lines with managers *speaking freely*. These were not standard data-gathering conversations or interviews which could be analysed but *dialogues between two human beings sharing an interest and a concern*. Some of these conversations left a few residues of thought which eventually gathered more mass forming ideas as I moved along my academic career. In mapping this landscape of business practices I share with you such thoughts and ideas blended with a generic understanding of practices as revealed in regular *sources*. The effort therefore will be not only to provide an overview of practices but also to draw attention to some issues inherent in these practices. I begin by looking at popular surveys, moving to specific models and finally the issues.

Survey speak

In CSR surveys two vantage points are usually available to us. One looks at the firm from the outside and treats the firm as a singular actor interfacing with society, the other looks at the inside of the firm, its managerial practices and managers as the actors. In reviewing CSR we will first treat the firm as the actor using the external vantage point and then look at the internal position.

CSR as seen from outside the firm

With growing consolidation of CSR as a field of practice, there have been several periodic and annual surveys and reports on CSR in Indian business by donor agencies such as GIZ and consulting firms such as KPMG, Grant Thornton, and Mercer. An external vantage point has been most commonly adopted by these surveys. Relying on externally available information about the firm such as disclosures, an external vantage point is used to help investors and business partners make decisions about the relative extent of a firm's responsible behaviour. All these assessments utilise disclosure information on websites, annual reports, business responsibility reports, sustainability reports and assess company performance with reference to global norms, especially GRI. I will however depart from the assessment paradigm since our primary concern is to identify the notions and practices of responsibility in Indian business. Given that it has been just 2 years since Section 135 came into effect, I will begin with surveys looking at the implementation of Section 135 CSR legislation and then examine other aspects.

Data obtained by *Factly* the data journalism and public information portal, from the Ministry of Corporate Affairs through a query under Right to Information Act shows that 460 companies had provided CSR spending details for financial year ending 2015.[1] Of these a total of 194 companies had spent INR 63.37 billion as against the expected aggregate 2 per cent amount of INR 83.47 billion. While the overall picture suggests that the commitment was missed by about 25 per cent, actual spending figures of companies reveal a wider variation. Only 81 companies spent the requisite 2 per cent, while 22 companies spent 50–100 per cent more than the mandated 2%. Reliance Industries exceeded the 2 per cent requirement and spent INR 2.27 billion making it one of the biggest spenders. 91 companies spent upto 24 per cent, over and above the requirement. On the other hand, 165 companies underspent between 50 per cent and 100 per cent of the budgeted amount. 101 companies fell short of the spend requirement by less than 50 per cent of the amount. Overspending by a few companies masked underspending by many others. Interestingly, ONGC was one of the highest spenders and also one of the biggest underspenders. The sectoral spend distributions threw up no new surprises. Education, health care and poverty alleviation remained the prime areas with each receiving more than 10 billion rupees. Geographically, a large part of the money was spent in Maharashtra and Gujarat.

Another analysis of publicly disclosed information by rating agency CRISIL found that of the over 3,800 companies listed on Bombay Stock Exchange, about 1,300 companies met the criteria outlined by Section 135 for the fiscal year 2014–15.[2] Of these 1,300 companies, spend details were disclosed by only 75 per cent of the firms and they together spent about INR 68 billion or 1.35 per cent of their profit. It also found that mid-size companies fared better than the large companies in achieving spend goals. Education and health care took up 60 per cent of spend, while rural development took up another 10 per cent.

Another survey of 150 members, this time by the industry association FICCI, went beyond spend analysis and looked at other aspects of the legislation.[3] It found that most CSR committees had atleast one independent director. Company CSR strategies and plans were also aligned with government projects and priorities. About 40 per cent and 36 per cent of companies used company foundations and internal departments respectively for implementing programmes. 24 per cent of the companies used NGOs. It also found that following the legislation 77 per cent of companies had increased their CSR spend during 2014–15. Many others expected a further increase in coming years.

Yet another analysis of top 100 listed firms with regards to their compliance to Section 135 by consulting firm KPMG showed that even though legally mandated, atleast five companies had not posted their CSR policy online. KPMG had until 2015 used GRI reporting standards as the basis for their annual analysis. But in 2015, they changed to Section 135 standards revealing the success of government's attempt at self-identification and creating space for an Indian version within contemporary CSR discourse. According to KPMG's analysis, 75 per cent of the firms had described their modes of governance as required by law. Their analysis showed that 10 per cent of the companies exceeded the statutory 2 per cent requirement and 60 per cent of the top 100 firms spent less than 2 per cent. They too found that health and education were the areas attracting most of the CSR spend.

Common to all these reports and analyses is the finding that companies vary in the amount of CSR spending and levels of compliance to the new legislation and certain sectors like education and health care are favourites among companies. While, variation in compliance has generally been attributed to the newness of the legislation, one cannot rule out other factors like ownership and origin effects that might also be at play. In fact, the KPMG report belies expectations that Indian and foreign firms would respond to CSR mandate differently. These expectations could be because public sector enterprises and many Indian family-owned businesses have been engaged in community welfare or philanthropy for several decades. It is therefore possible that these firms are better able to implement the mandate of Section 135 compared to others.

While findings of KPMG report on differential compliance to spending focus within Indian and foreign firms, and public sector and private businesses, are in no way conclusive of origin and ownership effects due to sampling constraints; it is interesting that this category actually makes a comeback to the analytical schema after several years. Back in 2009, the Times of India survey, one of the early surveys in the current spate of CSR in India had used origin and ownership as an analytical category. At that time for companies of Indian origin and public sector enterprises, strategic CSR as articulated by the global discourse of modern CSR was a novelty. The 2009 survey had shown that quite a few companies (including MNCs) had started their CSR programmes after 1991 after India had embarked on liberalisation. In a sense that survey implied that public sector and Indian origin companies understood their philanthropic practices and modern CSR as two different things. The Times of India survey reflected an inflection in the trajectory of Indian notions and practices of responsibility, a schism between historical practices of responsibility and contemporary practices of modern CSR.

Evolution, Consolidation or Blooming Diversity: With regards to reporting, a key feature of modern CSR, most surveys of CSR agree that reporting rates have consistently been rising in India and attribute it to mandatory requirements of SEBI and other legislations. These surveys also converge in suggesting sector-specific differences in disclosures and CSR practices. For instance, they all agree on the high quality of compliance and disclosures in information technology (IT) sector. KPMG surveys suggest that natural resource sectors are probably more affected by CSR issues and hence appear to be more compliant. Similarly, Economic Times surveys suggest that manufacturing firms appear to be paying more attention to sustainability-related issues. Such specificity is prima facie logical, and sometimes supported by other empirical research (Jammulamadaka and Kollegal, 2009). However current inferences made by surveys are a cause of more confusion than clarity. These inferences are based on extremely limited sample representations (in some instances as low as one or two companies for a sector appear in the top 100 firms) creating a false sense of convergence and sector effects in CSR practice. What we need is a deeper examination of firm practices to establish convergence, sector specificities and explanations thereof.

Information technology is one sector where we are in a position to draw some confident inferences thanks to the 2015 NASSCOM-BCG survey on CSR. Like most Indian businesses, this sector too has a huge focus on education and skill building, health care and sustainability. The survey shows that a distinctive feature of IT companies is that 83 per cent of companies follow an employee volunteering model. 76% of them also provide funding support. 50% of the companies partner with NGOs to implement their CSR. Volunteering is perceived as a strategic CSR initiative since it enables the company to use its core IT capabilities and also contributes to employee morale and engagement while contributing to social good. Some quick analysis I had done with my students showed that even though volunteering was followed, many IT companies carried out activities that did not utilise their IT competencies but used their general skills. Our analysis of 30 IT companies for the period 2008–13 before Section 135's curbs on pursuit of shared value came into effect revealed that there was hardly any difference in business impact parameters like attrition rates between firms who used IT competencies in volunteering, i.e. strategic CSR versus those which used their general competencies, i.e. general CSR. Anecdotal evidence from some of the companies suggests that several young engineers in firms pursuing such volunteering were probably first-generation graduates and industrial employees, and particularly valued the opportunity to give back to others from similar less privileged and modest backgrounds. The NASSCOM report probably reflects this sentiment when it finds that 'there is a strong interest in wider development goals'.

Several surveys done in recent years show that over time, motives for pursuing CSR have transformed. While the three surveys mentioned below are not exactly comparable due to different methodologies and samples, what is interesting is the shifting language of motives and a predominance of economic justification. CSR becomes increasingly talked about as a market- and/or regulation-based phenomenon and not a leadership philosophy. If being a good corporate citizen, founding philosophy and improved local community relationships were found to be most important motives in a 2002 survey by UNDP-CII; the 2009 Times of India survey found that business benefits in the form of good will and branding had become important. By February 2016 FICCI survey, the dominant reasons became pursuit of shared value and social good compliance.

Significantly, a review of recent surveys and rankings seems to suggest that questions of motive and perceived benefits of CSR and sustainability are no longer of relevance. Whereas, in 2009, concerns such as *why* were they doing CSR, *which* were the companies pursuing modern CSR, *what* were they doing, from *when* were they doing and *how* were they doing, were significant; presently, such *why and when* questions have slowly disappeared due to legislative, market and/or investor compulsions. In their place *content* of CSR appears to have become more important. This shift indicates a movement away from philosophical aspirations. It also shines a spotlight on the messiness in Indian CSR practice. Consider this. The top 10 companies for 2014–15 ranked as per CSR spend (data from Factly) and top 10 companies ranked with CSR defined as disclosures, governance, sustainability and stakeholders' management (as per Economic Times survey) have just two companies in common (see Table 5.1).

This simple fact suggests interesting implications: (a) Companies that spend on the ground may not necessarily disclose. (b) Those that have extensive disclosures and reporting may not necessarily spend on the ground promoting community development. (c) Some companies may be doing both. (d) Some companies may be doing neither. If we are to interpret the community development and CSR spending approach as a continuation of a traditional approach and disclosures and governance as modern CSR, then it would imply that companies are exercising choice in being traditional, modern, an amalgam of both or neither.

Table 5.1 Ranking as per different CSR meanings

CSR spending top 10 in descending order, 2014–15	CSR performance top 10 as per Economic Times-Futurescape-IIM Udaipur survey 2014–15, descending order
Reliance Industries	Mahindra and Mahindra
ONGC	Tata Power
Infosys	Tata Steel
TCS	L&T
ITC	Tata Chemicals
NTPC	Tata Motors
NMDC	GAIL
Tata Steel	BPCL
Oil India	Infosys
Wipro	Jubilant Life Sciences

Source: Author

CSR as seen from the inside

Shifting our vantage point to inside the organisation and examining managerial actions for CSR, reveals new dimensions and throws light on the status of CSR as an organisational function. The growing institutionalisation of CSR as a field of practice in India prompts us to expect that CSR would be occupying significant managerial attention and organisational resources. In fact, newspaper reports suggest that there has been an increase in hiring of senior-level executives specifically for CSR.[4] Some recent research we had carried out aimed at getting inside the organisation to assess this expectation and what we found showed that CSR is still a long way off from achieving a standardisation and fixity of practice within organisational management. We found that managers did not make strict distinctions between sustainability initiatives, CSR and community development initiatives but used these terms interchangeably. In several cases, sheer compliance to codes of conduct was perceived as a CSR activity. There were several different types of codes and reporting standards that were being followed, but most of them preferred the standards and reporting frameworks of the Indian government. An examination of decision-making practices showed that most CSR decisions were made by top management on a case-by-case basis. Such decisions were usually informed by a consensus approach. To the extent a company policy on CSR existed, decisions were informed by a search for fitness with company policy and priorities. Such top-down decision-making process required 2–6 months to launch a new project. Interestingly top-down decision making was found even though as managers themselves reported, CSR initiatives were not considered to be of significance to the business strategy and CSR initiatives themselves lacked an internally coherent strategy.

Our research also showed that CSR communication practices were externally focused and usually one way. They included things like annual reports, sustainability reports, website disclosures, newsletters and notice boards. They were broadcast oriented and aimed at informing external public instead of fostering internal dialogue, employee conversations and actions. This was in spite of several companies having employee volunteering programmes and opining that CSR helped in improving employee engagement. No wonder, companies felt that employee participation in CSR was something they wanted to improve. Among the important barriers that managers identified in implementing CSR within organisations was the time constraint. 52% of our sample of 50 firms identified lack of time. One in two firms cited lack of time as an important barrier to CSR. This indicates that managers frequently combined CSR activities along with other job responsibilities and struggled to allocate time for CSR. The other two barriers were lack of human resources (38%) and lack of employee motivation (34%). When seen along with the finding that 'compliance to codes' is CSR, these results indicate that managers required a separate skill set and incentive structure for fulfilling such CSR responsibilities and that they currently found themselves underskilled and underincentivised for the same.

58% of the sample, i.e. 28 firms said that they had a separate CSR department that managed the CSR activities of the firm. The coexistence of a separate CSR department to carry out activities along with time constraint as a barrier suggests that even though CSR department may in principle be responsible for initiatives, specific projects could be requiring participation from various line functions. When specifically asked about which function managed CSR activities in the absence of CSR department, human resources was found to be the most common function responsible. Fund utilisation and number of people impacted were the most common indicators that were tracked for measuring and monitoring CSR activities. Both of these reveal a preoccupation with reporting the activity rather than assessing its appropriateness or effectiveness.

These findings suggest that managerially speaking, pressures exerted by external and internal drivers of CSR are not in alignment. Instead variations amongst external drivers like legislation and investors, and, internal drivers like leadership, employees and industry demands are forcing managers to approach CSR function and activities in an adhoc way that responds to different pushes and pulls as they come along. Had they been in alignment, it would have been possible for managers to articulate coherent and consistent approaches to CSR. As such we see that communication systems are oriented towards external drivers even though all constraints and barriers are referring to internal drivers. Significantly, managers do not see their CSR communication and decision-making practices as responsible for barriers. Apparently, businesses are following their own interpretations of CSR in which modern and traditional CSR do not merge seamlessly but lead to fragments of efforts in various directions.

Models of CSR: foundations

We now turn our attention to various models in vogue in practising CSR. Surveys show that foundation approach is the most common practice adopted by companies to pursue CSR. A recent study by Charities Aid Foundation showed that of the top 300 companies, 142 of them had foundations which were used for doing CSR activities (Mukherjee et al., 2015). They were commonly registered as trusts, but some were registered as not-for-profit companies or societies. While the parent company ensured sustainability of funding, foundations' identity became synonymous with company. Many foundations directly carried out operations in communities making them markedly different from grant-making foundations of the West. Unreliability and/or high overhead costs of NGOs prompted some companies to pursue direct action on ground through foundations. Several also partnered with NGOs for grassroot implementation. They also partnered with government to access critical support for various initiatives. Among the other models of CSR some companies used internal departments and others worked directly with NGOs. Companies used more than one model in carrying out CSR.

As mentioned earlier, the foundation approach dates back to pre-independence times. A closer examination of the foundations and companies suggests at least four variations within foundation approach and two variations within internal departments approach. I outline these below and also provide some examples (see Figure 5.1). The choice of examples is totally idiosyncratic and does not reflect any implicit ranking or value judgement. We will discuss partnering with NGOs in a subsequent chapter.

Institution builder approach

The first kind of foundation-based CSR, which we can call here the institution builder approach has its genesis in pre-independence and early post-independence period and the commitment of these businesses to nation-building. Some distinctive features of this approach are as follows:

- The business group collectively vests shares or allocates profits to a family owned trust.[5] Often this is not a single trust but several interrelated networks of trusts in memory of various family members.

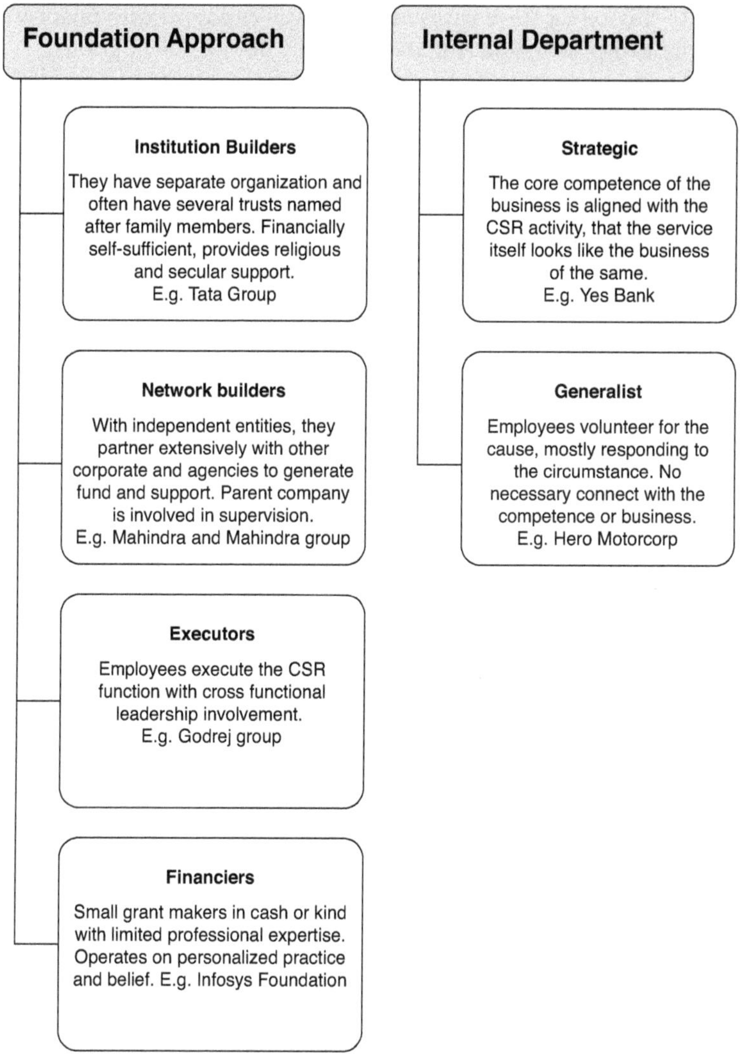

Foundation Approach	Internal Department

Institution Builders

They have separate organization and often have several trusts named after family members. Financially self-sufficient, provides religious and secular support.
E.g. Tata Group

Strategic

The core competence of the business is aligned with the CSR activity, that the service itself looks like the business of the same.
E.g. Yes Bank

Network builders

With independent entities, they partner extensively with other corporate and agencies to generate fund and support. Parent company is involved in supervision.
E.g. Mahindra and Mahindra group

Generalist

Employees volunteer for the cause, mostly responding to the circumstance. No necessary connect with the competence or business.
E.g. Hero Motorcorp

Executors

Employees execute the CSR function with cross functional leadership involvement.
E.g. Godrej group

Financiers

Small grant makers in cash or kind with limited professional expertise. Operates on personalized practice and belief. E.g. Infosys Foundation

Figure 5.1 CSR models: foundations and internal departments

Source: Author

- To this extent these trusts are often well endowed with finances, are rather self-sufficient and normally do not solicit grants.
- Trusts' operational portfolio includes running independent institutions and/or sponsoring and executing large projects by supporting various grassroot implementation agencies and NGOs. The activities and charters of these trusts are informed by founding priorities and subsequent assessments by social and development experts.
- The trusts are administered by fully separate administrative and functional organisations. These organisations are distinct from business group's main organisation itself. Their day-to-day operations are completely delinked from the everyday affairs of the business organisation itself. Trusts are staffed by professionally qualified development experts. The business group owners, exercise governance oversight and symbolic participation in trust activities. Trusts also help execute CSR activities generated through business group's employees. Trusts liaise with government and international donor agencies in their own right as bodies independent of the business organisation.
- The trusts of Tata group, Bajaj group and Birla group are examples of this approach. While these institution builders share a common interest in building and developing the country's institutions, supporting communities and employee needs, there are several differences in specific activities including secular or religious pursuits. They also vary in the extent to which they provide elaborate reporting and Triple Bottom Line disclosures.

Bajaj Group Trusts: The 90-year-old Bajaj group with presence in automotive, home appliances, lighting, iron and steel, insurance, travel and finance businesses and revenues of US$6.3 billion exemplifies the institution builder approach. The first trust of the Bajaj group, Jamnalal Bajaj Seva Trust was set up in the year 1942 in Wardha to take up Gandhian pursuits and rural development. This trust is active even today and is engaged in a wide variety of activities. Since then, other trusts and institutions like Janakidevi Bajaj Gram Vikas Sanstha, Jamnalal Bajaj Foundation, Marathwada Medical and Research Institute Trust, Institute of Gandhian Studies, Gandhi Gyan Mandir, Gitai Mandir, Gita Pratisthan and Fujii Guruji Memorial Trust have been set up. The common thread running through these is the carrying forward of Gandhian values and legacy of rural development. Pursuant to the spiritual beliefs of founders, the trusts also support Vedic studies and Bhagavad Gita studies. They also maintain museums and other historically relevant establishments like Bajajwadi where Gandhi used to stay.

Between them these trusts manage hospitals, medical, nursing and other professional colleges and training institutes. They have financed the setting up of research departments in various universities and carried out activities for all around development of rural areas. They carry out non-formal education and skill-building programmes for children, youth and women empowerment programmes. These trusts also provide social welfare services for employees of Bajaj group. The group also manages industry bodies and has instituted awards for promoting quality and ethical business practices. Interestingly though, we find that the group does not spend resources in developing state of the art disclosure reports by adopting the GRI guidelines. This is not to imply that they do not pursue sustainability. Sustainability informs not only shopfloor operations but even product development in this group. They also take diversity and affirmative action a step further and actually report not just about women and physically disabled but also about the number of SC/ST and other category employees they have on their rolls.

Tata Group Trusts: The 150-year-old Tata group, India's largest family business group, with revenues in excess of US$100 billion, 30 publicly listed companies and many other subsidiaries also illustrates this approach. The Tata group's trusts Sir Dorabji Tata and allied trusts, Sir Ratan Tata Trust, Nawajbai Ratan Tata Trust, J.N. Tata Endowment set up before or immediately after independence together control 66 per cent of the shares of the group holding company Tata sons. The income from these investments finances developmental activities of trusts in building and managing institutions, supporting causes, grassroots organisations and individuals. Some of the country's foremost educational and research institutions like Tata Institute of Fundamental Research, Tata Memorial Center, Tata Institute of Social Sciences, Indian Institute of Science and hospitals are supported by this trust group. Tata Trusts support several rural and social development organisations across the country.

While all these are managed by independent professional staff and organisation, the group is also extensively involved in other kinds of business sustainability and CSR activities. Trusts work closely in facilitating the initiatives of various group companies. The group also supports several competitions to spot and encourage solutions and talent within country's youth through programmes like social enterprise challenge, national entrepreneurship network and skill-building initiatives. In addition there are other employee volunteering programmes and community support projects which support local communities through NGOs and focus on empowering underprivileged. Such projects do not necessarily have a business linkage or strategic benefit for the company. Tata group engages in detailed and extensive sustainability measurement, reporting and disclosures.

Network builders

The second kind of approach in working through foundations is what we can call the network builder approach.

- This approach generally has one lead trust, sometimes a second trust supports these activities.
- These trusts generate their income mostly from corporate endowments and investments vested in them. Nevertheless, they partner extensively with other corporate, donor and government organisations in raising funds for specific projects/programmes.
- In this approach, trusts implement some of their own initiatives, and partner extensively with other grassroot organisations for other programmes. They are thus extensive network builders.
- The trust organisation and projects/initiatives are run as entities independent from regular business of the group. They are staffed and managed by development experts and professionals and causes are identified by supplementing founder preferences with systematic development data. The projects themselves are mostly of a secular character.
- The parent group provides board level guidance and supervision. The parent group companies also have senior cross-functional leadership for handling CSR within group companies and these teams work closely with trust organisation to derive mutual benefits. The parent group companies also actively adopt sustainability reporting and other triple bottom line based responsibility initiatives internally within their ongoing business. Foundations of Mahindra and Mahindra group and Dr. Reddy's group are examples of this type.

Mahindra and Mahindra Group: Mahindra and Mahindra group is a US$17.8 billion, 71-year-old multinational family business group headquartered in Mumbai. With presence in over 100 countries, it operates across aerospace, agribusiness, aftermarket service, automotive, construction equipment, defence, energy, farm equipment, finance and insurance, industrial equipment, information technology, leisure and hospitality, logistics, real estate, retail, and two wheelers businesses. The KC Mahindra Education Trust set up in 1953 by Mahindra group illustrates the network-builder approach quite well. One part of the activities of the trust in education and skilling, i.e. running and managing *Prideschools* for skilling and securing employment of country's youth are managed internally. An extensive scholarship programme is also managed as an internal operation of the trust.

The second part of the activities through the flagship *Nanhikali* project demonstrates the network model. The *Nanhikali* project aims at improving education for girl child. The project has an extensive fund raising mechanism and reaches out to other corporations, donor agencies and government funding. Fund raising for this project assumes strategic significance within the trust organisation. Several programmes and fund raisers are also organised. The other company organisations like Mahindra foundation and Mahindra UK and US foundations also raise funds for this project. The project is implemented through partnerships with several grassroot NGOs across the country. They also partner with similar-minded foundations and organisations in taking the project forward.

In addition to such social developmental initiatives through trust/foundations the business group companies themselves pursue resource sustainability and employee volunteering programmes. For instance, given their presence in automotive space, they carry out driver trainings or other activities like a crowd sourcing initiative with matching company grants for helping farmers in distress given the company's presence in the farm sector. They also produce extensive sustainability and Triple Bottom Line reports. According to Anand Mahindra, the chairman of the group, a few years earlier an investor had asked them for a Triple Bottom Line report. They had then realised that it was not enough to do work but reporting and talking about it was also important. Since then the group has been actively producing detailed sustainability reports.

Dr. Reddy's Group: The 32-year-old US$2.3 billion, Hyderabad headquartered pharmaceutical multinational is an instance of this type. The livelihoods advancement business school of Dr. Reddy's Foundation now rechristened as GROW is another example of network-builder approach. Dr. Reddy's Labs founder Anji Reddy set up the foundation in 1996 by allocating a certain portion of profits to this foundation. The foundation's focus was and continues to be on education and livelihoods. It was one of the early companies who had taken up the cause of livelihoods. It developed expertise in identifying youth, designing and delivering skill training and providing placement assistance. Mahindra pride schools also follow a similar model. These projects network extensively for raising funds securing grants from donors, governments and other businesses. Networks are leveraged for funds, implementation and final placement of trainees. In addition the group also manages some activities internally such as neighbourhood schools and a vocational college. The group also supports another foundation, Naandi which promotes livelihoods across the country and partners with *Nanhikali* project. Senior leadership of group companies closely pursues CSR and sustainability within business operations also. Being in health care, the group uses another trust Dr. Reddy's Foundation for Health Education to provide patient education and counselling. It also works towards making medicines affordable and accessible, and improving resource sustainability within the business. Extensive sustainability reports are another feature of the group.

Executors

The third kind is what we can call the executors. This approach to foundation is about using it as a fund source instead of creating a separate trust organisation.

- The foundation itself does not have an elaborate administrative organisation. Group owners and top leadership provide governance guidance. Senior cross-functional leadership of the group company drives CSR within the firm. The foundation's activities are managed by executives of the group companies through volunteering. For specific activities, expert assistance and outside partnerships are put in place as and when necessary.
- Employees of the company are closely involved in foundation activities, some of which may have a direct business benefit, others not. While some companies pursue business-linked CSR,

resource sustainability initiatives, along with sustainability reporting using GRI guidelines, others may pursue activities primarily in the community development space.

- The Godrej and TVS group's CSR activities can be seen as exemplars of this type.

Godrej Group: The Godrej group is a US$4.1 billion diversified family business group founded in 1897 with presence in sectors such as real estate, consumer products, industrial engineering, appliances, furniture, security and agricultural products, managed and largely owned by the Godrej family. 24% of the shares of Godrej group holding company are held in trusts – Pirojsha Godrej Foundation, the Soonabai Pirojsha Godrej Foundation and Godrej Memorial Trust. Through these trusts the group supports health care, hospitals, schools, skill building and education, and environmental sustainability. Mangrove conservation at Pirojshanagar, a 1,000 acre bustling mangrove forest is an important activity carried out by Godrej group. The management of mangroves is integrated into environment management system of the manufacturing plant and company staff oversees activities. Senior management at Godrej leads these programmes through a cross-functional team and employees at various levels in the organisation participate and ensure implementation. Given the emphasis on managing internally, scaling up the initiatives happens through opinion building in wider public rather than a direct expansion of programme implementation. The group regularly hosts public interactions among prominent individuals on relevant issues to create awareness and inform public discourse. The group produces Triple Bottom Line report but the detailing is far less compared to many other companies.

TVS Group: The 100-year-old TVS group, with interests in automotive and other businesses and over US$6 billion turnover has set up the Srinivasan Services Trust. The group's employees are engaged in implementing the activities of the trust around its factories. Activities like providing better infrastructure, piped water, roads, schools, adequate medical facilities and skill training are all carried out by the company through the trust. The company hires other people like animators, where necessary for carrying out community development work. TVS believes that these activities carried out in the vicinity of the company cut out the hostility at factory locations and also reduce the uncomfortable disparities that result from a modern business flourishing in the midst of poverty and collapsing infrastructure. The group does not involve itself much in producing elaborate sustainability reports.

Financiers

The fourth kind of approach is what we can call the financiers. In this model, the company sets aside a specific part of the profits for the foundation.

- The foundation does not directly manage grassroots activity but supports grassroots partner organisations through donations of cash and kind. They essentially act as small grant makers.
- Specific partners and activities which the partnerships cover are a function of management policy and preferences.
- Programmes and partnerships operate in a more or less detached way from the companies. Company provides governance guidance through Board participation.
- These foundations do not raise funds from public at large, other donor agencies or corporations for any activities, but are focused on using their own funds to support initiatives.
- Foundation administrative structure is usually small and made up of generalists with limited and/or no development professional expertise.
- This approach is not committed to pursuing scale but excels at reaching out and serving neglected and not so popular sectors and thematic areas.
- Similarly, their partner identification is not driven by expert knowledge either of the managerial type or of development type but by more personalised practices and beliefs. They thus avoid some of the blind spots generated by expertise. The Infosys Foundation illustrates this type.
- The parent company's CSR activities usually operate as a distinct activity unrelated to the foundation's activities. The parent company may pursue varying levels of other kinds of CSR with regards to employee volunteering, resource sustainability, community engagement and finally sustainability reporting.

Infosys Foundation: Established in 1996 by committing 1.5 per cent of profits from the group companies, Infosys Foundation has been supporting various grassroot NGOs, hospitals, schools, special interest institutions and cultural institutions in executing specific projects and upgrading their infrastructure through project financing. They have helped construct school buildings, hospital wards, hostels for students and destitute, provided scholarships to underprivileged and deserving students, artistes and others. This foundation is managed by a separate board without an elaborate administrative and programme management organisation. Infosys also has an elaborate employee volunteering programme which is run internally within the company. It also produces an elaborate sustainability reporting initiative. In fact, it was one of the first Indian companies to adopt the reporting framework.

Models of CSR: internal departments

We now turn our attention to implementing CSR through internal departments. We can distinguish atleast two kinds of approaches – strategic and generalist.

Strategic approach

The strategic approach involves initiatives in core areas of business. These initiatives are anchored and managed just as any other business or activity of the company. Given the functional relevance of these initiatives to company business, unless the company specifically articulates them as CSR, it would be difficult to identify them as socially responsible activities. They merge seamlessly with the organisation's product-service portfolio and use the organisation's core capabilities to pursue the activities. They directly help in positioning the company in a certain way and/or provide other market and business benefits. The CSR initiatives of NDTV and Yes Bank are examples of a strategic approach.

NDTV: New Delhi Television Network is a media company and almost all its initiatives involve using its news broadcast media for social purposes. It has several campaigns under its portfolio like Coco-Cola NDTV support my school, NDTV Godrej green champion, NDTV Nirmal marks for sport, NDTV Aircel save our tigers, Diageo NDTV road to safety, *Shikhsakiore* with Kalinga Institute of Social Sciences, Philips breath clean, Dettol b*anega swacch* campaign etc. Each of these campaigns involves cobranding with another organisation and uses competencies of NDTV to organise shows, create news documentaries or even run ad campaigns. These campaigns are at times not distinguishable from ongoing programing of news channels. At other times such as the Greenathon, a fund raising programme for alternate energy, ongoing programming is suspended for promoting a social cause. But either way, it is the use of competencies in news media that are brought to bear on CSR initiatives. At the same time, NDTV does not produce elaborate sustainability reports.

Yes Bank: The banking company Yes Bank's CSR initiatives too largely draw upon core competence and capabilities of the company. The CSR initiatives of Yes Bank involve identifying investment opportunities in socially relevant sectors like renewable energy, agribusiness, financing MSMEs, cleaning river Ganga etc. and publicising these opportunities through seminars, meets and sectoral reports. The bank uses its regular business skills and expertise in both identifying and promoting these opportunities. As a sign of further strategic integration of its CSR, its risk assessment includes social and environmental parameters as well. Yes Bank provides detailed sustainability reports and is on some international CSR committees.

Companies such as Future Retail also share this approach. Future group one of the front runners in launching retail revolution in India has an initiative that trains and skills people from underprivileged backgrounds to work in retail sector. What is distinctive about Future group is that, this training practice has been housed in a separate education business of the group, and not as a charitable activity. The group does not engage in elaborate reporting of its CSR activities.

Generalist

The generalist approach is one where company uses its internal departments and managers to pursue community development initiatives. However, these initiatives do not bear any connect with ongoing business or competence of company. They are of a widely diverse nature responding to circumstances. At times they are also just tasks that are performed in addition to regular business functions.

The 32-year-old Hero MotoCorp is the world's largest two wheeler manufacturer. The CSR initiatives of Hero MotoCorp are of a generalist nature. It carries out all its CSR initiatives internally. Some of these are aligned to its business in the sense that is offers road safety training programmes. In addition to these it carries out activities aimed at empowering girl children and young girls, afforestation, community development, preventive health care etc. Several of these activities are carried out both internally and through partnership with NGOs. They do not produce a detailed GRI compliant Triple Bottom Line report.

Similarly the pharmaceutical company, Cadila, runs a hospital. But it also supports several other initiatives like rehabilitation of disabled, scholarships for students, afforestation, spiritual events etc. through its internal department. We do not see a Triple Bottom Line report for Cadila either.

The CSR initiatives of public sector enterprises like ONGC, NTPC, BHEL etc. carried out jointly by CSR, and rehabilitation and resettlement departments also fall under this category. These departments are managed like any other department in the company. For instance in NTPC, Rehabilitation and Resettlement Department manages compensation, reconstruction of colonies etc. and the CSR department is engaged in activities in primary education, rural electrification, women's empowerment and self-help groups, primary health care, technical education, rehabilitation of disabled, water supply, scholarships for meritorious students and so on. As a public sector enterprise, they are also mandated to assist the government in implementing its welfare policies and programmes.

Sometimes, the generalist approach coexists with other forms like foundation-based CSR. Employee volunteering initiatives such as Mamta at Infosys and Maitri at TCS are examples of this. Both these initiatives are driven by employees who identify causes of their interest. Company facilitates their participation in the cause/ NGO by allowing employees to volunteer. At times, such participation also involves some financial support. Such financial support is usually rooted through formal CSR department/foundation of the organisation. The activities, organisations and causes that are covered under Maitri or Mamta programmes are a reflection of employee preferences and hardly have anything to do with company business or strategy.

Issues in CSR

It is now time to look at some issues in practice of responsibility by large businesses in India. These are issues that are salient to practice of responsibility but are often neither the subject of public debates nor scrutiny of responsibility in India. These are issues which are mentioned in unofficial conversations but hardly acknowledged in official discussions and debates either within organisations or in business press. I identify three such issues here – reporting problems, competence problems and spending choice problems.

Reporting problems

A few years ago a friend from a highly reputed IT company was sharing what had transpired in a regional association meeting. The meeting was called to discuss and share best practices in CSR. All participating companies had begun presenting their models, projects and impact numbers. The reports were glorious. One of them casually started adding up numbers on people impacted for the whole group. Suddenly, they realised that they had collectively impacted more number of people than the actual population of the region where they were all working. This anecdote points to one of the most common oversights in CSR practice and reporting.

Often companies work with partner NGOs who work with multiple companies. NGO partners working on the ground use funds received from multiple sources together. Administratively they find it rather impossible to maintain donor-wise details. They share the same total impact figures with all partner companies, in effect leading to double counting when the companies report these figures. The preoccupation with reporting, especially the number of people impacted, makes companies overlook the actual impact. This also impacts choice of CSR projects. As one CSR senior executive recently shared, we are so concerned about measurement today that we are actually unable to take up important activities simply because some of them cannot be measured in discrete terms. We have so few companies willing to work on gender violence because it is difficult to measure impact there.

Competence problems

Another issue relates to increase in hiring specifically for CSR positions. The head hunting firm Third Sector partners placed 65 senior-level CSR professionals in 2015–16 alone. This firm says that corporates generally wish to hire professionals with grassroots or development experience but they have limited choices. As such, they promote the hiring of cross-over professionals who are willing to let go of their regular corporate jobs and focus on development activities. These cross-over professionals are even willing to take pay cuts for the same. In many cases, there is even poaching of such professionals.[6] While this trend reflects serious commitment in terms of growing top management interest in institutionalising CSR, it also points to a disturbing understanding of competence.

In spite of good intentions, the corporate managerialist approach which seeps into working with communities reduces complexities of development and empowerment processes to simplistic managerial plans and measures. The preoccupation with impact numbers is in fact a sign of the search for an equivalent to profits, revenues or costs. It also leads to companies claiming far more than their just contribution into the complex process of development. Since managerial logics thrive on finding synergies with the business, it also poses a related problem of sustaining the activity initiated in the community in the absence of business synergy. While there has been a rise in the number of community-based projects initiated by companies, it remains unclear whether companies have the skills and competencies necessary to work with communities and whether regular managerial training is adequate for working with communities. Some companies are trying to overcome this problem by recruiting social work and rural management graduates to managing these projects.

Spending choice problems

Spending choice pressure is another issue CSR legislation has given rise to. The problem is not just about the quantum of spending. Companies, especially the very large ones are regularly subject to unofficial pressures from government and politicians to spend in pet projects and pet areas. While it is difficult to get anyone on record given the scandalous nature of this issue, senior executives do admit that they receive requests asking them to spend the budget in certain constituencies or in certain projects. For instance, after the launch of Swacch Bharat Abhiyan, businesses have been expected to contribute to this government programme.

Irresponsibility: the other side of the coin?

In a lay person's notion, the rubric of responsibility includes actions that are both good and not good, i.e. responsibility and irresponsibility exist as two sides of a coin. Our attempt to understand the borderland would therefore remain incomplete without reviewing this other side of the coin. Hence we will look at practices of business irresponsibility and try to figure out what it suggests about CSR. While there could be several domains of (ir)responsibility we will examine practices in two such domains for illustrative purposes, namely, land acquisition and pollution. We will look at some instances here to identify specific practices adopted by businesses to tease out the (ir)responsibilities therein. The instances are listed in no specific order but simply point out the diverse ways in which (ir) responsibilties are practised.

Unlike CSR we do not have extensive reporting of such instances. Business press often does not talk about these, to the extent it does, it is usually in terms of the impact on stock performance or production performance of the said company and the legal challenges the company is facing. Businesses themselves are usually silent or on the defensive, defending themselves from activist claims. To the extent irresponsibilities are actually discussed it is by activist groups and activist press. The instance and practices described below have been culled from public sources and interactions with activists and managers over the years. Though in some instances company names have been mentioned, the point here is not to call names or embarrass any company. It is basically to draw attention to some of the structural issues that enable such practices.

In one of the more widely known instances, Vedanta group after acquiring lease rights for mining and refining at Niyamgiri had applied for approval from Ministry of Environment and Forests for diverting the use of forest land for mining. However, instead of applying for approval for the entire project, which would have implied a greater scrutiny, they used certain administrative provisions to break it into two separate applications. The 1,400 hectares with over 700 hectares of forest land was broken into 723.343 ha and 721.323 ha applications to make it easier to get approvals (Jammulamadaka and Bhattacharjee, 2013). This is a practice which is often followed by businesses. It is only recently that regulatory changes have mandated fresh impact assessments and approvals for expansion projects. There are umpteen instances where mining companies have used an administrative provision of automatic renewal to avoid scrutiny that requires detailed social and environmental impact assessments.

In another extremely well-known and historic case of Singur project of Tata Motors where land was acquired for Nano factory, the company maintained that it had nothing to do with acquisition since legally the government was responsible for the acquisition. It completely ignored the fact that it had asked the government to acquire an extremely fertile land that was being used for agriculture. While we know that land is a scarce resource, fertility is an even more scarce resource and the company refused to take cognisance of this in its location choice.

When Adani acquired land for its port and airstrip at Mundra, it had intelligently acquired village commons and not private land. It had transacted with the government and to that extent it had avoided public compensation struggles that were an integral part of Singur episode. Upon acquisition, it fenced its land and restricted entry of local fishing community. Entry restrictions effectively cut off fishing folk's access to sea. It was only after several days of protest by community that the company allowed fisherfolk to walk through its property. In a related instance Adani had acquired rights and approvals for constructing and operating the port at Mundra. It had completely ignored the fact that local fishing community was also traditionally using the same port for its fishing. Once port operations began, entry and exit of ships led to tearing of fishing nets and loss of livelihoods. It took prolonged protest and activism by fishing folk to secure compensation from the company. In both instances, the company lost sight of the fact that commons are so called not only because they are state owned but because they are used *commonly* by several groups for diverse purposes.

The claims made by companies on water sources are also similar. One company setting up operations near Visakhapatnam had requested municipal corporation of Visakhapatnam to supply water. The company required over 50 per cent of the capacity of the municipal corporation. Serving the company thus meant letting domestic taps run dry. A local activist had approached the court to stop this. What is interesting here is that even though technology was available and the location being a sea coast presented the possibility, the company chose not to set up a desalination plant but to draw water from municipal corporation. Similarly power plants in Mundra area chose water cooling technology that drew in huge quantities of sea water destroying marine flora and fauna impacting natural environment and fisherfolk livelihoods. It took prolonged protest and legal battles with companies to get them to change to gas cooling technology that spared environmental destruction. In both cases, companies' technological choices ignored ecological and community impacts.

In another instance, a company, this time from public sector had successfully acquired land for its mining operations. One of its managers managing rehabilitation nursed a personal resentment against one of the displaced communities in the area. He ensured that no one from that community got a job, even though they were demographically a significant group there.

Utilising the opportunity presented in weak and dysfunctional monitoring machinery, companies blatantly engage in pollution through dumping of effluents, or disposal of waste by-products. Even though technologies and guidelines exist for safe disposal, few companies actively engage in scrubbing their gaseous emissions. Similarly companies are notorious for disposing untreated effluents.

Sadly, the small list is not exhaustive. Instead the instances reflect a lack of sensitivity to stakeholder, whether community or environment. Often refuge is taken in a legal loophole or administrative provision. Companies and managers exercise their legal rights, at times even relying on state's power for violence ignoring or even denying principles of natural justice, and/or plain and simple social decorum. The Kalinga Nagar firing which killed sixteen people on the spot, when Tata Steel chose to go ahead with a boundary wall construction even though it had not yet addressed demands of tribals in the area is a telling reminder of the thin line between legally right and just behaviour. Another reminder is the violence which ensued in a public hearing being organised by a coal mining company simply because decent and respectful seating arrangements were not made for local community leaders. In that public hearing, chairs were provided only for company officials and district administration. Community leaders were asked to sit on the floor. The community had taken this as a wilful affront. This instance exposes deep-seated biases against community, social decorum and natural justice in managerial action.

This review also appraises us of a very significant aspect of the practice and notion of responsibility in Indian context. Responsibility and irresponsibility appear to exist as separate categories. It is as if responsibility and irresponsibility are not two sides of a coin that are inseparably bound, but two separate worlds. In fact companies that have been cheered and awarded for excellence in CSR are also some of those who have been quite irresponsible.

Conversations with senior executives point us in the direction of a managerial explanation. They suggest that often departments dealing with CSR, land acquisition, community issues and ongoing business operations are different. These departments do not work in tandem. Instead they are driven by their own independent managerial logics. Land acquisition department functions under the rubric and ideology of project management and it focuses on keeping costs low and meeting deadlines. Project orientation and time pressures of managers make them disregard the political process of community engagement. Similarly, operations department focuses on production schedules, keeping costs low and quality high. CSR department on the other hand focuses on doing good for communities and spending money. These independent managerialist logics have limited scope for countervailing power and provide limited scope for a political process of engagement with stakeholders, even though such processes are of great significance in organisations. The organisational feedback process that finally connects all, is rather slow and indirect, allowing companies to ignore engagement. Consequently, protest becomes the only way of exercising countervailing power through which communities are able to make their voice heard within companies.

Communities who perceive pseudo commitment of the company to a political process continue to protest against company's actions even as they cunningly use company's need for their own purposes. In one case, a power project had acquired community grazing land. In the public hearing villagers questioned the company about how they would graze their cattle in the new situation. In response, the company committed to setting up a shed and providing fodder. The villagers accepted this. In a matter of a few years, the company was burdened with a huge expense being incurred towards maintaining the cattle shed. Villagers now had no cost to maintaining animals and did not think twice about buying cattle. They just bought new animals and put them in the shed. Cattle population had almost doubled. Project managers in their hurry to get consent had not thought through the essence of villagers' objection. Villagers' concerns were anchored around overall disruption to life and livelihoods that the project posed, as such villagers continued protests even after the cattle shed was in place. The question of cattle was just one of the several dimensions of community concerns that was easily articulable and hence raised in the public hearing. The company instead of grasping these deeper concerns, focused on fodder because it was a quick and easily solvable fix. Nevertheless it proved to be to the disadvantage of the company. Company developed a false sense of having addressed community concern and ill prepared them for subsequent protests.

This juxtaposition of (ir)responsibility suggests that in contemporary Indian business, responsibility in the sense of legal correctness is not sufficient for business and managerial action. Mere charity alone in the sense of contemporary transmutation of custom is also not sufficient. Conduct of business in the earlier customary sense of being 'just' is still very significant, even though feedback processes are quite slow and often take years for the protest to pan out. Those businesses which continue to follow personalised management practices are better placed to manage such conduct. Some managers and business leaders who are sensitive and personally motivated have realised the importance of conduct and have sought to engage with communities, employees and other stakeholders on an ongoing basis, even though this might even mean non-adherence to certain laws or global CSR discourse.

However, it would be erroneous to conclude that all those with personalised practices are better placed. Lack of legal compulsion for these processes has made it easy for many to restrict personalised practices to self-serving ways that maximise their profits and opportunistically use laws for dealing with stakeholders both within and outside the firm. Usually this manifests as using personal networks for lobbying and indulging in securing permissions or other resources through illegal means and then citing legal compliance to overcome objections from stakeholders like employees and communities. Many other businesses are learning the hard way with stalled projects. Some businesses are learning to work with groups who operate from non-managerial logics. They are learning the importance of the political process to ensure that their business remains socially acceptable. Some of them are also learning that closer integration within the organisation is required and silos between departmental logics and practices need to be overcome not just for technical reasons but also for political reasons. In a sense, it is déjà vu. In the past responsible business meant doing the business itself in a socially acceptable way and building a reputation for the same. Whether modern CSR or not, businesses apparently lost this ability and are now slowly learning it all over again.

Life in the borderland: loyalists, modernists, hybrids and contortionists

The brief review of CSR practices and the notions implicit in them show that Indian businesses adopt their own idiosyncratic approach to being responsible, some of which aligns with national legislations, some with global discourses and much of it remains distinctive to the company. The different approaches – institution builders, network builders, executors and financiers all cater to different needs of the company and country and reflect different capabilities including wealth potential of the companies. In the specific activities and means used, having foundations does not preclude internal departments working on CSR or employee volunteering, sustainability and resource efficiency initiatives. To this extent, it reveals an amalgam of historical tendencies of societal building, modern compulsions and emergent opportunities. Even though we have ourselves used the terms strategic and general as categories in our analysis here, the actual practices clearly defy a neat categorisation of CSR into strategic and general.

Attitudes towards customary and modern CSR are also revealed in company compliance to and reporting as per GRI standards. GRI reporting might be important from a global perspective, and surveys have been reporting a consistent growth in compliance and reporting. However, in actual practice, Indian companies have shown varying levels of interest in reporting and compliance. Setting aside legally mandated business responsibility reports and Section 135 reports, companies have vastly differed on reporting according to GRI parameters and producing sustainability reports. Avoiding rankings and reporting allows the company to pursue its own notions and practices of responsibility which can range from spiritual activities, community welfare and institution building to business sustainability. Many such activities do not have space in a Triple Bottom Line approach. Abstaining from reporting thus could even imply that companies are relatively free to choose their projects without worrying about impact figures.

Embeddedness in global markets could also influence reporting compliance. Companies with a strong Western/developed country interface – either in markets like pharmaceuticals and IT or the emerging Indian multinationals appear to be actively engaging with GRI. In some cases, these business leaders have even found themselves on boards of global associations. In other cases where the foreign markets seem to be in global south, companies do not appear to be rigorously adopting GRI. Many other companies have ignored both. We would require greater research in order to firmly conclude about effects of foreign institutional environment and founder beliefs.

Even though CSR may be becoming more standardised and convergent from an external perspective, the actual practice is far more diverse. It reflects specific beliefs of the founder groups, including their religious, nationalist and/or modernist beliefs. They could thus include loyalists to custom, modernist, hybrids of modern and custom and contortionists defying both custom and modernity. They thus present a bouquet of notions and practices rather than a stark juxtaposition of custom and modernity along the border. At this juncture, we may not be able to systematically classify Indian business into these categories, but that is beside the point. What is relevant is that these four variations of life in the borderland do offer useful ways of understanding the border experience from the perspective of large Indian businesses.

Loyalists firmly anchored in custom carry out activities without regard to either disclosures or reporting. As such it becomes very difficult to even identify them in the usual schema of things. Modernists embrace not only modern CSR notions and practices but also modern managerialist logics. The hybrids seem to adopt a big tent approach and engage in several different kinds of activities. And the contortionists show disregard to custom and/or law seeking to slip away from spaces between both. Consequently, we see a certain kind of choice being exercised in the specific approach towards responsibility within large Indian businesses.

Notes

1   https://factly.in
2   www.crisil.com/pdf/corporate/The-CRISIL-CSR-yearbook-20Jan2016.pdf
3   http://ficci.in/Sedocument/20361/csr_survey_ficci.pdf
4   http://economictimes.indiatimes.com/jobs/hundreds-of-jobs-opening-up-as-companies-sharpen-csr-intent/articleshow/51819011.cms?utm_source=contentofinterest&utm_medium=text&utm_campaign=cppst
5   The word trust is used here as a generic reference to foundations and not to its legal status.
6   http://economictimes.indiatimes.com/jobs/hundreds-of-jobs-opening-up-as-companies-sharpen-csr-intent/articleshow/51819011.cms?utm_source=contentofinterest&utm_medium=text&utm_campaign=cppst

Chapter 6

Partnering for responsibility

Business perspective

> Corporate-NGO partnerships are evolving. No longer are they simply a reputation building or fund raising exercise. It's now about sparking innovation and spurring on societal and environmental missions through the sharing of contacts and knowledge.
>
> (Chahal, 2016)[1]

In continuing our exploration and review of enactments of responsibility in Indian business practices, we look at partnerships between corporations and NGOs. A detailed examination of partnerships is warranted because partnerships have been common to various models of responsibility being pursued by businesses for several decades now. In addition, partnerships have been vigorously promoted by Section 135 legislation. Business-NGO partnerships involve collaboration across two different kinds of organisational and institutional logics. Whereas businesses represent a profit logic, NGOs represent a service logic. These different logics, which can even be contradictory at times, impact the design and outcomes of collaborations. This chapter therefore examines collaborations from a business perspective.

Partnership with NGOs has been a long-standing responsibility practice in Indian business. As we had discussed in the earlier chapters some *srenis* were endowed by merchants for specific purposes. In this chapter though, I will not revisit the distant past but focus on partnerships that have occurred in the context of the modern legal system which distinguishes between profit making and non-profit public welfare, thereby producing two different institutional logics that create the ground for partnerships between such profit and non-profit organisations. Some of the earliest partnerships of modern type occur in the form of early industrialists supporting libraries and hospitals for workers and general public in places like Bombay. These have come about primarily due to philanthropic objectives of business owners. The resulting organisations, i.e. hospitals or libraries had their own managements with varying degrees of participation by business families. These partnerships start in late 1800s and continue into early 1900s. Tata group's support to Servants of India Society in early 1900s is an early instance of modern partnerships between business and non-profits. Other early instances included funding support extended by businessmen to freedom struggle against the British, especially the Indian National Congress. Several large business houses and even small businessmen funded the activities of Congress. Some even maintained a regular donation account for this purpose, just like they had maintained donation accounts for religious purposes (Birla, 2009).

The 2013 legislation has made, funding partnerships with NGOs a central feature of CSR, by essentially defining partnerships as funding relationships. The law's stipulations have created a fund of at least INR 100 billion to be spent by companies in a project mode in pursuit of welfare of the nation's communities. Initial estimates of funding available for partnerships were in the range of INR 200 billion, the figures had been subsequently scaled down to around 100–120 billion since less than half of the listed companies met the stipulated criteria.[2,3] Given that on average government has provided about INR 9.5 billion per year to NGOs, funds made available through CSR become significant.[4] This has led to a phenomenal expansion of the scale and range of partnerships both within the company and across companies. It has also narrowed fields of engagement since the legislation has listed permissible activities. In the financial year ending March 2016 companies had spent at least INR 60 billion on CSR. This amount was spent either through companies directly supporting NGOs or through company-promoted foundations working with NGOs. With expansion in partnerships, selection of NGOs has become critical, bringing in other challenges in its wake.

In the seven decades between the early partnerships and the 2013 legislation, an assortment of objectives has characterised business partnerships with NGOs. Apart from shared philosophies, we can see objectives like rural marketing, cause-related marketing and funding relationships. Scanning this period, I broadly distinguish

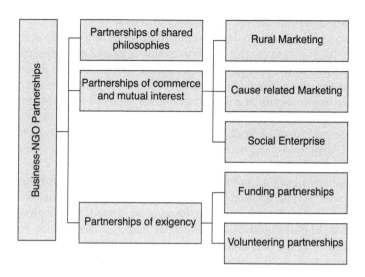

Figure 6.1 Types of business-NGO partnerships

Source: Author

three different business approaches to partnerships based on a variety of motives, modalities and management. They are partnerships of shared philosophies, those of commerce and mutual interest and those of exigency. In some sense, all the variations can be found in contemporary practice (see Figure 6.1).

Partnerships of shared philosophies

With independence in 1947, there was a lull in voluntary activity. Many leaders who had worked for social and community welfare formerly joined government and helped it pursue citizen welfare. As was already discussed in a previous chapter, business absorbed itself in pursuing India's economic growth. Some of the earlier activities of providing support to voluntary, community development and institution building work by business groups like Tatas, Birlas, Bajajs or Chettiars continued after independence. Disillusionment with government and numerous calamities in the 1960s and 1970s broke the lull in voluntary activity leading to a resurgence of voluntarism in the country (Jammulamadaka, 2009). Company owners and key managers, influenced by Gandhian ideals and resurgent voluntarism, supported NGOs through providing grants from trusts/foundations. The choice of partner and the cause was influenced by business leadership's philosophy and value system. To a large extent in this era companies approached partnerships on a completely voluntary basis. Instead of formal due diligence processes, the partnership was guided by shared philosophies and a desire to participate in a noble cause being pursued by a committed and impassioned activist/volunteer. Thus, this approach respected the commitment of grassroot NGO workers, and supported their work with funds, and management skills. It was not an era of monitoring and reporting.

Such motives and modalities informed the partnership between Mafatlal Industries and Bharatiya Agro Industries Foundation, a partnership that came about because of shared philosophies of Arvind Mafatlal and Manibhai Desai (Sundar, 2013). This trend continued as the only trend well upto the 1990s. Not all companies did this though. It was not the in-thing to do, even though from time to time business leaders exhorted companies to engage with communities.

Partnerships of commerce and mutual interest

In the period since the 1970s, voluntary organisations grew in vast numbers. Government actively engaged with NGOs as partners since the sixth Five Year Plan in 1980s. The period witnessed entry of several international, bilateral and multilateral donor agencies eager to operate in India (Jammulamadaka, 2009). During 1980s and 1990s microfinance and self-help group movement was also discovered and gained momentum. With support from government, the World Bank, and the United Nations agencies microfinance movement grew at a phenomenal pace across the country leading to the creation of a massive organisational infrastructure at the grassroots (Jammulamadaka, 2016c). Accompanying these developments in voluntary space was the wave of economic liberalisation which started in 1991.

Post-liberalisation, increased competition, emergence of a consumerist market, and public-private partnership model led to several corporates entering into areas that were hitherto considered non-lucrative or public service. The forays were initially made by IT and marketing companies. IT firms were building and managing software for government departments and marketing companies were assisting government in social marketing of healthcare products, most importantly family planning, and maternal and child health products. Initially the public sector enterprise Hindustan Latex Limited (now changed to Hindustan Lifecare Limited) was executing several projects of central government, state governments, United Nations Population Fund, United Nations Development Program, Department for International Development, United States Aid for International Development and other bilateral and multilateral agencies in social marketing of condoms, intrauterine devices, contraceptive pills, iron and folic acid tablets and the like. These projects aimed at improving distribution and access in rural, remote and interior areas which had generally been underserved by retail distribution system until then. The logistics challenges posed in serving these interior markets led to the discovery of NGOs as viable logistics and social marketing partners.

NGOs and the network of self-help groups, community associations and microfinance institutions (MFIs) promoted by NGOs provided a potent network of accessing the remote rural consumer. They served as stockists and their volunteers/workers functioned as sales agents. They also served as agents of communicating the desired behaviour change. Hindustan Latex's AIDS prevention project in Tamilnadu supported by USAID-VHS had partnered with NGOs to make condoms available with sex-workers and on highways. The company partnered with NGOs in Uttar Pradesh to foster behaviour change communication promoting contraception. This experience of successful partnerships opened the floodgates to rural marketing, an area that had otherwise been limited to agricultural input companies, public distribution system and Indian postal department.[5]

Rural marketing

Rural marketing provided an excellent solution for the desires of both companies and NGOs. Towards the end of the millennium, companies had learnt that bulk of India's markets was in rural areas and that they had to enter these markets if they wanted to succeed in India. Growing SHGs, MFIs and NGOs were actively looking for alternate sources of income and financial independence since the development grant space had become extremely competitive. These realisations paved the way for numerous corporate-NGO partnerships.

Partnerships were now based on detailed market planning and a careful selection of the NGO partner. NGOs with excellent credibility (understood as a recognised dominant player in the field) and a good grassroot organisational infrastructure were chosen as partners. Companies provided training to NGO partners in selling and reporting skills. A regular information monitoring system that tracked sales, behaviour change communication activity and other project management approaches accompanied these partnerships. These were highly instrumental and commercial partnerships subject to termination by either party due to dissatisfaction. They had very little to do with leadership philosophies or value systems of the company or NGO leadership. Instead market potential and organisational/community infrastructure drove them. An incentive structure in the form of sales commissions was worked out for NGO/MFI/SHG and its volunteers who served as channel partners in the rural areas. Both companies and NGOs positioned commissions as a means of income generation and financial empowerment. After humble beginnings as pilot projects, some of them were scaled up. The emergence of modern CSR discourse during this period enabled companies to showcase several such initiatives as CSR partnerships that promoted empowerment of rural, poor women.

While the idea of NGO partnership for entering rural markets caught on quickly and helped companies showcase CSR through these partnerships, the practice showed differential impact across industrial sectors. In the financial services space, there was a natural alignment with the growing microfinance sector. Insurance products were in demand from rural areas and government policy had put in mandatory service obligations. Several financial companies like Bajaj Allianz, ICICI partnered with NGOs and MFIs to sell specific financial products. Products were developed and designed based on specific inputs received from NGOs and then made available in rural areas. Birla Sun Life had developed the *BimaKavachYojana* as a single premium affordable insurance policy specially designed for rural underprivileged. It was working with several NGOs to sell its insurance policies. NGOs in fact contributed to a majority of its rural sales.[6]

Hindustan Unilever's project Shakti provided training in basic accounting, selling skills, health, hygiene and relevant IT skills to SHG women and called them *ShaktiAmmas*. They were also provided smart phones with mini ERP packages which helped them sell the company's products in their villages. By 2015, the project had

70,000 *ShaktiAmmas* and was reaching out to 162,000 villages.[7] Though there were several initiatives in the FMCG space, the volumes generated by NGO volunteers were not similar to those generated through regular channel partners like stockists. Only a few volunteers achieved such volumes and they transformed themselves into formal retail channel partners. With the potential of these markets becoming clearer, companies were also investing in developing regular marketing and distribution channels for rural areas.

NGO partnerships provided not only last mile connectivity but also brand building support to companies. Working with NGOs helped companies build their brands, and create product familiarity and trust in the rural areas. As Nita Kapoor of Godfrey Phillips pointed out, 'We learnt very quickly that if we tried to build trust on our own, we could not have it beyond a pilot. NGOs are your biggest bridge in building that relationship in that community.'[8] NGOs by virtue of their presence in local areas offered a higher frequency of brand communication than companies could achieve through sales personnel. Being associated with a locally credible NGO meant that company benefited from the credibility of the NGO in the eyes of rural consumer. A few companies used NGO partnerships to also source their products. For instance, ITC partnered with NGOs like Self Employed Women's Association in Bihar for production of incense sticks. It also used the NGO's network of women to source other agricultural commodities in Gujarat. This initiative was positioned as one which empowered the women through income generation. It also provided ITC a basis for product differentiation as a socially conscious producer. This in turn triggered the emergence of cause-related marketing as another mechanism of partnering with NGOs for CSR.

Cause-related marketing

The transition from rural marketing to cause-related marketing in the context of NGO partnerships was quick. It appeared to be a means of connecting with the urban consumer and improving brand communication. Brand communication meant that companies had to carefully identify a social cause and in turn the NGO they would be associated with. Identification of causes was driven by diverse motives. Sometimes partners were identified based on strategic alignment with the brand. At other times it reflected the beliefs of key business leaders. Such cause-related marketing was used to raise funds. These funds were then used to support other grassroot NGO partners working on specific issues. Grassroot NGOs were usually identified for support through a formal process by the main implementing NGO partner of the company. Support provided to grassroot NGOs was project based with specific deliverables and measures of impact and/or outcomes. Elaborate reporting systems were in place for working with grassroots NGOs. Funds raised and spent through such cause-related marketing were carefully audited since it involved raising a kind of public contribution. This approach became quite prominent in fast-moving consumer goods space.

Companies like Proctor and Gamble and brands like Tata Nihar used this to raise awareness and funds for supporting social causes, especially education for girl child, and health and hygiene campaigns. The cause partner was usually a large well-known NGO like TERI in climate change and sustainability, WWF and IUCN in wildlife conservation and biodiversity, CRY in childcare etc. NDTV had partnered with TERI for its environmental campaigns. Often large national NGOs like CRY or foundations like Naandi and KC Mahindra Trust coordinated the process between companies and grassroots NGOs. The *Nanhikali* project run by the KC Mahindra and Naandi foundations mentioned earlier had received funds through several cause-related marketing campaigns by other companies. The financial services company HDFC contributed INR 100 to *Nanhikali* project for every loan application made by a woman customer. These funds were then disbursed by KC Mahindra foundations to several NGOs working with girl children. In the year 2013–14, there were 20 different grassroot NGOs which received financial and capacity building support from *Nanhikali* project.

Social enterprises

Social enterprises provided another approach to corporate partnerships with NGOs. Growing realisation that newer kinds of products and services were required to effectively cater to the needs of rural people, prompted companies to partner with research institutions, NGOs and social entrepreneurs, to promote social innovation and social entrepreneurship. Several big business groups and venture capital funds today support social enterprise competitions and invest in social enterprise start-ups in sectors like health care, education, agriculture, income generation, skill development etc. In most cases NGOs are involved with these social enterprises as knowledge partners, pilot testing partners and/or marketing partners. There are many examples of eco-friendly stoves that have been developed by researchers with financial assistance from corporations and social venture capitalists, and are being marketed by NGOs and MFIs. Vilgro marketed First energy's Oorja brand of stoves developed by Indian Institute of Science with support from British Petroleum. Such multipartite partnerships are also found in health care, primary education and agriculture. In these kinds of partnerships, the corporate partner usually serves as the financing partner who funds opportunities that are seen as having potential for success and scale up. Specific social enterprise partners are identified through open competitive processes like the ones conducted in business schools and/or one-on-one evaluation of the business ideas by social venture capitalists.

Social enterprise and social innovation space presents a lot of hybridity in organisational logics. The conventional divides between NGOs, businesses and research institutions collapse. Instead one finds a collective of individuals and organisations pursing a shared goal with organisational type as a fluid category which transforms according to the financial and legal opportunities that are available. These three different types of partnerships currently in vogue are differentially presented as CSR initiatives by companies. They are positioned as CSR partnerships with NGOs for consumption by global CSR discourse. With regards to national CSR and reporting to government, these partnerships, especially rural marketing are often underplayed given the stipulation that companies should not seek business benefit from CSR.

Partnerships of exigency

These are partnerships that have emerged in the shadow of global and national compulsions of CSR. Since late 2000s, growing pressures for responsible behaviour from both within the country and outside investors, buyers and activists have impelled businesses to engage with NGOs and pursue activities of broader social relevance. We will not rehash the discussion on foundations and models of CSR here but look at the partnering angle specifically. Partnerships of exigency are most often funding relationships with the corporate partner providing grants to NGOs either directly or through foundations. One aspect of cause-related marketing is the disbursal of mobilised funds which also leads to such partnerships. Whereas in cause-related marketing the actual disbursal may be carried out by the NGO cause partner, in partnerships of exigency it is the company or its trust that does this.

In spite of having own foundations which partner with NGOs, many companies have been partnering with NGOs directly for grassroot activity. For instance, TVS Motor Company has its own foundation Srinivasan Services Trust which carries out welfare activities around its plants. In the year ending March 2016, it spent 26 per cent or INR 1.91 million of its CSR spend through this trust. But it had also supported four other organisations like Voluntary Health Sevices of Chennai and NIMHANS of Bangalore with the remaining fund. Within the Bharti group, companies like Bharati Axa Insurance and Centum Learning have supported local NGOs working on different issues in addition to the group level CSR activity which happens through Bharati Foundation. While TVS group spent bulk of its funds through the NGO partners, for Bharti group, the NGO support of these companies represented a peripheral activity with most of its CSR funding being managed by company foundation. Thus companies have differed in the emphasis they have placed on external NGO partners. Legally company foundations are separate non-profit organisations, therefore these have also been reported as corporate-NGO partnerships in some cases. For instance, Finolex talks about partnering with Mukul Madhav foundation which was set up by the founder of Finolex. Similarly Dr. Reddy's Labs talks about working with Naandi foundation which was set up by the company founder Dr Anji Reddy.

Partnerships of exigency have ranged from the purely transactional kind focused on achieving spend targets and producing reports to a meeting of minds variety where the exigency served as the opportunity that enabled two different organisations to interact and develop long-term relationships. At times they have also been exploitative partnerships. Whatever the reasons, the selection of NGOs has become a critical decision in implementing the project mode of Section 135 CSR.

How are NGOs selected for funding?

NGO selection has become critical because the NGO sector of India has been a field of contradictions. Recent reports of the Central Bureau of Investigation say that there are officially 3.1 million registered NGOs in the country and less than 10 per cent of them have even filed any returns with the government.[9] The government also blacklisted several hundred NGOs in 2015–16 and there are reports that atleast 15 per cent of the fund is used by NGOs in bribes.[10,11] This has heightened credibility and trust issues vis-à-vis the NGO sector. For companies this poses a challenge because firms face penalties and even imprisonment for taking unfair advantage of law according to the Company's act. Thus, companies are extremely cautious about inadvertently supporting fraudulent NGOs. Be that as it may, India also has a thriving non-profit sector with several illustrious people and models. Studies suggest that there are atleast a few thousand such reputed and respectable organisations (Kudva, 2005). Barring a few popular and large national NGOs, many of these committed NGOs work in the interiors of the country and not much is known about them in general public domain where corporates participate. This has led to major problems of information asymmetry and matchmaking thereby making the selection of a trustworthy partner critical. Given the enormity of spend volume and a general unfamiliarity of corporates with social and community development, companies have often bemoaned in several roundtable discussions and public fora on CSR in the last 3–4 years that they cannot find good partners.

To alleviate problems of information asymmetry, various agencies including government, industry associations, academia and NGOs have come together to bridge the information gap and set up validated databases and directories of NGOs with whom companies could partner (see Figure 6.2). There is a national CSR

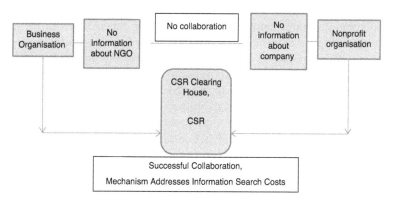

Figure 6.2 Approach to selecting an NGO: business perspective

Source: Author

hub – an online portal at Tata Institute of Social Sciences.[12] The Bombay Stock Exchange, Confederation of Indian Industry and the Indian Institute of Corporate Affairs (IICA) have together launched another online platform called Sammaan.[13] This platform which is operational on the Bombay Stock Exchange lists vetted projects. Within three days of its launch more than 600 vetted projects from NGOs which collectively require about INR 20 billion and 200 corporates registered on this platform. The vetting of documents and verification of activities for Sammaan is being done through the IICA and other NGO partners like Dasra, Credibility Alliance etc.[14] The website of the IICA also lists NGOs vetted by six different ministries of the government. This listing ensures that NGOs are not terror suspects or are under scanner for any illegal activity.[15] There are other online matching tools created by non-profits such as karmayog.in, ivolunteer.in or samhita.org. Several CSR consulting organisations and think tanks like Business Community Foundation, Dasra and Common Purpose, CauseBecause specialise in reviewing the field, identifying partner NGOs and assisting companies in spending CSR budget.

While such matchmaking improves information availability, the actual selection of the NGO still involves significant effort within the company. And several micro-practices have emerged depending upon the seriousness of the company and its intent in investing resources into the process. Many of these practices bear little resemblance to parameters used in rural marketing assessments or social-enterprise assessments. Unlike partnerships of commerce, there is very little training support that is extended to NGOs in spite of greater compliance and reporting expectations in these partnerships of exigency. Anecdotal evidence from company executives, NGO managers and a perusal of company and/or foundation websites indicates that some companies have identified priority and focus areas like education, health care, environment, girl child, rural development and seek to support NGOs in these areas only. For example Finolex is involved in education, health care, social welfare and water. Dr. Reddy's Foundation focuses on education and skill building. Many other companies do not explicitly spell out focus areas, instead they support a whole variety of causes. For instance Cadila supports rehabilitation of disabled, financial sponsorships for poor students, hospitals and also spiritual discourses on Bhagavad Gita. Another company Infinity Infotech supports Bhagavad Gita discourse week, Akshaya Patra Foundation for nutrition of children, green buildings and CSR meets. Or take the case of Apeejay which supports volunteering awards along with other things.

We had seen in Chapter 5 that surveys had pointed out that company's top leadership was the key decision maker in CSR. We also saw that decision making was often on a case-by-case basis and responded to emergent demands from below and outside. Those findings juxtaposed against the identification of thematic areas suggest that it is the owners' philosophy and attitude towards CSR which informs the extent to which an organisation seeks to engage in responsible practice, systematise its CSR practice, identify and articulate CSR priorities and measure and align it with global and national discourse. In the case of both Cadila and Infinity the spiritual beliefs of the owner family informed the organisational mandate. Both companies also did not show too much interest in measuring and reporting CSR. The same was the case with TVS, whereas in Mahindra owner beliefs emphasised focus, measurement and reporting. Mahindra's focus areas were a combination of business interests and general societal concerns: agriculture being a prime sector for the company, farmer initiatives were taken up, education and skilling appeared as a general societal concern and expectations impelled them to pursue reporting.

If leadership attitudes have influenced thematic areas and approach, the actual selection of NGOs is a more adhoc managerial process governed by caution and convenience. Many a times, employees identify the NGO based on their familiarity with the organisation through their personal networks. This practice serves as a proxy for assessing the trustworthiness of the NGO. For instance, in NGO partnerships that are done through Matiri programme in Tata Consultancy Services; employees identify the NGOs and recommend them to the company. In another instance a compressor maker from Western India started supporting an NGO working with mentally challenged because one of its employees had been associated with that NGO in his personal capacity. At times it also happens that the NGO is among the only ones located in the company's vicinity and thus the company ends up partnering with it. Mining company partnerships with NGOs in the vicinity of mining operations are often of this kind. At times, when the NGO itself has been suspect in the community's view, it adversely affects company image in the eyes of the community, even though it might help the company report about the partnership in its CSR reports.

Often NGOs are unable to make contact with company managers due to non-availability of contact information. Under these circumstances, sometimes, the NGO that is eventually supported happens to be one of the few ones that was able to make contact with company managers and persuade them effectively. In yet another practice, company managers get referrals about the NGO from others in the industry. And last but not the least an NGO happens to be one of the well-known organisations in the field. Organisations like CRY, Goonj, Akshyapatra Foundation, Deepalaya are quite well known and consequently have several corporates who are willing to work with them. Our survey of 50 companies had shown that 45 per cent of them worked only with reputed NGOs. 21% of the companies worked with either NGOs which were in their vicinity or NGOs which approached the company directly. Three companies out of the fifty worked only with those NGOs who were referred to by other colleagues in the industry.

In spite of the cautionary approach of companies, we find that the actual screening and vetting of the NGO partner is usually an informal process, exceptions occurring with the involvement of large foundations or big companies. Some of the minimum criteria used in the formal vetting process are availability of 3-year financial statements and experience of working with other donors. In some cases, personal visits are made to assess the capability of the NGO in the field. Companies also assess the extent of governance and transparency systems, and administrative effectiveness within NGOs. As the CSR head of Tata Motors says:

> reporting ability of non-profits is a crucial point when striking a partnership. . . . We want NGOs . . . to have a system to capture continuous progress and we want to know the progress in a prearranged schedule, and that's important to us because it gives visibility of how things are progressing.[16]

At times, companies have also used other criteria like the ratio of administrative overheads to programme spend in assessing the operational efficiency of the NGO partner. Tata Motors seeks to partner with those non-profits that do not have overheads above 10 per cent, as their CSR head explains, 'Overheads over 10% show that they are not spending their resources efficiently.'[17] The area of operations of the NGO and its geographical spread is yet another factor, particularly significant in the case of companies with a national footprint.

As the vice-president of sustainability at Mahindra and Mahindra, who needs to carry out operations at five locations explains, 'We look for this capability or the desire to expand when we look to partner with NGOs on large projects. Finding these types of NGOs is challenging as there are very few of them.'[18] With regards to the specific projects being implemented by NGOs we see some impact of partner's ability to negotiate. In situations where the partner NGO is large, well respected and provides significant associational advantages for the company, there is a room for improvisation and needs of the NGO are also taken into consideration. In other cases where partner NGO is often small and in need of support, corporate partnerships have often been fixed straight jacketed projects that reflect corporate needs for branding, visibility and reporting much more than the ground realities and needs of the communities or NGOs.

For instance Cognizant Foundation's partnership with LVPEI came about because, health care was an identified foucs area for the foundation and the non-profit was a hospital. It helped that LVPEI Institute was in Hyderabad because the company had decided to focus on geographies where it had its operations. In addition to the financial statements and other vetting, the actual identification of the project required working together and flexibility on both sides because the foundation supported purchase of assets like medical equipment and LVPEI did not need any medical equipment. They finally agreed upon an audio library project since this too involved the creation of a long-term asset. In another instance an IT company had partnered with an NGO working in the field of primary education. During discussions, the company learnt that the NGO's leadership had been struggling with weekly monitoring of its vast field force at the school level. The IT company then used its expertise to develop a software application that simplified the monitoring process for the NGO.

But not all partnerships are mutually beneficial; there are also instances where lack of corporate commitment to the partnership even in a rudimentary legal sense had resulted in adverse community and NGO outcomes. Changing company priorities, management systems and leadership transitions have also adversely affected project commitments and in turn NGOs. In one instance an engineering and power major began supporting a grassroots NGO working with rural women in West Bengal through its foundation. The project envisaged training and improving the skills of women in applique and *kantha* work (a local handicraft) and connecting them to markets thereby generating incomes. Accordingly, the foundation had sent a city-based designer and women were asked to prepare goods worth INR 0.1 million. However, both the designer and the foundation disowned responsibility for marketing and left the NGO high and dry with inventory on its hands. The company's internal turmoil and change of leadership at the foundation aggravated the problem for the NGO.

Volunteering

Volunteering is another approach to partnerships of exigency. Unlike funding relationships, the volunteering relationships are not subject to elaborate screening, since the employee himself/herself decides to work with the NGOs. Volunteering has been an important employee engagement practice in many companies. Volunteering in schools, after school education centres, rehabilitation centres for disabled etc. are quite common. At times, the trust established through volunteering relationships also leads to grant and project-based NGO partnerships from companies. They are given specific number of hours and sometimes matching donations by companies. Volunteering hours often conflict with other business priorities of companies and are impacted by the availability of a bench workforce or the employees' willingness to devote non-office hours for such work. Most large companies, especially those in the IT sector today encourage their employees to volunteer with NGOs. For instance, Mindtree Consulting has used such volunteering to improve the emotional intelligence of its employees and groom talent for leadership positions.

Current state of affairs and challenges

All the above kinds of partnerships are visible in CSR practices of Indian businesses, often within a single company itself. Responsibility practices of a company as seen from the outside might appear as a singular activity carried out by a company. In practice though, multiple functions and departments within the company pursue multiple points of engagement with communities and NGOs for their own immediate purposes. Be this as it may, effectiveness of partnerships with NGOs is impacted to a greater degree by managerial behaviours and attitudes towards these partnerships. Human resources function interfaces with NGOs for volunteering opportunities, employees interact with NGOs in their personal capacity, marketing function interfaces with NGOs for rural marketing and brand communication, strategic investments and planning function interfaces for investing in social enterprises, CSR departments interface with NGOs for community welfare projects and so on. Silos between various departments may impede internal coordination thereby undermining effectiveness of partnerships.

A short term quarterly orientation is usually prevalent in business management. Often companies are interested in short-term projects since profits vary over time, as do the strategic priorities of the firm. Project management approaches also emphasise clear structure with specific time lines and deliverables. The philosophy of investment also encourages quick returns and short-term orientation. Consequently this orientation is likely to spillover and inform managerial approaches to community development and CSR projects as well. However, development work is a highly complex process with unclear causalities involving a wide range of stakeholders and long time lines. NGOs thus prefer a less structured and more emergent approach to projects that allows them to take into account both problems and opportunities arising from the local context. Further, local contexts in which NGOs work are highly diverse. From a development perspective, the absence of strong wide-ranging planning and informality of NGO systems actually serves as an advantage that helps them retain community-centricity (Chakrabarty et al., 2017). When these two distinct approaches of companies and NGOs meet it leads to a tense situation. Often the company view prevails since it is the more powerful one and is providing funds. Business approach advocates strategic planning and fund raising even within NGOs. In a way this advocacy traps NGOs into becoming more donor oriented and reduces their ability to respond to community needs effectively. This adversely impacts the effectiveness of the project.

Often business managers are more educated, qualified and have higher incomes than NGO staff. Their higher status often could lead to an attitude that undervalues the expertise of NGOs. This makes managers susceptible to believing that they are more capable of finding solutions to community problems. Usually, business managers' inadequate appreciation of challenges of development and the dynamics of working with communities makes them propose and advocate ineffective solutions leading to disappointment and frustration both within companies and NGOs. Business managers are also used to quick decision making based on well-defined lines of authority. The political process in the NGOs thus is likely to appear as a distraction in the pursuit of efficiency. But for NGOs working with communities, the political process of community-based decision making is crucial to capability building and empowerment, even though it is likely to compromise efficiency. This divergence in preferences leads to project delays and friction with company. Of similar kind are the frictions that come from the participatory language in use in NGOs and a directive language in use in businesses.

These differences in managerial cultures and preferences have the potential to adversely impact partnership experience. Managerial practices of NGO selection usually eliminate several small but able NGOs from consideration. Practices of project management frustrate business managers and undermine NGO effectiveness. Thus, in order to promote fruitful business-NGO partnerships information availability alone is not sufficient. It becomes imperative for businesses to develop competencies in working with emergent phenomena over which one has little control, such as development. It is possible that the capabilities developed in this process could even feed back into improving effectiveness in routine business management and innovation.

Notes

1 www.marketingweek.com/2016/09/13/corporate-ngo-partnerships-wont-work-if-they-are-simply-a-cash-based-badging-exercise/
2 CRISIL handbook.
3 CSR PPT link.
4 www.achrweb.org/press/2013/IND01-2013.html
5 There were a few other battery companies which had been able to achieve supplies to the interior markets through retail networks. In the absence of electricity batteries were essential for torch lights in rural India.
6 http://linengage.com/core/rurallandscape/15.htm
7 www.hul.co.in/sustainable-living/case-studies/enhancing-livelihoods-through-project-shakti.html
8 Masters of rural markets in association with Accenture.
9 http://indianexpress.com/article/india/india-others/india-has-31-lakh-ngos-twice-the-number-of-schools-almost-twice-number-of-policemen/
10 www.business-standard.com/article/economy-policy/blacklisting-no-solution-ngos-pitch-for-a-reformed-capart-107061901019_1.html

11 India's Funds to NGOs Squandered, Edited by: Suhas Chakma, Director, Asian Centre for Human Rights; Published by: Asian Centre for Human Rights C-3/441-C, Janakpuri, New Delhi 110058.
12 www.ngoportal.org/funding-agencies-811-Emapanelment+of+NGOs+-+National+CSR+Hub+-+TISS+-2.html
13 www.bsesammaan.com/
14 http://timesofindia.indiatimes.com/business/india-business/CSR-platform-goes-live-on-BSE-projects-worth-Rs-2000-crore-listed/articleshow/50158997.cms
15 www.dnaindia.com/money/report-ngos-to-help-companies-undertake-csr-work-2070591
16 www.livemint.com/Companies/6nAPxHAA0s8P0EhA3Mx1kL/The-uneasy-relationship-between-corporates-and-NGOs.html
17 Ibid.
18 Ibid.

Chapter 7

Facilitating responsibility

NGO perspective

The importance of collective impact has been made clear in the legislation itself, which calls for and encourages companies to utilise the expertise of non-profits . . . being complemented by the corporate's wherewithal, . . . collaborations and associations make for an effective business case with respect to achieving maximum impact for a given CSR capital investment . . . apprehensions and concerns [have been] raised . . . [but,] the reporting requirements have ensured [transparency]. . . . NGOs on their part have never been better positioned than now to be the consumers of a large quantum of capital . . . not only fuels their cause directly but also increases the visibility of their work, thus building trust and credibility for them.

(Nexgen, 2014)[1]

It is very important to set the expectations right, since the beginning itself, in terms of requirement of resources, activities under the project, intended outcomes and impact. While it is important to aim for a positive impact for the target community, NGOs must let the donor know that timelines also matter a lot. Social change is certainly not an overnight process and many other factors come into play in this context.

(Arora, 2016)[2]

Having looked at CSR and partnerships from the corporate side, I continue our examination of partnerships from the NGO point of view. Before elaborating upon NGO approaches and experiences towards partnerships with corporates, it will help us to briefly examine the contours of India's NGO sector and the position of NGOs. This will help us in better appreciating the nuances of the NGO perspective.

Contours of NGO sector

Two features, i.e. non-profitness and voluntary founding have defined the perceived advantages and strengths of the NGO in the Indian NGO sector. Various advantages like ability to attract altruistic resources, provide for unmet and heterogeneous demand for public goods, protection against contract failure and freerider problem are attributed to these two defining features of NGOs. These features have given rise to a stereotype of an Indian NGO as convivial, participative, innovative, cost-conscious, locally rooted, responsive and thus a valued partner in development (Jammulama-daka, 2007). The growth of such an NGO sector in India has been subject to a variety of influences.

The period immediately after independence witnessed many social activists and development workers join government and help in reconstruction of the country. Consequently there was a lull in voluntarism. The subsequent rise of NGOs in post-independent India can generally be traced back to the 1970s when socially minded people disillusioned with government efforts in the face severe adversities, left their academic/business pursuits and entered villages to partake in development. Noted NGOs like Urmul Trust, BCT, Pradan and RDT all started during this period (Jammulama-daka, 2009). Initially these initiatives identified themselves as voluntary organisations. Development in this period was understood as *a passion and a commitment to the community, and sincere work,* rather than a specific set of skills and competencies aimed at specific goals. In fact, development skills and competencies evolved later from the lessons of experimentation within such voluntary organisations. The work of these voluntary organisations was funded by some committed corporate philanthropists and more generally by international donor agencies.

By the sixth Five Year Plan (1980–85), government of India started becoming a small but important source of funds for NGOs. Grassroots organisations had also expanded their presence, size and activity. There were local, regional and national-level organisations and networks of organisations. Simultaneously, there also emerged a differentiation within voluntary sector between social activists leading social movements and development workers carrying out constructive programmes. The gamut of constructive programmes became diverse with environment, income generation, women's empowerment, microfinance, watershed, primary education, capacity building, primary health and many other fields of intervention. A literal boom in microfinance occurred during the 1990s and 2000s.

Towards 1990s, the term NGO started to replace the term voluntary organisations with significant implications for the sector. In spite of criticism that formal management shifted the focus away from communities towards donors, the sector was getting formalised with an increasing emphasis on professional development skills, project planning, implementation and monitoring frameworks. Professionalism seemed to be gaining in value over passion. With burgeoning numbers of NGOs, the sector had become highly competitive. National and international funding was becoming increasingly difficult.

International donor agencies were among the single most important source of funds for Indian NGO sector. India was the largest recipient of NGO aid in 2005 at Euro 261 million as per OECD/DAC (Koch et al., 2009). As per Indian government statistics, foreign funding was over INR 51 billion in 2003–04 (approx. $1 bn) vis-à-vis a state support of INR 3 billion (approximately US$63 million) for the non-profit sector, for the same year (Kudva, 2005). Over the years, international donor funding for development started getting scarce. While the absolute quantum of funds being received from foreign donors had been rising, data from Ministry of Home Affairs on foreign contributions received by Indian non-profit organisations showed that there was a steady decline in the average quantum of funds received by each non-profit over the years (Jammulamadaka, 2015a).[3] This was due to an increase in the number of non-profits seeking and utilising funds. It was also due to changes in donor priorities stemming from increasing competition from other countries for the same funds. Sub-Saharan Africa and the Middle East consumed a greater share of development funds unlike previous decades (Kharas, 2007). International donor agencies were also faced with changes in their domestic giving environment, and they increasingly turned to local fund raising within recipient countries to generate funds for disbursal to NGOs (Greensmith, 2002).

Along with declining foreign aid, NGOs also experienced a reduction in funding from government under the influence of neoliberalism. An analysis of CAPART data showed that in spite of increase in absolute funding for NGOs, there has been a general decline in per NGO quantum of funds in the 1990s (Jammulamadaka, 2007). As mentioned earlier, recent pressures on Indian government to reduce its fiscal deficit, including warnings of sovereign credit rating downgrade implied that welfare spending had to be reduced (Jammulamadaka, forthcoming). These reductions in welfare spend meant that the pool of funding available for non-profits was reducing considerably since NGOs spearheaded the implementation of most government welfare programmes. It is in this context of the emergence of *development* as a professional competency and skill, growing formalisation of the sector, a microfinance boom, funding scarcity and mushrooming of NGOs that contemporary corporate interest in NGOs emerged and the government enacted the CSR legislation.

Historically, NGOs had been quite distant from corporate activity focused on communities. NGOs got their funds from the government and international donors. Philanthropy of some businesses was one point of interaction between businesses and NGOs but such interactions were few and far between. Interaction usually happened only when NGO founders had access to business owners/leaders through some networks and shared a mutual appreciation. The other point of interaction was when activists within NGO community started protesting against corporate abuse and environmental pollution. But, even such protest was usually directed against government and very few companies were targeted. With such sparse corporate engagement history, NGOs have entered the space of modern CSR and partnerships and struggle to navigate corporate expectations. In making sense of the NGO side and their experience of CSR partnerships, we shall continue with the broad categories of partnership we had identified in Chapter 6.

Partnerships of shared philosophies

As already mentioned this type of partnerships pre-dated modern CSR partnerships. Mutual appreciation characterised these relationships. These relationships were characterised by trust and a shared passion for the cause. Companies provided funding and, at times volunteers. But monitoring, reporting and measurement of impact were not a pronounced feature. To this extent, these relationships did not result in additional demands being made on NGOs. They provided space for NGOs to continue their activities without feeling overwhelmed or interference from corporate supporter-partner.

Partnerships of commerce

The coming of rural marketing placed very different kinds of demands on NGOs. NGO workers typically carried out a variety of activities in the field. Their success in working with communities was dependent on the NGO being perceived as unselfish and interested in the well-being of the villagers. Some of the chief capabilities which influenced NGO success were community animation, mobilisation, participation and grassroots institution building. While rural marketing presented NGOs with an opportunity to supplement their income and prompted many NGOs to actively consider assisting companies in reaching consumers, they soon realised that the NGO's skills and resources were insufficient to meet the needs of companies. NGOs realised that they were expected to promote company products with villagers. This conflicted with their position of unselfishness. They were also expected to *sell* the product but they did not have such selling skills. Merely stocking the product and letting villagers know that the stock was available was not sufficient. During NGO interaction with communities, they needed to spend time in both skill training and actual selling. Either way, time required for these activities diverted them from other serious and more important development activities.

Thus NGOs started showing reluctance towards their staff selling products. It was overheads, diversion of NGO time and critical human resources into corporate activity that disincentivised direct corporate-NGO partnership. Instead NGOs encouraged companies to directly interact with community members like SHG leaders for product selling and promotion. This way, NGOs freed their workers' time and also provided an income alternative to communities. Unlike the previous type, these partnerships had very little to do with passion, trust and mutual respect, instead they sought to use NGO infrastructure to pursue corporate objectives and NGOs addressed this corporate interest by attempting to directly link communities with business. In this sense, such partnerships were essentially between company and the community and NGOs served as a coordination and communication conduit between company and community.

Unlike selling, NGOs involved in behaviour change communication directly implemented company activities. These activities were usually social marketing activities and were done in a project mode where the NGO was expected to carry out a certain number of street plays, video shows, meetings etc. For instance behaviour change communication for contraception projects of Hindustan Latex and other companies enabled NGOs to develop assets and competencies in street plays and video shows leading to mutually beneficial circumstances.

Partnerships of exigency

The two variations in partnerships of exigency, i.e. volunteering mode and project funding mode have been experienced by NGOs differently with varied ramifications. Some ongoing research I have been doing on this along with my students and conversations with NGOs inform the accounts described here.

Volunteering partnerships

For volunteering partnerships, companies and employees approach NGOs seeking volunteering opportunities. This model of corporate-NGO partnership has been highly popular and successful abroad and many companies in India also follow this. To the extent the company and not individual employees in their personal capacity have approached NGOs for such opportunities; it has yielded mixed impact and experience for NGOs. NGOs often found that such partnerships did not benefit them significantly because of non-commitment and lack of skills within companies and their employees. They found that often the activities which company employees were willing to undertake had little relevance for NGOs or their communities. On other occasions, timings and schedules for volunteering did not match NGO needs and even if they were aligned after careful planning, the company did not follow through the plans due to exigencies.

For instance, a reputed hospitality firm sought out an NGO in West Bengal. The NGO was running an experiential school, a shelter for girls from high-risk families, a library and a 'School on Wheels' – a bus equipped with learning material and a small library, and a children's clinic for poor communities. This company had mandated that their employees spend 10 per cent of their time in volunteering. The chefs in the company accordingly went to the NGO and demonstrated healthy cooking recipes to students' mothers, while other company employees spent their time teaching students, assisting teachers etc. The chefs who had no prior idea about the socio-economic background of the students, taught making cakes and pancakes. These recipes needed expensive equipment such as microwave oven, grinder etc. which was not even remotely affordable for students' mothers, consequently the recipes did not appeal to most of the parents. Further there was no coordination between employees teaching the students. A person coming and teaching on one day had no clue what the person coming in an earlier week had taught. Thus there was no consistency in teaching, making it ineffective for students.

This NGO had also partnered with another large respected media firm. Here too the NGO was approached by the company for volunteering opportunities. Company desired to participate in a teaching programme. Though targets had been set initially between NGO and company, these were not adhered to. Out of 400 employees who opted for volunteering in the beginning, only 40–50 turned up, 20 started teaching and about 10 volunteers remained till the end of the 3-month programme. Continuity of volunteers was not ensured by the company. This adversely affected the ability of the NGO to implement its plans. Several other companies had approached the NGO for volunteering and were interested in sending their employees outside office hours. But this NGO's work was limited to day time activity at that time and hence these volunteers were not needed. Eventually, this NGO decided against partnerships for volunteering and preferred limiting them to funding.

There are also situations where the specific activity taken up by the NGO makes it difficult to find volunteers or even use volunteers effectively. For some NGOs working in the area of rehabilitation of differently abled, old people or orphans, it has been easy to find volunteers and find ways for mutually meaningful contributions. For instance, an NGO working with visually impaired maintained an online database of all those who had volunteered with them and used this to seek support for specific purposes. It posted requirements for writers, readers, audio recorders etc. to this volunteer list and company employees depending upon their professional commitments came forward and helped the NGO. Another NGO which was working in the area of leprosy could not find volunteers nor use them because of the highly infectious nature of the disease, clinical role of therapy and the stigma of the disease. Similarly, NGOs involved in rehabilitation of sex workers find stigma as a deterrent in attracting and using volunteers. Some such NGOs which have not been able to find volunteering opportunities for ongoing engagement have discovered that using volunteers to design management systems that improve the NGO's administration has been a far more effective and efficient utilisation of volunteering programme. Many NGOs have used volunteers to develop specific IT systems, control systems, streamline their accounting practices, developing corporate pitches, marketing strategies etc. However, here too NGOs have had mixed results. In some cases NGOs benefitted but in others, the system that was finally developed had limited utility since it had ignored several contextual and practical factors. At times, the elaborate systems proposed by volunteers meant that NGOs had to invest in new capabilities and assets which they were unable to do. Further, companies varied volunteer resources committed to these projects impacting quality.

Funding partnerships

Some research I had done along with my students on funding partnerships showed that relationships were impacted by issues related to corporate preferences, management systems and power. NGOs often found that projects were defined by business preferences which often conflicted with needs and interests of communities. As one NGO founder from West Bengal who had worked with highly reputed companies on CSR projects said, 'We have often seen that CSR projects are designed keeping in mind the business perspective so situation arises where the need of the community gets neglected. As NGOs work at grass root level keeping in mind the need of the community, it has been always a tough task to make the corporate understand this perspective.' He also added that in future if any corporate shared an interest with them and committed to consistent support, he would work with them on a long-term basis otherwise he was doubtful about partnering with businesses. An NGO founder from Andhra Pradesh added,

> Another major problem in these partnerships is the non-alignment of goals between NGO and company. Without common objectives in mind it is tough to function together as a partnership for each of these entities. It becomes tough to appease the companies which are looking at CSR activities as passive marketing campaigns. NGOs who also have to push the company by showing the branding benefits find the going tough when the context is a rural area.

Fortunately or unfortunately most of our work is done in the rural area where only a limited number of brands extend their reach due to high distribution costs. There is a tacit tension over the credibility of the service event organized. In our rural awards initiative, a company had approached us to give a big pile of money in return for branding the event completely as their own. But we could not agree to that. We had local supporters who were associated with us for many years even though the amounts were small. We also had our own identity. We were not a front for the company. Eventually, we decided not to take the money from the company but do it ourselves.

NGOs add that companies ask them to work in areas that are company priorities. Often such priorities diverge from local requirements of communities and NGOs and therefore alignment of cause is difficult. Even highly credible and respected NGOs have said that they have had difficulty in persuading companies for support because their activities did not align with company priorities or interests and passions of business owners. Often company projects are straight jacketed with little room for adaptation undermining project effectiveness. Founder of an NGO working in rural empowerment says, 'Budget is not as per as program need. Hence so many changes take place while implementing the program that the project ultimately gets hampered.' Often ongoing adjustments and revisions to the budget are hampered because many companies do not have mechanisms of interim review. NGOs add that generating impact on the ground requires a longer time frame and commitment for a 3–5-year period. However, companies are not very keen on giving such longer term commitment. Adding to all these challenges is the perception of the community. NGOs say that communities understand that an NGO is getting corporate support, consequently community expectations from that NGO go up and adversely affect participation.

NGOs say that even though corporate funding forms only a small part of their overall portfolio of funds, expectations of corporates are disproportionately high. The director of resources at Child Rights and You, popularly known as CRY, said that only 15 per cent of their revenues were from CSR spend. In spite of this, corporate expectations from NGOs were overwhelming.[4] Often these demands appear in the form of elaborate monitoring and reporting systems and budgetary constraints. Producing these reports means

NGOs need higher-quality people and have to pay greater salaries adding to their costs. As one NGO founder says, 'The financial and other reports have to be created with the utmost sensitivity and transparency. An NGO does not have a second chance to redeem themselves once a mistake is made.' CRY is one of the larger, well-established NGO that raises funds and supports smaller NGOs across the country. If CRY found company expectations on reporting overwhelming one can easily imagine the burden this demand would place on smaller NGOs. As CRY's director points out:

> On the one hand, there is this expectation that NGOs should live a hand-to-mouth existence and should be frugal. On the other hand, companies expect the same organization to be very professional. . . . Professionalism comes with investment. If companies want top class reports and videos, it costs a lot of money. If no one finances that how can we bring it about?[5]

Another NGO manager says, 'It is a chicken-and-egg situation really. They want us to be professional, but will not give us the necessary financial resources to bring about that professionalism . . . it would cost Rs. 2–5 lakh for a professional project report, which corporates expected from NGOs.'[6]

Another implication of such expectations and reports is the emphasis on measurement. There is too much emphasis on quantitative impact measurement. Corporate business managers running these partnerships, sometimes take pride in their ability to quantify and deploy specific success indicators and measures. NGOs find that such quantification assumes a simplistic view of the complex process of development, empowerment and impact. As a consequence, 'qualitative part gets neglected as results are mostly quantified'. With limited administrative resources for tracking company-wise support utilisation, NGOs are also forced to report the same overall figures to different companies. This often leads to double counting and perceptions of the NGO as fraudulent. Often NGOs concentrate on specific areas or regions in order to better respond to peculiarities of the local context. But this strength of the NGO itself becomes a disadvantage because they cannot provide the scale that a company working at a national level wants.

NGOs thus say, often companies call us partners but it is not a relationship of equal partners. Because they give the money, companies expect to have the upper hand, control and dictate to us.

The corporate anxiety of accountability manifests as close control and imposition on an NGO. As an NGO founder said, 'we are called partners but not treated as one. Mostly plans are imposed and not discussed prior with us. As another says, balance of control is central'.

How do NGOs find corporate partners?

With a limited historical background of corporate engagement, NGOs also face information asymmetry problems just like corporates. NGOs do not know which company is interested in spending how much on which projects. Whereas for a company, information asymmetry implied establishing trustworthiness of the partner, for NGOs this has implied identifying projects and financiers willing to commit. With differing concerns, the challenge of CSR partnerships has affected NGOs differently from corporates. Given that very little is known about the means by which NGOs find corporate partners, I dwell upon this aspect using some of my recent research on two comparable NGOs. I identify these two NGOs as Vision and Touch (names have been changed for confidentiality).

Both Vision and Touch are in healthcare space. Vision is a non-profit eye care provider with extensive clinical, research, outreach and community-based rehabilitation programmes. Vision is known as a pioneer and a centre of excellence in the field. Touch is also a non-profit service provider in treating an infectious disease that is seen as a scourge of the developing world. Touch too is a pioneer and a national centre of excellence in its field. Touch provides a range of services including clinical services, rehabilitation, counselling and advocacy in its domain. Both the NGOs are headquartered in the same city and have a network of centres in other parts. Both NGOs were started at around the same time in late 1980s. While Vision was set up with philanthropic contributions by individuals and government grants, Touch was set up through a dedicated funding from a British donor agency. Vision uses a cross-subsidisation model of charging fees to meet its operational requirements and provides free service to about 50 per cent of its clients. Touch provides free service to all its clients. Vision is a large organisation with a budget of about INR 1 billion whereas Touch is smaller in size with a budget of about INR 9.3 million.

Since both NGOs operate in the healthcare space, the environmental conditions are likely to be similar. Both of them are recognised leaders in their field, therefore neither of them would suffer from a credibility problem rendering the organisation unattractive to a corporate partner. Both of them have a dedicated person responsible for managing the process of approaching businesses seeking collaboration. Both NGOs have been pursuing businesses for partnerships since 2012. Vision was successful in securing corporate partnerships and had over INR 20 million worth of partnerships, whereas Touch had hardly secured any partnerships. It was still struggling with a few thousands of rupees worth of event sponsorships from corporations. There was one stand-alone project for a few hundred thousand rupees from one company. Most of the project amount went to the beneficiary in the form of a house. Touch served as a mediator in this case.

Identifying companies

The first aspect involves identifying companies. Both NGOs focused on companies within the same city. Similarity in the approach ended there and they both followed vastly different processes in the identification and targeting of companies. Touch did very basic google-based research on the internet about companies in the city. Initially they simply searched company websites for contact information without any specific targeting. After a few months, Touch slowly adopted basic targeting to confirm whether health was included in the CSR policy of the company. 'We do some research on the internet, are they funding health, is health in their CSR policy?' (Fund raising manager, Touch). At this time, Touch also began targeting pharmaceutical companies because they believed that their healthcare domain was a natural fit with pharmaceuticals (they had access to free medicines from companies under global CSR policies and government programmes). However, Touch reported that they did not get any response whatsoever from pharmaceutical companies. After a year of unsuccessful efforts, Touch did some rethinking and looked back into its history to identify businesses that had supported it in the past, irrespective of the size of funding. It then decided to revisit those businesses and initiate an interaction that had gone cold. Touch did not particularly consider targeting a company or researching its policy. It sought to contact any and every firm. The 75 firms Touch contacted through letters and emails included companies of all sizes, from all sectors and with all kinds of credibility problems.

Vision on the other hand, appeared to be very systematic in its search process right from the beginning. It targeted the large firms in the city first. It thought that if it could persuade the large and highly reputed firms, it would have a demonstration effect and establish Vision's credibility with all the smaller firms as well. It first targeted IT companies since its patient data showed that employees of IT companies are prone to eye health problems. It did this even when it had large pharmaceutical companies as members of their governance board. Pharmaceutical companies were approached much later. It was clear from the discussions that Vision was cognizant of the effects of credible partners and thus targeted large credible companies to begin with. In addition, Vision's manager carefully followed corporate activity and CSR news, and tried to target those firms which publicly professed interest in CSR.

> I will keep my eyes open and ears open and try and see if there is any forum happening, if it is, what is it? Is it connected with CSR, who are the participants, we would know that they are the ones who are interested, that is one segment. . . .
>
> (Assistant Director, CSR Initiatives, Vision)

Contacting companies

Once companies were identified, the second step involved securing contact information and contacting them. Both NGOs expressed difficulty in securing contact details of CSR point person from company websites, annual reports or sustainability reports. Touch attempted to solve the contact problem in a direct, simple and naive way that relied on the goodness of a company's manager. Touch used email, telephone and on a few occasions personal meetings in contacting prospective partners. In most cases, Touch ended up sending out emails to company mailboxes and managers from other unrelated functional areas requesting CSR funding assistance. On many occasions, in the absence of proper contact information, emails were simply sent to 'investor relations office' or even to 'info@' email ids. These emails carried standard text which basically introduced the organisation and sought project assistance. Most of these emails were ignored by companies. On occasions, specific material support like generator sets, televisions were sought through these emails. Phone calls were also made. They were unable to secure even an initial interaction, telephonic or email, with prospective companies. Most of Touch's emails went unanswered and phone calls unreturned. A company was contacted atleast 6–7 times before Touch gave up on pursuing the company any further. Often these phone calls were stuck at the main 'telephone reception level' or with some other person and they would be kept on hold without getting any appropriate response. In the few face-to-face meetings that Touch managers were able to materialise, they would generally be met with inattention and annoyance by company managers. After waiting out the inattention and annoyance, the managers of Touch would be told that the current year's budgets were used up, or that their internal processes did not permit such a partnership at the current time. On very few occasions, they would manage to get a few thousand rupees worth of support from the company.

'Around 6–7 times

RESEARCHER: 6–7 times you were going there personally?

TOUCH: personally!

RESEARCHER: personally and then emails and phones and then nothing has come yet?

TOUCH: yes . . . for 2 years i have been . . . you know kept on writing to,'

On other occasions, the person with whom Touch managers had begun liasioning would change and they would have to repeat the whole thing.

'Basically what happens is these Maharatna companies and NTPC, the officials keep changing. So again it's a new process. Every time we approach it's a new process because that person will not know us and again we have to start up again saying this is the thing . . . last year so and so has done this. And he has to get convinced. It takes a lot of time.'

Vision on the other hand dealt with this problem of lack of contact information in many interesting and innovative ways. First, the manager in charge mobilised personal networks to get some information on CSR point persons in IT companies. Second, the outreach clinic of Vision was located in an area very close to where IT firms were located. Vision's manager kept a close watch on patients who were coming into this clinic, to identify any potential persons from IT companies who could provide contact details of

CSR managers. The organisation did not collect employment information per se from patients, but the manager tried to interact with patients to understand customer satisfaction and in the process sometimes got lucky with contact information. The manager also used volunteer data maintained by their rehabilitation department to secure corporate appointments and references. In addition to all these innovative methods, the manager with support from Vision's leadership started participating in events related to CSR. His logic was that big companies would come to these events. These would be companies that were interested in CSR. Another advantage with events was that the leadership and senior decision makers of the company would be present in there. Thus Vision believed that meeting these senior managers during the events, introducing itself and initiating a conversation was a way of bypassing the problem of lack of contact information.

> It is basic gut feel . . . when you meet about 10 people . . . you realize 2 or 3 are very excited to speak to you and . . . you would establish a conversation with these two three and it all depends on how this conversation goes . . . so when you start talking, one guy says ok, let's connect again, so then you exchange numbers and get in touch. Or someone would say, no I am into something bigger. So it tells me . . . if I think bigger, I need to go to this guy later on. . . .
> (Assistant Director, CSR Initiatives, Vision)

> There are typically 2 or 3 kind of people you meet when you see these kind of events. One is who has lot of money to spend because they have targets or whatever. Second is the passion, they are really interested in doing something good and then they have the responsibility and the authority so they would like to channelize that. Third is they would like to know how you as an NGO are doing, so they have their own agenda to talk to you. So I would go with the person who is actually passionate and also has money in his pocket. I would spend more time talking to this person or giving away details which might say, 'ok this guy sounds interesting so let me talk next time'.
> (Assistant Director, CSR Initiatives, Vision)

Vision continued to innovate in its approaches. About 6 months earlier, this manager had joined social media and started participating in various fora and speaking about his organisation and their partnerships to elicit interest from businesses. One such forum presence led to a conversation with the head of an industry lobby.

Thus careful participation, planning and processing of events, and conversations during the events to generate prospective partner data were features of Vision's approach. There was a lot of preparation that went into the seemingly spontaneous off the cuff conversations that the manager of Vision was having with companies.

> . . . so it is a very conscious effort that I do that . . . I make him or her know that these are things we have done, these are things we would like to do. . . .
>
> Because we would know . . . I do go through the sustainability reports of these companies and then figure out how much they spend. Their budget, what have they done . . . what are they looking at and how they make the reports as well because that will tell how they will look at you also and what are they expecting from you as an NGO. . . . So are we prepared . . . if not . . . we can look at ourselves . . . and develop them . . . so there is a lot of homework that goes into it . . . yes . . . so you need to be clear about yourself, the facts, the past, what's happening and then the trends and the solutions. It is very significant because suddenly if somebody a top guy asks what do we do . . . you should be able to say something, rather than saying I will check with my colleague.
>
> So while speaking you throw in names, 'like while we were doing that Chief Minister was there'. So he will think. 'Ok, this guy is associated with big guys, so there is no problem, I can associate with him.' If they think this guy is not upto a level where I should get my name tagged on, then they back off. Of course because then their credibility is at stake. But when you tell them, 'you don't worry. If you tag with me, then there are bigger guys who are tagged with me, so you won't have problems'. I think that is more important. I think that is the stealer.
>
> The designation that your card carries matters a lot. For me fortunately I never had a problem because a lot of the people think that I am a director. I told the executive director about the designation. I told my HR guys also, but they did not do much and especially if I am meeting someone for the first time and I do not know that person very well designation matters. It very well matters, a CEO of a company would not want to talk to

an Assistant Director right. He would prefer to talk to a Director or a Chairman or whatever. That is the ego issue.

Just contacting companies without any prior contact, the hit rate may not be good or it can be negative also. It is like doing a sales call, it will not augur well for the brand. Honestly I think it is 50–50 [brand and personal effort]. The brand does matter a lot. For them [company] the safety of their funds is important. Their reputation is important. From that point of view they would look at the brand and say, 'there won't be any problem here'. So it helps.

(Assistant Director, CSR Initiatives, Vision)

Vision on the other hand relied more on face-to-face contact. They were already following the event route to get contact information, therefore they were able to meet the concerned persons face to face after some persistence. Upon meeting face to face, Vision's manager did not use any standardised material for presentation and communication. While he had such material ready with him in the form of brochures and presentations, the manager relied more on conversation. Further, the initial contact was in the form of an eye check-up service which Vision could offer the company employees rather than a request for funds. Interesting nuggets of information about the capabilities of Vision and the expertise it had shared with the company during these conversations in order to sustain the company's interest and curiosity in Vision.

The manager prepared for his corporate meetings, by studying sustainability reports and other publicly available material on the company to get a sense of what the company was looking for in a partner. He would use this understanding to strategically share information with the company. The company's curiosity was further encouraged by Vision's manager to eventually lead into a visit by the company to Vision. Usually around this time, discussions on funding and projects would begin. Vision too had to face many refusals where after the companies had heard him out with interest and patience, refused to partner on the grounds of 'lack of strategic alignment' with the company's strategy. On other occasions, certain idiosyncratic reasons also led to a decline in collaboration. The manager of Vision narrated an instance where the CSR head of a large firm had in principle assured collaboration and then arrived at Vision's facility to avail some treatment for family members. Vision was unable to attend to this person on time due to heavy patient load. This prompted the CSR head to withdraw the offer of support to Vision citing lack of trust and reliability.

Purpose and nature of partnership

Reviewing the purposes for which assistance is sought also provides interesting insights. Vision very clearly sought support only for capital expenditure for new projects. These funds were used to expand existing facilities or create new services. Thus, capital expenditure and/or asset creation that expanded Vision's ability to serve final beneficiaries were the purposes for which a company's support was sought. Several projects in rehabilitation department of Vision received support through CSR projects. This appeared to fit well with companies' diversity and giving priorities. Touch on the other hand was either very specific or very vague in seeking support. Depending upon the needs of existing facilities and activities, it sometimes asked for specific things like generator set, food packets, television sets etc. At other times, it sought generalised assistance.

> The project needs support from you to continue extending helping hands to the most neglected people living with disease. We believe that by coming together in partnership, we can make a real difference. We look forward for a favourable response.
> (Excerpt from an email sent by Touch)

Discussions further revealed that Touch believed that securing partnership was a gradual and prolonged process. It believed that if it could persuade a company to give a few thousand rupees in one year, in the following year, a slightly larger amount could be sought and thus a growing relationship could be built. Thus, Touch mainly focused on securing INR 5,000–10,000 from a company. Further, it was interested in securing open-ended donations which Touch could use to meet its operational needs.

Another interesting aspect that was thrown up during discussions with both NGOs and corporate managers was the role of employee engagement. They mentioned that companies were interested in having opportunities for their employees to volunteer. This helped the company in immediate ways by providing employee engagement opportunities. Further, such volunteering arrangements eventually led to a familiarity with and acceptance of the NGO within the company. Since fund raising for CSR initiatives often included employee giving initiatives, one of the corporate procedural requirements for supporting NGOs was that company employees vouch for and recommend NGOs which should be supported by the company. Lack of volunteering opportunities meant that this route of gaining corporate acceptance was not available to Touch. Touch was working in the area of infectious diseases and thus there were very limited opportunities to volunteer for serving patients/beneficiaries' care. This had impacted their corporate acceptance. A few companies had refused Touch because they could not be recommended by company employees. Since Vision worked in the field of visual impairment, it was easy to provide significant opportunities for employee volunteering in the form of readers and writers for visually impaired.

As such one can see that a number of factors act as enablers and hindrances for NGOs seeking corporate partnerships. These are given in Table 7.1. One of the main hindrances relates to the unavailability of company contact information. Since the contact information of the person responsible for CSR was not available on company websites or annual reports both NGOs did not know

Table 7.1 Enablers and hinderances in NGO-business collaborations

Enablers	Hinderances
Familiarity	Lack of contact information about CSR managers
Opportunity for generation of trust	Inability to present in a corporate friendly way
Existence of prior support for the NGO from others	Operational/administrative funding
Ability to present oneself in a corporate friendly way	Small value funding
Project funding	Idiosyncratic views
Demonstrated implementation capability	Not figuring in strategic priority of the firm
Prior preparation and targeting	Lack of prior preparation and targeting
Adequate opportunity for corporate employee volunteering and employee engagement initiatives	Limited or non-existent opportunities for corporate employee volunteering and employee engagement initiatives

Source: Author

whom to contact. NGOs use innovative ways to bypass this lack of information. The innovation was possible for Vision because its manager seemed to have an understanding of how companies operated and what their priorities were. Vision's manager recognised a corporate authority structure as well as CSR strategy, and reporting requirements of companies. He also had the necessary etiquette and presentation skills that made him and Vision appealing to companies. Touch did not have any of these characteristics, and was therefore unable to develop creative ways of tackling the contact information problem. Its unfamiliarity with corporate priorities, systems and culture was further evident in the emails being sent to unconnected email addresses, request for small and micro fund amounts for support and absence of company targeting among other things.

Among the other hindrances were the kinds of funds sought. To the extent that funding directly benefitting final beneficiaries was sought, it appeared to have greater chances of success. Support for ongoing, administrative expenses appeared a no-go for companies. The strategic priorities of companies and idiosyncratic views of those responsible for disbursing CSR funds within companies were also important hindrances for securing successful partnerships. On the other hand, Vision's familiarity with corporate etiquette, priorities and culture, and their reliance on face-to-face conversations, absence of overt and direct requests for support, and gradual development and steering of interaction towards a partnership appear to have created enough familiarity and trust vis-à-vis the NGO inside the company. This trust appears to have triggered large-scale collaborations which are currently in place between companies and Vision.

Pursuing this line of argument further, and examining the reasons for the apparently high degree of familiarity with corporate management practice that Vision's manager has vis-à-vis the manager from Touch, leads us to recognise the significance of corporate managerial behaviours, skills and competencies in the person responsible for such collaborations in materialising successful CSR partnerships (see Table 7.2). The manager responsible for securing such collaborations was designated as Assistant Director, CSR Initiatives at Vision. He was an ex-corporate vice-president who had managed sales in a large multinational. He was remunerated comparatively well and his previous corporate experience gave him insight into the workings of companies and their management

Table 7.2 Comparison of skills and competencies of NGO managers responsible for collaborations

	Vision	Touch
Designation	Assistant Director, CSR Initiatives	Manager, Fund Raising
Educational qualification	Master of Commerce	Masters in Social Work
Prior experience	Corporate Sales in a Multinational Company	Human resources management at NGO B
Demeanour	Confident, Aggressive	Apologetic, lacking confidence
Personal attitude	Highly ambitious	Satisfied with current performance
Familiarity with CSR	Knowledge of best practices, company priorities, legislative developments	Hardly any familiarity
Familiarity with corporate management and etiquette	Highly familiar	Not familiar
Communication and selling skills	Very good	Very poor

Source: Author

concerns and priorities. The experience also provided him with the necessary socialisation and etiquette that made him acceptable to corporate decision makers. On the other hand, the manager looking after corporate collaboration at Touch was designated as manager, fund raising. He had been working with Touch since the beginning of his career. He had worked in various human resource functions at Touch prior to becoming a fund raising manager. Thus the manager at Touch did not have any exposure to corporate management, authority structure, selling, CSR or even corporate etiquette. The one new understanding he seemed to have developed after getting into the role of a fund raising manager was that he could not meet corporate managers without prior appointments! It is possible that Vision manager's familiarity with corporate management not only gave him an advantage in seeking partnerships but also made him more believable and relatable to company managers. His ability to speak corporate language and understand company concerns, and his confident demeanour apparently assured companies that their interests would be protected. Whereas, Touch manager's lack of corporate understanding led to a diffident demeanour that not only made it more difficult for Touch to identify companies but also made them less desirable to companies. Lack of employee engagement opportunities at Touch further reduced their chances of success.

As we see from the cases of Touch and Vision, it makes no difference that Touch is also a national centre of excellence and a credible partner just like Vision. Touch simply could not find a seat at the corporate table because of a naïve approach to CSR, business organisation and decision making.

Business decision making in dealing with information asymmetry problem appears to be driven by a fear of adverse selection and moral hazard. Adverse selection refers to the possibility of choosing an unfit or incompetent partner, moral hazard on the other hand refers to the possibility that the partner may renege on the contract, and, not deliver as promised. Seen in this context, the refrain about 'lack of information about NGOs', made by companies is probably, only that, a refrain. If plain and simple information availability was the problem, the companies could have simply solved it by disclosing their CSR manager's contact information on their websites. This would lead to the company being inundated with applications for support. The company would then have to incur significant costs in appraising each of these applications to establish the credibility of the application before it finalised a few partnerships. Thus, we see that in practice, companies do not usually disclose this information. NGOs have to go through great trials to secure audience with corporate managers as our investigation has shown. These hurdles and trials that an NGO is going through serve the company as a mechanism to screen NGOs against adverse selection and moral hazard in a cost-effective way (see Figure 7.1).

Many NGOs either due to resource constraints, lack of information or inability to persist for long periods would not be able to go through all the trials. NGOs which successfully clear all the hurdles would be self-selecting themselves as credible non-profit partners for the corporate entity. Not acknowledging phone calls and emails from NGOs can also be understood as another corporate measure in this overall strategy of cost-effective screening. Hence the company reduces significant costs in screening NGO applicants. The credibility of the company is taken for granted in this case. NGOs credibility is suspect until proven otherwise. The costs and onus of

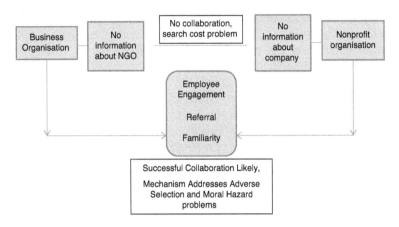

Figure 7.1 Model of pre-selection in NGO-business collaboration

Source: Author

proving their credibility lies to a large extent on the NGO and not on the company. The reference that Vision's manager made to the credibility enhancing effect that association with big names makes in seeking corporate collaborations attests to the prevalence of a fear of adverse selection and moral hazard.

NGO views on facilitating responsibility

In the current scenario, all three kinds of partnerships-shared philosophies, commerce and exigency can be seen, though there is an increasing prevalence of funding and volunteering partnerships. These trends are carrying with them a gradual shift in the character of the relationship. Whereas, earlier, partnerships were characterised by mutual respect for each other's abilities and interests, they have since mutated into instrumental relationships. In spite of a rhetoric of partnership, these relationships are imbued with power, inequality and domination.

Embedded within this narrative of ways of gaining familiarity, trustworthiness and eventually partnership is a subtext of 'desirable' skills and competencies in securing partnerships. The partnerships are currently in the nature of impositions of business managerial superiority that devalues and derecognises local competence. From an NGO's point of view, securing partnerships with NGOs are not just about post-funding project effectiveness or reporting overload. They are also about possessing skills and capabilities that are isomorphic to corporate organisations which enable NGOs to navigate not only absence of information about CSR point persons but also the corporate decision-making hierarchy. However, smaller NGOs do not have the resources to hire people with such skills and this puts them out of contention right away. They could seek to hire altruistically minded business managers, but finding such people who would work in small NGOs is again a remote proposition. This bias in favour of a certain style of working, presentation and competencies automatically disadvantages smaller NGOs which might be otherwise competent and well-versed in their line of work. It sets up a very high entry barrier for smaller NGOs to participate directly in corporate partnerships. Though in principle all NGOs should be able to partner, the actual practices and dynamics of the partner search process itself privilege larger and more managerially enabled NGOs in accessing funding, which inevitably implies higher administrative costs.

CSR partnerships with businesses from an NGO's perspective are not benign efforts to build a better world. Instead they are new sources of domination where NGOs are the silenced actors. The interest shown by NGOs in partnering with corporates in spite of this, points to the financial stress in the NGO sector. It also points to the changing nature of business-society and state relationship in India.

Notes

1 www.forbesindia.com/blog/the-good-company/collective-impact-when-government-corporates-and-ngos-collaborate/
2 www.fundsforngos.org/developing-countries-2/india/how-indian-ngos-can-mobilize-funds-through-csr-a-guide/
3 Under the Foreign Contribution Regulation Act (FCRA) organisations receiving foreign funding have to be registered with the Ministry. The aggregate figures provided by FCRA include religious, educational and scientific trusts and societies in addition to social development non-profits. It is therefore likely that the actual amounts available to non-profits are much lesser than the averages arrived at using FCRA figures.
4 www.livemint.com/Companies/6nAPxHAA0s8P0EhA3Mx1kL/The-uneasy-relationship-between-corporates-and-NGOs.html
5 Ibid.
6 Ibid.

Chapter 8

Borderland's underbelly

Medium, small and micro enterprise practices

> As India gears up to retrace the high growth path, the MSME sector assumes a pivotal role in driving the growth engine. The MSME sector in India continues to demonstrate remarkable resilience in the face of trailing global and domestic economic circumstances. . . . With its agility and dynamism, the sector has shown admirable innovativeness and adaptability to survive economic shocks, even of the gravest nature. The significance of MSMEs is attributable to their calibre for employment generation, low capital and technology requirement, promotion of industrial development in rural areas, use of traditional or inherited skill, use of local resources, mobilization of resources and exportability of products.
>
> (Deep Kapuria, CII Trade Fair Council and CII National SME Council in 2015)[1]

> 'Development' has an underbelly, which is quite large and precarious. Like other 'shining' industrial belts in India, the burden of the so-called 'development' . . . falls directly on the low-paid and insecure workers.
>
> (Jha and Chakraborty, 2014)[2]

In continuing to describe life in the borderland of responsibility from the exterior, I now turn our attention to the underbelly of Indian business – MSMEs. The phrase *Indian business* often evokes images of large business houses and firms. Lying outside these evoked fields of vision – often ignored in popular debates on economy – are MSMEs; individually insignificant, but collectively, a crucial pillar of India, propping up its economy and society, and carrying the burden of development, livelihoods and growth. In the case of MSMEs the borderland of responsible practices is further constrained because they not only operate along the regulatory border but also are extensively implicated in global value chains.

Literally speaking, the term CSR in a sense precludes small and medium enterprises, the assumption being that these small enterprises with limited capital, technology and access to resources and power, are individually insignificant and unable to impact society adversely or favourably at the same scale as large corporations. Effectively even Section 135 legislation places MSMEs outside its ambit since most of the enterprises would not meet net worth, turnover or profit criteria. Therefore advocates and experts have proposed the term enterprise social responsibility instead of CSR to draw attention to responsibility practices in smaller businesses (UNIDO, n.d.). Whereas instances of green supply chains and product innovation have been discussed as CSR in the context of European MSMEs (Jenkins, 2004; Moore and Spence, 2006; Morsing and Perrini, 2009) in translating the idea to the specific context of India and its MSMEs, a developing nation with limited resources, a supplier country for global value chains; the supplier code of conduct approach has come to signify modern CSR. MSMEs risk being branded as irresponsible if they do not comply with MNC buyer codes of conduct.

In fact, we could even argue that MSME participation in global value chains and global CSR is far more disadvantaged than that of a large Indian business given the nature of competition, and weak bargaining power of MSMEs. MSMEs in different sectors driven by purchasing pressures and practices of MNCs are engaged in a global race to the bottom competing against each other from within the sector and across sectors from different countries. Therefore in some sense, they constitute the *exterior of the exterior*. Not only are they disadvantageously placed in global value chains; MSME position and voice vis-à-vis large Indian business within domestic polity and economy is also extremely tenuous. So how do these doubly disadvantaged, but extremely crucial, MSMEs enact responsibility? Before we start examining the enactments, it would be prudent to lay out the peculiarities of MSME sector so that we can begin to appreciate their disadvantaged status and lack of voice.

MSME underbelly

The MSME ministry's annual report for 2015 estimates that there are around 48.846 million MSMEs in the country. More recent estimates put it at 51.1 million.[3] The sector has been growing at 10 per cent per annum. MSME ministry estimates that less than 5 per cent of the enterprises are registered, the sector being over-whelmingly unorganised. Collectively MSMEs are active in 6,000 product categories from the low-tech to high-tech end of the spectrum and operate in a range of industries in manufacturing and service sectors. They contribute to 8 per cent of India's manufacturing GDP, over 40 per cent of India's manufacturing output, over 30 per cent of service sector GDP and 40 per cent of exports of the country. The sector provides employment to over 100 million people.

The 2006 MSME act classifies micro, small and medium enterprises as follows. Medium enterprises have investments of INR 50–100 million, small enterprises of INR 20–50 million and micro enterprises of INR 1 to 2.5 million.[4] The unregistered enterprises are even smaller and often employ less than 10 people. According to estimates of government, these enterprises have an average investment of INR 2.87 million per unit in the registered sector and INR 0.12 million in the unregistered sector. MSMEs usually occur as clusters or local agglomerations of enterprises producing and selling related and complementary products. Estimates are that there are 350 industrial clusters and up to 2,000 artisanal clusters in India (UNIDO, n.d.; Russof, 2001). The employment provided in these clusters ranges from as less as 100 workers to as high as thousands of workers. This is the second largest sector after agriculture in terms of employment (Gupta, 2009; Grant Thornton India, 2010).

Clusters sometimes emerge due to historical process of trade agglomeration. In some other cases, clusters develop as ancillaries of large manufacturing firms. Such clusters are visible in the auto components and hitech electronic goods industries. Clusters often account for a major portion of the total production of that product in the country. About 80 per cent of cotton hosiery is produced in the Coimbatore cluster and Ludhiana produces 95 per cent of the country's woollen knitwear. The West Bengal leather cluster accounts for 25 per cent of the country's leather exports. In fact 60 per cent of leather goods export and 90 per cent of hand gloves export is from this cluster.

Usually, it is the medium-sized tier 1 firms in a cluster which are in direct contact with the final TNC buyers from Western markets.

But tier 1 firms and the total employment they have form only a small percentage of the total worker and firm population in these clusters. The small and micro enterprises take the lion's share. For instance, in the Bangalore garment sector, there are two large firms, Gokuldas Exports and Bombay Rayons which together employ about 25,000 to 30,000 workers, whereas the sector as a whole provides employment to 500,000 workers (Mani, 2013). Similarly, in the Kolkata leather cluster, there is just one large-scale company, a couple of hundred small- to medium-sized manufacturer cum exporter firms and several thousand micro and even household level fabricators engaged in production (EDI, n.d.). There exists a widely dispersed process of subcontracting to tier 2, 3 and even tier 4 and 5 firms. For instance in Tirupur it is said that a garment moves between 20 and 30 units before it is exported (De Neve, 2009).

Such a large MSME sector is a consequence of Indian industrial policy's special focus on MSMEs on the one hand and a regime of international export quotas under GATT and subsequent export-oriented neoliberal growth on the other. The Second Five Year Plan said, 'small scale industries provide immediate large scale employment, offer a method of ensuring a more equitable distribution of national income and facilitate an effective mobilization of resources of capital and skill which might otherwise remain unutilized' (cited in UNIDO, n.d.). With such a view, the industrial policy of 1967 reserved certain sectors for SMEs. Over decades this reserved category was expanded and by 1996, 836 products were reserved for small-scale production. MSMEs during this period were generally a means of improving domestic manufacturing capacity and achieving import substitution.

In the 1970s, global trade was regulated using a quota regime. Exports from developing countries to developed states like the United States and Europe was governed by country-specific quotas in different products. For instance, the Multi-Fibre Agreement that governed global trade in textiles was signed in 1974 between the United States, Canada, Europe and 65 other developing countries. Such a regime and a favourable domestic policy enabled MSMEs in India to grow under reasonably certain markets. For example, textile exports from India grew from virtually nothing in 1970 to US$1 billion by 1980 (Hirway, 2010).

The phasing out of quota regime from 1995 and introduction of WTO exposed this sector to global competition. In the new competitive environment of global value chains, countries started competing with each other in multiple ways to become attractive outsourcing destinations in what is now characterised as a 'race to the bottom'. Indian MSMEs were competing with every other low-cost manufacturing destination in the Third World. With the neoliberal focus on export-driven growth, most developing country governments were reducing regulatory oversight on industry. For instance, Philippines excluded garment sector workers from minimum wages; Dominican Republic and El Salvador excluded textile worker wages from indexing to cost of living. Mauritius increased work week to 7 days and so on (Hirway, 2010:168). As with most other developing countries, India too encouraged such export-oriented growth with the creation of SEZs where firms were exempted from regulations.

From 1997 under influence of liberalisation Indian MSMEs became viewed primarily as sources of export and the problem has been described as one of inferior technology and lack of financing which compromised the competitiveness of Indian MSMEs. Growing concerns about SME growth, capital adequacy, technological capability and competitiveness led to products being dereserved. The last 20 products were dereserved in April 2015 with the commerce ministry adding, 'There is no prima facie justification for continuation of reservation of manufacturing in the MSME sector since such reservation may inhibit the possibilities based on technologies, economy of scale etc. vis-à-vis the imported items.'[5] Other initiatives like scrapping of licensing requirements, foreign investment for export-oriented units, technology and skill upgrading programmes, import duty waivers and cluster development initiatives have all been part of a special emphasis on integrating MSMEs into global value chains so as to enable realisation of national economic growth and employment objectives (UNIDO, n.d.). Much state support for MSMEs has been now anchored in export performance of these enterprises. Government even introduced a concessional finance scheme to enable MSMEs procure ISO certifications so that they could access export markets (Jammulamadaka, 2015a). This post-liberalisation fillip by government to MSME exports led to phenomenal expansion of the sector. For example, from almost non-existent exports in 1970s the garment sector has now grown to become one of the largest sectors in India (Hirway, 2010; Barreientos et al., 2010; Mani, 2013). India's textile exports alone grew to $6.8 billion in 2003 (Hirway, 2010:170). But the policy also made MSMEs precarious and susceptible to footloose buyers. The ready-made garment industry shifted from Sri Lanka to Bangladesh in this search for low-cost producers (Alamgir, 2014). This race to the bottom of ever-reducing costs implied extremely fragile employment within MSMEs.

Encountering modern CSR

MSMEs usually begin operations with minimal investments. One of the most important social purposes they fulfil is providing livelihoods. At the same time, with limited capital investments, they depend on freely using natural and public resources and civic infrastructure of the area for disposing their wastes. Thus many MSMEs in tanning, dyeing and chemical clusters freely draw water from nearby rivers or municipal corporations. They also dispose off their effluents into open drains severely polluting water and land in their vicinity. These practices have led to dangerous levels of pollution over the years. Local activists and NGOs active in these areas approached courts for redressal under India's environmental laws. During the same period, in the context of growing awareness of environmental sustainability in export markets, products made in environmentally hazardous conditions met with boycotts and bans from Western buyers. For instance, in the early 1990s, Indian leather was banned in Germany and other European countries for use of unsafe azo dyes. Foundaries in Kolkata came under greater scrutiny of the Pollution Control Boards following Supreme Court directives.

In response to these twin pressures from domestic court directives and international buyer boycotts, common effluent treatment plants were set up in several clusters. Other improvements and modifications in production technologies were also advocated. Common effluent treatment plants operated by treating the effluents from all the small units at one central place, and, releasing the treated water into natural sources. This reduced the cost of treatment and brought it within the reach of MSMEs. MSMEs were also encouraged to set up associations and pay-per-use systems to manage these common effluent treatment plants.

On the other hand, MSMEs also were being noticed for their poor working conditions, labour rights and child labour. With limited abilities to invest in safety, work was being carried out under hazardous conditions harming the health and well-being of workers often including that of owners who worked alongside workers.

Widespread poverty along with entrepreneurial greed contributed to children working in these units. Children often worked alongside their relatives.

With growing public awareness of labour conditions in supplier factories, MNCs who procured from such clusters faced consumer boycotts. Nike was one of the first MNC to face such criticism but it was soon joined by many others (O'Laughlin, 2008; Bair et al., 2014). The critique was framed as one of securing accountability from MNCs who because of their global nature could slip through being accountable to any sovereign government. Faced with severe criticism and consumer boycotts, and seeking to alleviate brand reputations MNCs began ethical sourcing, i.e. sourcing from suppliers who complied with MNC codes of conduct for labour and environmental standards in the production processes (Lund-Thomsen and Nadvi, 2010; Lund-Thomsen, 2008; Jammulamadaka, 2013a, 2015a). They terminated purchase agreements and blacklisted suppliers who failed to measure up to the code. Some of the early codes can be traced to 1970s, but it is the proliferation of codes in recent years that has come to constitute the dominant model of modern CSR (Jammulamadaka, 2015a). Faced with the prospect of loss of business, Indian MSMEs started complying with these buyer CSR codes thereby bringing in modern code compliance CSR into MSMEs. This pressure driving CSR in MSMEs has continued and grown since mid-1990s. As the 2011 National Voluntary Guidelines on CSR said,

> Due to increasing integration of the Indian economy with the global economy, especially during the last decade, enterprises of all sizes have been gradually exposed to global competition. Global buyers are basing their sourcing decisions not only on traditional commercial considerations such as price, quality and delivery commitments, but also on compliance with social and environmental norms in the workplaces, covering for instance, health and safety, social equity in employment and production, and ecological compatibility of products and processes. Many Indian buyers too are beginning to incorporate these requirements into their purchasing decisions. MSMEs not sensitive to these expectations run a serious risk of isolation and rejection by buyers as well as consumers, whereas those that are responsive to these expectations might find new business opportunities opening up for them.

CSR Surveys in MSMEs

With compliance to standards and modern CSR as the backdrop we turn our attention to surveys of MSMEs. Given the general invisibility of MSMEs in popular business discourse, understandably, we do not have extensive annual surveys of MSMEs like large businesses. Instead we have a few academic studies and sectoral reports. Some of the early studies (Revenkar, 2004; Kumar, 2004) indicate that MSMEs find it very difficult to carry out CSR due to their limited resource base. Some also think that complying with laws in itself is sufficient CSR practice (Revenkar, 2004). They are generally unaware of modern CSR, and are at a loss to see the business case for it (Kumar, 2004). Consequently, studies have usually made a case for popularising modern form of CSR among MSMEs. They also suggest that these enterprises do not distinguish between philanthropy and CSR. They add that irrespective of code compliance, to some extent, most MSMEs are engaged in some form of philanthropic activity or the other; and being closely subject to owner control, the specific activities are determined by owner's value system, and priorities. Another study by UNIDO (Sachdeva and Panfil, 2008) on five different MSME clusters in India finds that most MSMEs contribute some of their earnings to carrying out some form of socially responsible activity or the other. Enterprise size and position in the cluster specifically influences the level of activity. Most of these enterprises have activities for labour welfare and health care. The report adds that these activities however do not meet the minimum requirements of labour standards and fall short of CSR. Later studies continue to find support for prior observations, in spite of growing awareness of CSR. They find that it is generally the relatively larger firms or those which are located in clusters that are more familiar with modern CSR. Nevertheless, due to financial constraints and lack of support from government many do not wish to comply with codes. (Gupta et al., 2012; Gupta and Khanna, 2011). To the extent they do, a combination of moral duty, competitive and buyer pressures impel them (Gupta et al., 2012; Gupta and Khanna, 2011).

Thus we see that MNC buyer pressures are instrumental in launching modern CSR in MSMEs. At the same time, casting our sights beyond these surveys directly onto the MSME sector we notice that the field of responsibility is much wider than the binary choice between compliance and non-compliance. In spite of predominance

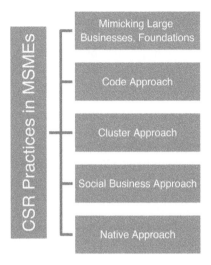

Figure 8.1 CSR approaches in MSMEs

Source: Author

of codes, enterprises differ in their enactments of responsibility. These differences are due to industry and market peculiarities and owner preferences. In describing these enactments of responsibility in MSMEs once again I will fall back on the conversations I have had over the years, even as I look at the writings of others. Based on these understandings, atleast five different variations can be identified in MSME enactments of responsibility-mimicking large business, code approach, cluster approach, social business approach and native approach (see Figure 8.1).

Mimicking large business

In this approach, enterprises mimic practices of large businesses by setting up foundations and partnering with NGOs. This approach is not very common because of high and consistent flow of funds required to run the foundation. Thus it is seen only within medium-sized enterprises whose volume of operations permits them to allocate a percentage of their profits to the foundation. The foundation in turn implements various initiatives directly or through partnership with NGOs. Such foundations are closely managed by business owners and their staff; however business operations are kept outside the ambit of the foundation's sponsorships. Enterprises also show varying levels of engagement with compliance to standards depending on the nature of industry and market. The foundations of Bruckhardt Compression, Sohrab Enterprises and Sashwat Systems are examples of this type of approach.

Bruckhardt Compression began in India as a wholly owned subsidiary of a Swiss company. In 2004, it became an independent entity. This industrial compressor manufacturer located in Western India set up a trust in 2008 and decided to contribute 2 per cent of profit before tax to the foundation. The trust was managed by a cross-functional senior executive team of the company. This trust encouraged company employees to submit proposals for supporting NGOs and local communities. After careful screening the senior executive team funded proposals from the trust funds. The company also encouraged volunteering by its employees.

The Sohrab group started in 1987 in Punjab as a textile mill making nylon tyre cord fabric. The group since has diversified into other textile businesses and furniture manufacture. Unlike Bruckhardt, Sohrab is an export-oriented company and subject to greater compliance to standards. Maintaining safe and healthy working conditions and securing regular third party audits to comply with Ethical Trading Initiative, Forest Stewardship Council and SEDEX Global standards are an important feature of responsibility. The group also complies with commonly followed codes of conduct with employees being paid a basic minimum wage along with facilities like Provident Fund, Employee State Insurance, Gratuity, bonuses, earned leave, sick leave etc. In addition to such compliance measures, in 1995, Sohrab group set up the HARF Charitable Trust to manage its CSR activities which include running educational institutions, scholarships for students, marriage assistance for orphan girls, stipend for widows and free medical dispensary. The group's employees also receive subsidised education for their children at the school and college being run by the trust.

Shaswat Systems, an Ahmedabad-based manufacturer of structural metal products and winner of numerous MSME awards set up Shaswat Foundation. This company is not heavily dependent on exports, but services domestic markets. It has limited reference to complying with codes of conduct though it mentions ISO certification for quality. Its foundation is used to promote entrepreneurship. The company is woman headed and the foundation works towards encouraging women entrepreneurs of the state by guiding and mentoring them.

Code approach

Code approach is the second and more popular variety of CSR. Labour codes of conduct is the primary mode of CSR in most export-oriented MSMEs like garments, textiles, leather, sporting goods etc. These codes are used by foreign buyers to ensure compliance to social and environmental standards in supplier firms. The code approach essentially involves a social auditing and monitoring mechanism used by buyers to assess responsible behaviour of suppliers. This approach is usually restricted to registered MSMEs, that too the tier 1 suppliers of global buyers. But the clusters themselves have a large number of unregistered MSMEs which form the tiers 2, 3, 4 or even further down in the value chain. It has been estimated that of the more than 30,000 garment enterprises in Delhi as of 1999–2000, only 675 were registered factories (Barrientos et al., 2010). Another estimate says that 90 per cent of Indian textile workers are in the unorganised sector (Hirway, 2010). Taking the case of Tirupur cluster, even though Tirupur garment cluster had been operational since 1970, codes of conduct became an issue only from 2000. Until then buyers only looked at quality, price and delivery schedules. In this cluster which averaged $2 billion in exports in 2007, buyer codes of conduct are used as mechanisms to regulate employment conditions and ensure social compliance and responsibility. Supplier firms are expected to invest in improved working conditions and foot the cost of certification without any support from buyer firms. In addition other standards like Social Accountability 8000 and Worldwide Responsible Apparel Production certification are also followed in the Tirupur cluster. While compliance to company codes is checked by company auditors, compliance to the general standards is checked by third party auditor firms. Buyers insist on regular updates of such certification. Failure to demonstrate compliance leads to blacklisting of supplier firms and termination of buying agreements. The codes themselves are usually a fixed set of regulations that are informed by Western values towards employment and global conventions. Some of the common themes of the codes are as follows:

- Compliance with local labour laws and workplace regulations
- Prohibition of child labour
- Regulation of contract labour
- Non-discrimination
- Prohibition of forced labour
- Freedom of association and the right to collective bargaining
- Human treatment
- Minimum wages, living wage and other benefits
- Regulation of working hours
- Working conditions (health and safety)

Source: (De Neve, 2009)

Compliance to codes has visibly improved outcomes for some workers especially permanent workers (Barrientos et al., 2010; Utting, 2008). Some authors have suggested that wages and working conditions have improved for skilled regular workers due to skill upgradation and technological and product-mix improvements in the textile and auto component manufacturing clusters (Awasthi et al., 2010; Tewari, 2010) giving raise to what has been termed as 'regulatory enclaves' (Posthuma, 2010).

At the same time, codes are usually applied to only the tier 1 producers directly interacting with buyers codes. Consequently, the risks of business uncertainty and reducing margins have been passed on to suppliers in the lower tiers (Awasthi et al., 2010). Codes have increased vulnerability of self-exploited suppliers in tier 2, 3, 4 and other levels. They have also led to flexible casualisation of workforce. Piece rate workers find their earnings being squeezed. This has worsened conditions for contractual workers, home-based workers and women, sometimes even depriving them of safe work (Barrientos and Smith, 2007; Barrientos et al., 2010; Damodaran, 2010; Khan et al., 2010; Tewari, 2010). Thus codes have limited effectiveness in controlling practices which MNC buyers and Western consumers commonly consider as irresponsible, namely, 12-hour working day, lack of benefits, cramped working spaces etc. (De Neve, 2009).

Codes approach has added a new layer of burden and exploitation on suppliers by subjecting them to numerous codes of conduct and heavy costs of certification. For example, a leather micro enterprise with a turnover of INR 15 million spent INR 1.5 million on compliance and certification for SA 8000 and SEDEX of the United Kingdom. This unit had 15 people on rolls and another 15 people on piece rate and hardly had any orders in the pipeline. Even though inventory management practices and purchase practices of international buyers squeeze supplier firms on price and margins, forcing suppliers to pass on vulnerability to lower levels in the value chain, such buyer practices are placed outside the purview of modern CSR practice and discourse. MNC buyers are known to use CSR codes to force disclosures simultaneously improving their value extraction from the supply chain even as they reduce the earnings of suppliers (NTUI study, cited in Tewari, 2010). Managers and business owners from MSMEs say buyers consistently bargain for lower prices, higher quality and higher compliance requirements pushing suppliers into an impossible situation (Barrientos and Smith, 2007; De Neve, 2009). As one MSME owner says, 'Buyers want a Mercedes Benz car but they want to pay only for a Maruti car.' In spite of this, there has been an increase in adoption of such company codes approach to CSR since it has now become a condition of business. As manufacturers at Tirupur say, 'In Tiruppur we say that people won't change until the pain overcomes the fear. More and more companies try to get SA 8000 and WRAP certified because they realize that otherwise they can't get any order anymore' (De Neve, 2009:66).

Cluster approach

This third approach too has its origins in pressures faced by MSMEs from global buyers and national courts on labour and environmental conditions. The essential difference between code approach and cluster approach is that the latter accounts for the small size and resource base of MSMEs unlike the former. The cluster approach involves pooling together of resources of individual units through formation of an association and implementation of environmental and socially responsible activities through the association. This approach has been highly popularised by United Nations Industrial Development Organisation's cluster development programme. Various donor agencies also contribute to these cluster level initiatives of responsibility to supplement funds and capabilities of the MSMEs.

In the cases of Palar Valley tannery cluster, Kolkata's tannery cluster, Tirupur's bleaching and dyeing cluster, or Vapi's chemical cluster, associations were formed by individual unit owners to manage common effluent treatment plants with funding help from the government intervention. Member units pay usage charges according to the volume of effluents they send to the treatment plant. The associations also contribute a part of capital required for construction of the treatment plant. The remaining capital is provided by government through grant support. However, neither the associations nor the treatment plants themselves have been completely effective. In some cases like in Vapi, the growth of the industry has far outpaced capacity of treatment plants. In other cases, associations themselves have been dormant or fractious leading to delays in constructions and/or management of the treatment plants, like in Palar Valley even though eight plants had been planned in 1997, only one was functional by 2003 (Lund-Thomsen and Nadvi, 2009). Associations have also been ineffective in enforcing compliance to effluent treatment plant norms. These associations were formed as externally driven initiatives as responses to external business threats, but they did not have legitimacy within the business community to intervene in case of individual member deviations.

In the cluster approach to social compliance, association stands as a guarantor and implementer for social interventions designed and supported by multilateral financing. For instance local associations help implement child labour prevention and rehabilitation programmes in the sporting goods industry and the carpet weaving industry.

Faced with the prospect of losing business, the Sports Goods Foundation of India (SGFI) was launched in 1998 as a collective action forum. The sporting goods cluster of Jalandhar had been under severe stress following reports of child labour.[6] The cluster is also characterised by several micro-sized players. A 2009 report on this cluster says that there are 150 exporting enterprises. Of these 10 are medium sized, 40 are small and the remaining are in the micro category. There are about 15,000 stitchers and the workforce expands to 25,000 in peak seasons like Football World Cup. There are over 1,000 outsourcing contractors and over 3,000 home stitching locations in this cluster. The cluster's production accounts for 30 per cent of the revenue, 60 per cent of the employment in the area. The initial membership of SGFI constituted of 32 manufacturers and exporters of footballs, volleyballs and rugby balls. These members were exporting 95 per cent of their production. These members committed to contributing a fixed percentage of their export turnover to the foundation. The foundation in turn worked to prevent and progressively eliminate child labour in the manufacture of sports goods.

Even though it inconvenienced local workers, SGFI also progressively reduced home-based production and shifted to more centrally located and controlled production, because it enabled better compliance to codes. Remaining home-based workers were registered. The foundation regularly monitored work of stitchers, as did ILO and other international agency representatives. SGFI is entirely controlled by local industry and in 2005 it started cooperating with UNIDO to further strengthen social protection agenda. They started bridge schools, after school learning centres for children who were displaced from the industry, trained women from these families to take over work from children. They also started microfinance and self-help group initiatives for women and provided healthcare facilities for workers. In carrying out these activities, SGFI partnered with Lions Club and other NGOs, notably Reach which was started by the wives of the firm owners. The foundation's work was supported by grants from the Government of India, UNIDO, UNICEF, Save the Children UK etc. In spite of this there have been criticisms that the overwhelming use of piece rate and philanthropic approach adopted by SGFI do not facilitate compliance to standards (Lund-Thomsen and Nadvi, 2009).

The carpet cluster of Uttar Pradesh spread across Varanasi, Mirzapur and Bhadohi illustrates another use of the cluster approach. This cluster has been infamous for use of child labour and bonded labour. In the early days children casually worked along with their parents on looms at home along with other household activities. The export boom in the industry following 1970s led to labour exploitation and surge in child labour. When Kailash Satyarthi, the noted activist started work against bonded labour in 1980, there were an estimated 0.3 million child workers in the cluster and many of them in bondage.[7] Subsequently, bans in various Western countries like the United States, child rights activism by NGOs and pressure from Supreme Court of India led to concerted effort in preventing child labour. In spite of launching interventions at the cluster level for reforming production practices, the carpet cluster is not characterised by a centrally dominant and controlling association. This could possibly be due to interweaving of production process with community life in this artisanal cluster, unlike a factory-oriented production system. The carpet industry was generally a home-based industry. The weavers worked at home, not a central shed or factory making monitoring of child labour more difficult than in case of sports goods. Eliminating child labour implied changing complete family behaviours and providing alternate sources of income to families and education for children. Accordingly NGOs extensively participated in this process. They counselled families, provided schooling support to children and monitored compliance to zero child labour norms. NGOs were supported by government departments, international child welfare agencies like UNICEF, ILO and UNDP through multi-year projects for working with weaver communities.

Social labelling initiatives were introduced to create a market for ethical production. Rugmark was the first social labelling initiative promoted in 1994 by Kailash Satyarthi. It assured that the carpet was free of bonded and child labour. Later the Carpet Export Promotion Council, a body of carpet exporters formed under the ageis of the Ministry of Textiles, created the Kaleen label. Buyers also introduced code-based producer certification approach into this cluster. For instance, STEP was introduced by Swiss carpet importers. Some of the relatively larger exporters from the cluster adopted their own independent code of practices drawn from globally accepted norms and laws. IRLF report cites one such case of Obeetee, one of the oldest carpet companies of India.

Obeetee Company is one which doesn't subscribe to any of the labelling initiatives. Instead, the company has its own monitoring systems to ensure child labour-free carpets. Every detail of the loom that produces carpets for the company is recorded with the company. Before placing an order, the weavers are told about the rules and regulations of the company which forbid the loom owners from employing children. Violation of this law results in the rejection of the carpet. The company's representative takes note of the family members of the loom owner along with their age. All these details are logged into the computers. Supervisors working in the depot frequently visit the looms to monitor the progress and to check whether any child labourer has been employed. Apart from these supervisors the company has formed a child labour cell with the senior level staff. Members of this cell pay surprise visits to these looms. Initially there was resistance and weavers were inconvenienced. Before imposing these rules on the weavers the company gave them a month's time to stop employing children. Later on, senior Vice

President, Mr. Mithilesh Kumar stated 'we started implementing the rules, we withdrawn order in some cases. Initially it has
been a difficult task for weavers to get used to weaving carpets
without children. Slowly but steadily they got used to the new
system and now there is hardly any child labour in our looms'.[8]

(Venkateswarulu et al., n.d.:26)

Social business approach

This is similar to social entrepreneurship described in Chapter 7, the
key difference being the size of the organisation and nature of the
initiative. Even though currently several social businesses receive
venture capital financing, many early ones grew without such support. Their organisational conditions and growth have been very
similar to MSMEs. Often these social businesses differentiate themselves from regular MSMEs on an ethical and fair trade platform.
Regardless of international codes of conduct, such social businesses
choose to provide fair compensation to producers. They often work
with tiny and household-level craft producers in artisanal clusters
or farmers. Though not a natural corollary, it has also been seen
that, once these social businesses have been able to achieve success
and grow to a certain scale, they have branched off into setting up
foundations to promote the cause on a broader scale.

For example, Jaipur Rugs Limited which started in 1978 works
with carpet weavers across various parts of the country. It started as
an enterprise desirous of making a difference in the lives of weavers.
The company's vision is to allow artisans to have a greater share
of the wealth they produce. Eventually, they started identifying
impoverished areas and training people in weaving. Presently, the
company is vertically integrated and involved in product concept,
design, production and delivery to support its extensive network of
40,000 weavers. It is headquartered in Jaipur and has offices in various parts of the country and abroad. It seeks to provide them fair
compensation, and other benefits that improve quality of life like
healthcare, literacy and education programmes. The founder envi-
sions the company as a 'platform of connecting the end consumer
with the artisan so that they can both emotionally connect with
each other'. A foundation was set up in 2004, to further promote
education, literacy and training in weaving. The company works
together with the foundation as a single powerful mission-driven

entity focused on the empowerment of women and rural communities in India.

Selco Solar is another such social business set up in 1995 to provide affordable lighting using sustainable solar technology in rural India. By arranging credit support through connecting poor consumers with rural banks and microfinance institutions it has helped consumers with an average monthly income of INR 4,000 to purchase these lighting systems. The profits of this business are reinvested to expand access to solar lighting in rural areas.[9] Another example of a social business is Akshamaala Solutions that leverages technology to help farmers improve productivity and incomes. It provides interventions across the agriculture eco-system and helps farmers sell their outputs at a right price.

Native approach

Non-compliance to ethical codes of conduct within MSMEs has usually been taken as prima facie evidence of irresponsibility and worker exploitation in the form of low wages and benefits. Consequently, not much is known about the native approach to responsibility within MSMEs. I therefore dwell upon this in greater detail here drawing from some ongoing research at Kolkata's leather cluster as it enables us to appreciate challenges of the borderland better. To the extent possible, in order to give voice to these actors, I report here accounts from MSME owners and workers themselves on dimensions of work and employment that they value. I elaborate upon the practices and views within Kolkata's MSME leather cluster.

Kolkata's leather cluster has tanning units, leather finishing units, leather goods producers, leather garment makers, designers, subcontractors, merchant buyers, fabricators etc., all located close by in areas within Kolkata like Bantala, Topsia, Kasba etc. In addition to these micro, small- and medium-sized manufacturers, there are other support services like commission agents, whose job it is to get business from international buyers to the small and micro enterprises who cannot afford to directly participate in many fairs or pursue international buyers. Commission agents are those people who are aspiring to set up their plant, or had earlier set up their own unit either as a manufacturer or exporter and had failed in the business. There are also the knives makers, CAD machine designers, zipper cutters, accessories suppliers, machinery repairers and others. Together they support this cluster. There are several associations where cluster members participate like the Indian Leather Products Association, tanners association, Council for Leather Exports etc. These associations are used to make representations to the government. The association does not attempt to interfere in the individual operations of a company and companies themselves refuse and restrict the association's participation in employer-employee disputes as these are considered the internal affairs of a company.

Kolkata leather cluster operates in four different product categories: tanned leather, industrial gloves, leather goods and footwear. Leather goods subsector has 1,200 micro-level manufacturers and 236 export-oriented small-scale units. A few exporters have grown over the years and now have multiple units including tanning operations. Some of the larger operators in the leather-goods cluster have a turnover of INR 0.3 to 0.4 billion and operate in both export and domestic markets. One company had export earnings of INR 0.3 billion from leather goods, domestic earning of INR 0.04 billion and another 0.13 billion from tanning operations. A micro-scale operation typically has a turnover of INR 0.01 or 0.015 billion or even lesser.

Exporter firms typically seek to comply with the various codes of conduct and maintain direct buyer connections. These companies spend almost 10 per cent of their turnover to develop the shop floor to compliance standards. When firms obtain orders in excess of their capacity, they regularly subcontract it to fabricators. These micro and tiny enterprise, home-based fabricators do subcontracting work for exporters and domestic producers. Within leather goods, there exists a further categorisation into large goods like bags and small goods like wallets. Firms typically retained bag jobs inside the unit, since material costs are very high and neither exporters nor fabricators are interested in the material risk subcontracting of bags implies. Thus subcontracting generally involves small goods and bulk production jobs. Micro and small enterprises hire anywhere between 10 and a couple of hundred workers as salaried permanent workers. The rest of the workers work on piece rate. For instance, a small- to medium-sized set up would have about 250 workers on payroll and 500 workers on piece rate. Piece rate work is a practice that employers adopt to manage production uncertainties. It is also a preferred worker alternative. Regardless of compliance to codes, business owners in Kolkata leather cluster count three things as most important aspects of their employment relationship and responsibilities towards workers: (a) timely payment of wages/salaries, (b) providing interest free advances and/or bonuses to workers and (c) accommodating leave requests of workers.

On the face of it, timely payment of wages appears as a very silly and insincere way of thinking of responsibility. However seen in the context of the cash flows of these enterprises where they have several months gap, sometimes even non-payment from MNC buyers owing to certain delivery parameter violations; sticking to wage payment schedules requires great effort and commitment from firm owners. As one firm owner says:

> It is important that we pay the wages on time otherwise the worker will not get credit from the local groceries store and he will find it difficult to run his/her household. The grocery store keepers know that the worker works in such and such factory which pays its wages on time and therefore extends credit. It is important for us as factory owners to keep a reputation for timely and regular payment, otherwise we will not get workers easily.

The issue of advances is of similar import. Business owners agree that giving advances to workers sometimes even outside of company accounts from their personal income is an ongoing business norm. This norm makes the employer the first and cheapest means of social security. Thus their employment relationship is not just about purchase of labour value in an economic transaction. It is a community social security function. I summarise below a conversation with a business owner on this issue. As he explains:

> Workers want advances for all kinds of things, sometimes it is a medical emergency, sometimes it is a marriage at home, repairing house in rains, other domestic needs, sometimes for education of children. We have to give. We have to help.
>
> With growing size, we start facing many such requests, so we also need to make some rules. So now when they ask for large amounts of advance saying they want to build a house, I tell them I am not a housing finance corporation, go to a bank. Of late, we made another rule saying that a worker can get only one advance at a time. Only after repaying that advance can he get another. But we cannot follow these rules blindly.

There is a worker in our cutting department. He has been with us for 20 years. His daughter is doing chartered accountancy. I arranged for her articleship with our company's CA. The other day he needed INR 7000 for her fees. I gave it. He has prior advances due against him.

A worker's daughter doing CA, not easy you know. So I just gave him the money. Sometimes we do not bring these advances to company accounts also.

Yesterday one worker did not come. He called to say, he was admitting his father in the hospital and wanted advance of INR 10000. We first sent 5000 and a person, and told him not to worry, that we would help as necessary. It is not as if, we will give whatever amount as advance to whosoever asks. The rule does not work that way. It cannot be treated as a right, but we have to give. It is our duty. We will first confirm the genuineness of the request and then give it.

About repayment he had this to say:

Usually they repay back. If they are salaried they pay it back in 10–12 months depending upon their other expenses. Sometimes they request and we permit them to repay over even longer duration. But definitely we keep repayment as a policy because it creates a sense of exception when we waive repayment for some deserving cases. For piece rate workers, we usually avoid long duration advances. We have advances against orders. But if we give long duration advance, then we deduct 10% during every payment. There are several cases where workers take an advance and simply quit work. That is the cost of our business.

The third issue of leave and timings is equally significant. As firm managers explain:

While we have leave policies, we use a lot of discretion in implementing these policies. If cases are genuine then we do not mark their absence as leave or deduct any salary. They have other commitments at home and family and we accommodate them. They are of course free to avail their standard leave. Recently we had several cases of dengue among workers. We did not deduct any leave for them on humanitarian grounds, had we deducted, they would have used up all their leave and got salary deductions. Then there are cases of extended leave when workers go to their villages. Most of the workers are from outside Kolkata and during festival season they go back. They come back after several weeks. We simply have to accommodate this. This leave has hardly any connection to official leave policy. This is a taken for granted condition for work.

Workers in Kolkata's leather goods cluster also prefer a traditional understanding of employment relationship. They valued the system of advances and leave. Discretionary processes of management were suited to worker behaviour styles. They said, 'if I want a raise or need some money I will go and ask. If I don't like what I am offered, I will join another employer'. For the workers, good employers were those who provided regular work which enabled them to maintain their incomes at a particular level. Good employers also did not impose too many fines and deduct wages for unauthorised leaves, poor quality work and such other things.

Commenting on benefits, workers were reluctant to accept benefits which would accrue to them 20 years into the future upon retirement. Reluctance was evident in both piece rate and salaried workers. Instead they preferred higher current wages. They did want the employer to make deductions in their earnings. They were willing to consider savings and future investment practices on their own like depositing money in a bank account. The observations of Rani (name changed) a young woman who has been making leather goods for 8–9 years reflect some general worker perceptions. After becoming sufficiently skilled, Rani had always worked for a monthly salary and not piece rates. Her past employer had not provided any benefits but the current one was extending the same. She was nevertheless clear that it was proximity to her home which attracted her to the new employer and not benefits. She said:

My old company shifted me to a far off factory. I came here because it is closer to my home. Getting work is easy. I have worked in many places and I know my work well. So I have no trouble finding a job. Yeah, they said they will give benefits. Let's see, I have not yet given the documents so they have not begun salary deductions. Let's see, these benefits might restrict my freedom to easily move out from here, if I don't like it here.

Workers greatly valued their autonomy, their freedom to control their time and pace of work in the employment relationship. The experience of Islam, a leather goods worker, is illustrative of the preferences of an average leather goods worker. Islam had been a leather worker for almost 20 years. He had learnt the work accompanying his uncle as an adolescent. Islam had begun working as a piece rate worker. After gaining sufficient experience, he started off as a fabricator hiring 2–3 other workers.

He found that fabricator work was a little risky since workers could suddenly desert him and leave him with incomplete commitments and embarrassment. He therefore joined as a piece rate worker in an export factory. When another factory had been set up near his village, he moved to that factory. But a couple of years later that factory had stopped piece rate work and put everybody on monthly pay roll. That factory was aiming at full compliance to social codes of conduct and hence had stopped piece rate. Islam was not interested in monthly salary and therefore had come back to his previous employer as a piece rate worker. This time, he moved to a new factory of that employer because there were no vacancies in the old factory. He preferred this change even though this workplace was quite a distance from his village to avoid working on a monthly salary. He was very clear that he would not do monthly salary work, that he would not work where his time was controlled and earning was limited. If he did not like working here, he would consider moving elsewhere. Referring to my conversation with him, Islam said:

> I am able to talk to you now, because I am a piece rate worker, if I was a salaried worker I could not have talked to you. I would not be permitted because my production target would suffer. I would be reprimanded if I did something else during work hours. Food and rest time is fixed. But as a piece rate worker, I can work, rest or do something else as I like. I just have to deliver final goods by the delivery date. As a salaried workforce, I would be expected to work at a continuous pace with fixed production targets. I cannot adjust the pace according to my work load or my physical health condition or my other personal commitments.

I could notice a few piece rate workers having meals and then taking a nap at 11.00 during the day in the same premises. Islam continued:

> Salaried work is also unduly competitive. If someone on the floor finishes the number of pieces quickly, then I am pressurised into working at the same pace. If I fall behind I have to listen to criticism from the supervisor.

Clarifying the difference between competition in salaried work and piece rate work, Islam said:

> It is true that competition is severe in piece rate work compared to salaried work. But the difference is in incentives and dignity. In salaried work I really do not have an incentive to do more, but in piece rate there is the incentive of greater earnings with more work, consequently the competition is tougher among piece rate gangs. However, there is more dignity in piece rate competition. It is finally up to me whether I wish to compete with another piece rate gang on the floor or not. No one will criticise me for not competing. But in salaried work, I do not have a choice, and if I fall behind, I will be reprimanded.

Clearly autonomy, dignity and higher earnings were valued more than any wage security, fixed time or benefits. Such worker preferences are not limited to eastern India's Kolkata cluster, but they are found even in Tirupur garment cluster in the south of India. Just like Islam, workers at Tirupur also prefer autonomy over their work and time and dignity.

De Neve's (2012) ethnography of the workers of Tirupur cluster (which has been severely castigated for its non-compliant labour practices) actually shows that workers detest working in the fordist factories which offer wage and employment benefits. Such wages, benefits and fixed working hours have little attraction for them. They detest the control that the employer exercises on their time. Workers instead prefer to work as independent subcontractors or as piece rate workers where they are in a position to control their time and their earnings, mobilise their social networks effectively while attending to their other social roles.

A few recent surveys also suggest that these practices exist in other clusters like auto components. Surveys reveal that clusters have several informal practices which provide for labour welfare informed by a native understanding of an employment relationship. These are activities that begin on a small scale, do not require significant investments and create visibility and reputations through word of mouth in the local communities. These activities are triggered both by demands from employees and sentiments of owners (Gupta and Khanna, 2011; Gupta et al., 2012). By the term 'taking care of labour' most small firms mean making timely wage payment, providing workers with interest free loans, awarding bonus and sometimes just providing basic minimum wages. For the micro and tiny enterprises, it also includes providing refreshments for workers (Gupta and Khanna, 2011:271).

These views of owners and workers reveal the crux of the native approach to responsibility. What stands out in the owners' views and practices is an appreciation of their social roles and the normative sense of obligation that the owners feel when they say '*I have to*', '*we have to*'. Similarly, workers' views stand out in their desire to retain control over their time and their self. Both workers and owners refuse to view the employment relationship solely as an economic transaction. The actual practices of advances and leave, and preferences for autonomy are not mandated by any standards but by traditional norms of an employment relationship, which take into account the social and political in the employment relationship. Workers did not seem to miss a right to association or forming unions. They felt confident about their abilities to bargain and/or mobilise if necessary on the basis of the legitimacy of their claim and the strength of their social networks. In fact, there is hardly any effective trade union of leather goods workers.

The noise of silence

In our efforts to examine the enactments of responsibility in MSMEs, we have been able to identify five different kinds of practices. Three of them, namely code approach, cluster approach and social business approach are all linked to and justified by modern CSR's ethical code of conduct narrative. The foundation approach represents a mix of modern and traditional, in the sense of including charitable giving, but giving forms an activity that is distinctly separate from business. Giving coexists to varying degrees with compliance to ethical codes of conduct. It is however the native approach that presents a stark contrast to the modern version. Such native practices and understandings of responsibility were found in Bombay's textile mills in late 1800s and early 1900s. At that time, commentators said that these were residual agrarian behaviours. But a century later, in spite of being silenced and lacking in formal legitimacy both in national regulation and international responsibility discourse and increasing difficulty, native practices of being responsible continue to be followed. These are activities which continue in spite of downturn because of their intricate linking with the social structure of communities and the way of life (Gupta and Khanna, 2011). In the face of downturn in a particular business, owners try to mobilise other sources of funds to fulfil these responsibilities either from other businesses or from personal wealth since it is difficult for personal values, religious faith and social behaviour to fluctuate according to business cycles.

It is not the continuing native practice, but its treatment by MSME owners that is really surprising. Conversations, during a workshop with MSME owners in Kolkata leather cluster clearly showed that they did not look at their traditional practices as an alternate model of responsibility. It was simply the way business is done. At the same time, they also accepted that they lacked in responsibility, since they were unable to comply with ethical codes. As some leather factory owners say, 'They (MNC buyers, activists) have to understand that we are a developing nation. We have many more and diverse kinds of challenges. They can't simply expect us to follow standards of Europe.' Underlying this reference to India's developing status and poverty is an apology for refusing to comply. Somehow, owners themselves were unable to see their traditional practices as alternate ways of being responsible. Such is the domination in the world of MSMEs. While large Indian businesses and their owners have exercised choices in pursuing CSR and have had the opportunity to even adopt a big tent approach combining different models, MSME space has been far more subordinated. Compliance to ethical codes of conduct has become a condition of business, atleast for tier 1 suppliers, in turn, increasing the vulnerability of those in tiers further below. Modern CSR discourse somehow does not value these traditional notions and practices and

> producers are forced to engage with a set of values about how to produce and how to deal with labour that are not of

their own making and that they frequently see as an external-western-intervention that both ignores and devalues their own ways of organizing production.

(De Neve, 2009:64)

Non-compliance is generally treated as prima facie evidence of irresponsibility of MSMEs. There is thus hardly any discursive space for an alternate model. By discursively privileging codes as the solution to factory abuse, it prevents one from seeing how codes itself become another source of domination (De Neve, 2009) which denies these regions the legitimacy to practise their own indigenous form of responsibility that suits their social, cultural and economic moorings.

If the true essence of labour standards is to ensure that workers are treated in a just and humane manner, then traditional practices too work in the same direction. But there are three key differences, whereas fairness is a worker's right in modern labour standards approach, it is an owner's obligation in the traditional approach. Second, in labour standards, fairness is limited to an economic exchange of work value, but it encompasses the social and political individual in the native approach. Third, whereas restraining a deviant employer is a task left to external authority-monitors, buyers and trade unions in the former approach, by recognising and accommodating worker autonomy (Pettit, 1996; Jammulamadaka, 2016a), the traditional approach locates countervailing power in the hands of the workers themselves. By exercising the right to desert work and malign reputations, workers exercise a check over unilateral reneging of obligations/duties by business owners. If anything, leather workers in Kolkata cluster seem to dearly value their freedom to change employers at any time they wish even if it might mean losing a few days salary.

Notes

1 www.makeinindia.com/article/-/v/nurturing-a-manufacturing-culture
2 isid.org.in/pdf/WP172.pdf
3 www.cii.in/Sectors.aspx?enc=prvePUj2bdMtgTmvPwvisYH+5EnGjyG XO9hLECvTuNuXK6QP3tp4gPGuPr/xpT2f
4 *msme.gov.in/WriteReadData/ebook/MSME_at_a_GLANCE_2016_ Final.pdf*
5 www.thehindubusinessline.com/economy/policy/govt-removes-last-20-items-reserved-for-production-by-msmes/article7099156.ece

6 www.sgfi.org/

7 http://articles.economictimes.indiatimes.com/2014-10-11/news/
54899660_1_child-labour-carpet-industry-carpet-makers

8 ilrf.org/sites/default/.../child%20labor%20in%20carpet%20industry%
20122706.pdf

9 www.selco-india.com/about_us.htmlwww.businesstoday.in/magazine/
special/innovation-energy-selco-solar-lamps/story/186623.html

Chapter 9

So what do we know and where to from here

Imitations have their own limitations.

–J. L. Prasad, 1948–2015

We began our exploration with a few questions. Why did India have to legislate for mandatory spending on CSR, when in the popular imagination of the country, one continues to believe that contributing to social and public utility and purpose is part of the cultural fabric of the nation? Why does one legislate for something which is likely to be a deeper cultural practice? What changes to Indian *practices* do *we expect* this legislation will bring? What *anxieties of the nation* is this legislation addressing? Why do *we have such anxieties*?

What have we seen so far?

This book has been an attempt to answer these questions. We began our journey of exploring the notions and practices of responsibility in Indian business in the context of the encounter between indigenity and Western modernity, by going in and out of the past and present in Indian business, navigating through custom, modernity and coloniality. We gathered these experiences with the intent of teasing out and comprehending the struggles and silences, in the intersecting trajectories of the modern and indigenous, in a post-colonial globalising India and its business.

In seeking to critically anchor our explorations, rather than plainly review the pastiche of practices that go under the CSR rubric we have been informed by an ethico-political-epistemic imperative. Epistemically, the imperative is that given the specific colonial past and the socio-cultural history of India, the character of Indian business and its governance by state, society and global forces is likely to be different. This in turn is likely to have distinctive implications for practices of CSR. Yet Indian voices are far from being heard in contemporary CSR discourse. Politically, the imperative has been the limited ability of this location to intervene in global CSR discourse, and bring its specific epistemic understanding to bear upon an embrace of global CSR discourse. This is due to the subordinate status of India as a 'developing country'. The ethical imperative is to redress the inability induced by this subordination.

Let us briefly review where our journeys have taken us so far. In our explorations, we stopped along several sites and peeped into those moments. We saw a pre-colonial way of life, where responsibility in all its dimensions was embedded in the everyday conduct of the businessman, and sustained through individual reputations. We saw the colonial moment of struggles between native custom and modernity; between human ethics and amoral market logic; communitarian governance and colonial might. We saw how colonial jurisprudence served as the midwife, and gave birth to different notions of responsibility. One notion is customary conduct based and is presently illegal. The other notion is conduct agnostic but legally valid anchored in contractual notions and market logics. These notions with their attendant practices seeded the disruption of countervailing power, by fracturing life worlds of businessmen and communities, into discrete sets of exchanges in the social, economic and political spheres. We saw how the colonial encounter continued into the post-colonial moment and gathered new energy from the rising global neoliberalism dragging the nation into a deeper crisis of inferiority. We saw the spectre of the colonial past reach into the present through regulatory borders giving rise to the messy borderland of responsibility. In this messy borderland we noticed that notions of responsibility kaleidoscopically changed according to the perspective from which one looked at it. That according to perspectives such as domestic law, international governance practices, custom and managerial logic, the same practices could be either responsible or irresponsible or even hybrid. We also heard the silences of business owners large and small, of employees, of environment, of nation-state and of NGOs in contemporary practice.

Making sense of our exploration

So, how do we make sense of all these sights and sounds, i.e. our explorations and begin to articulate the answers to our questions? Let's turn to our old post-colonial scholar friends for some help again.

Ashish Nandy (1983:xiii–xviii) in describing the psychology of colonialism in the colonial arena, where the colonised has been assigned a subordinate place by the coloniser, asks the vital question about the manner in which a subordinated person preserves his/her sense of self and its coherence? How such a person overcomes his/her subordination? Analysing the psychological consequences and highlighting the role of individual agency, he says, the 'meek inherit the earth not by meekness alone. They have to have categories, concepts and even, defences of mind with which to turn the West into a reasonably manageable vector within the traditional world views'. He argues that even though structurally, the subordinated person faces a very powerful oppressor, he/she overcomes oppression, buy not completely buying into the images and positions created by the coloniser – both for the colonised and of the coloniser. This colonised person in constructing his/her view of the coloniser and surviving the oppression, however, is not confined to his/her assigned position – the inferior other of Western modernity – but accesses his/her cultural resources which are outside the scope of Western modernity (and its assigned position). Thus, the colonised has access to resources outside the scope and control of the coloniser and by using these cultural resources, he/she is able to find ways of managing the oppression. These cultural resources enable the colonised to preserve an inner sense of coherence even when outwardly silenced and subordinated. Some of the strategies deriving from cultural resources identified by Nandy are outward silence which lies in patient wait for friendly allies, overt compliance with inner disinterest, displacing meaning in practicing modern prescriptions, reinterpreting tradition and hybridising custom and modernity. All these are strategies of the colonised to cope with a hostile external reality. These strategies coexist, along with other strategies like servile imitation of coloniser and modernity, action being tamed by coloniser, admiration of the coloniser and tragic contestation of dominating modern West.

To Nandy's explanation of strategies for surviving in the post-colonial if we add Mignolo's elaboration of self-identification and enunciation in the post-colonial, we have the tools we need to make sense of our explorations and experiences. Mignolo (1995b:5) says that in the post-colonial condition, understanding the past and the present are not independent of each other.

> This understanding is a communal and dialogic enterprise, not solitary and monologic; the drive towards understanding arises not only from disciplinary and rational, but also from social and emotional, imperatives. The past cannot be rendered in a neutral discourse. Bound to a given discipline, any conception of it will be laid out according to the rules for scholarly or scientific reports within the discipline.

Mignolo thus argues that *understanding* is limited by the boundaries of a social science discipline. Therefore, both the *past* and in extension the *present* are subject to rules of engagement as prescribed within any academic discipline. Just as disciplinary boundaries, the concepts that can be used and their meanings are all located in the matrix of power. The matrix of power privileges some, especially the modern West and the metropolitan centre with an authorial voice and restricts the participation of others, i.e. the colonised along specified lines. This is exactly what we had referred to in Chapter 2 when we were struggling with trying to read historical practices and observed that they were usually driven by attributing primacy to an economic rationality and logic of capital. Mignolo says that the colonised by intervening into these disciplinary practices and seeking to speak, often, contravening the conventions of these boundaries, contribute to 'changing or maintaining systems of values and beliefs' as prescribed by the modern West.

It follows from reading the three things together – Nandy, Mignolo and the Indian borderland of responsibility – that *Indian practices of responsibility are all not only efforts at self-identification but also attempts at changing the disciplinary meanings of CSR through enactment.* We had discussed earlier about the denial of a denotative space, which is what social science disciplines and academic writings usually are (for the subordinated by denying them civilisation and knowledge) and how actions, enactments or enactive epistemic space is the only space that is available for the subordinated because these are in the form of cultures.

Thus responsibility practices in India are all attempts of India and Indian business at *domesticating* modern Western CSR into a *manageable vector (Nandy, 1983:xiii) and also create Indian CSR as a different set of practices.* From our journey, we can identify atleast five different actors attempting this self-identification – the nation-state, large Indian business, Indian MSMEs, Indian NGOs and this book itself. Each of these has used a different set of strategies based on its specific position with the matrix of power and its experience of subordination.

Self-identifications at work

The Indian CSR legislation is an attempt at overt self-identification by the nation-state as a responsible society displacing successive objectifications of India as poor, uncivilised, exploitative and uncredible. That this self-identification comes in 2013 more than 250 years after colonisation began is no coincidence. The ability of Indian nation-state: (a) to sustain itself as a vibrant democracy even seven decades after independence, (b) to use a geopolitical advantage vis-à-vis major global powers, (c) to achieve status as the third largest economy[1] of the world which continues to grow in the face of several global shocks, (d) Indian polity and economy's ability to withstand strong neoliberal pressures and (e) possession of a strong demographic dividend supported by a large educated workforce; all have contributed to a growing self-confidence of the Indian nation-state. This self-confidence has enabled the state to stake a claim at re-defining itself in the global arena through legislating for responsibility and seeking to come out of the inferior position assigned to it by global powers.

CSR practices of large Indian business are similar efforts at self-identification and self-preservation. They are attempts to overcome the binary brandings of responsibility/irresponsibility, and compliance/non-compliance imposed on them by modern West by enacting the business' own versions of responsibility using 'culturally rooted alternative social knowledge [that] is already partly available outside the modern' (Nandy, 1983:xvii). The pastiche of practices that large Indian businesses follow, under the rubric of CSR span the entire spectrum of strategies outlined by Nandy (listed above) on surviving in the post-colonial moment ranging from (a) admiration of modern CSR by internalising the Triple Bottom Line and UN Global Compact's voluntary code–based CSR (TBL and UNGC) approach, (b) imitative sycophancy in practising modern CSR to secure gains from the global neoliberal order,

(c) mere imitation of this modern TBL/UNGC approach without ideological complicity, (d) overt compliance to the TBL/UNGC approach with internal decoupling of everyday business practice, (e) displacement of meaning of TBL/UNGC approach to include philanthropy, (f) reinterpreting tradition to mean spiritually informed giving, (g) non-participation in modern CSR, thereby ignoring TBL/UNGC approach and (h) cunningly and opportunistically pursuing self-interest through slippages and cracks between traditional and modern CSR practices.

Depending upon the specific character of the business owner and the business/company some of these practices seek to preserve the self and custom, by rehabilitation and reinterpretation of *conduct-based practices*. Some more practices not only seek to cope with adversarial global neoliberal forces and competition, but also seek to wrest back local sovereignty of native businessman which the post-colonial nation-state has usurped during colonial jurisprudential fixation of boundaries – political, economic and social and the creation of a modern nation-state-based governance system. Yet others, amongst these practices seek to instrumentalise neoliberal pressures for a neoliberal expansion of Indian businesses across the globe, even as these seek to resist the post-colonial state's control of their (customary residual) autonomy by defrauding this nation-state and its publics.

Practices in small Indian businesses are another instance of self-identification and self-preservation. Overt compliance to codes of conduct with superficial implementation that attempts to slip out from the grasp of the code at the slightest pretext is a strategy for managing a dominating and powerful external force and securing survival inside this powerful grasp. Silently accepting defamation as irresponsible and exploitative is another such strategy that recognises limitations of the dominator's (or West's) ability to comprehend an alternate life world and way of life. Silence both within national discourse and global discourse enables these businesses to preserve the space for their customary life-world in a subterranean way and retain fidelity to the culture's inner voice. The particular efficacy of this strategy in the face of dominance is revealed when customary worker management practices of MSMEs are contrasted with those of large Indian businesses. In large businesses, these customary employment practices were initially on public display. Such display made customary practice vulnerable to constant challenges of legitimacy from a dominating modern managerialism.

Illegitimised as unprofessional, eventually these customary practices shrank and vacated most organisational domains in large
Indian business for takeover by the dominating modern managerial logic of extraction and efficiency. Whereas in Indian MSMEs,
in spite of being even more tightly implicated within global value
chains, customary practices have survived to a much large degree,
thanks to their invisibility and silence in public discourse.

Indian NGOs are also playing their supporting role in this broader
self-identification effort. Some of them are assisting the nation-state
and Indian businesses through CSR partnerships in fashioning an
alternate meaning of CSR informed by the cultural histories of *this*
location. At the same time, many NGOs are also contesting their
subordination to corporate pressures by mere imitation and silent
acceptance of corporate managerial expectations and dictats. Yet
others are serving as foot soldiers of global pressures by participating in code compliance monitoring efforts. Some more are serving
as a crucial line of community defence by fighting for community
rights thereby contesting neoliberal extraction that is at times aided
by the post-colonial state. These NGOs are also at the forefront of
restoring and rehabilitating silenced community rights.

A last but not the least attempt at self-identification is this book
itself. It is an attempt at geocultural identification, an attempt to
surface some of the silences in CSR discourse from an Indian locus,
an attempt to understand business practices and responsibility from
decolonial categories which reflect the Indian concerns more appropriately rather than subsuming them under definitions and methods
of modern Western CSR. By examining responsibility as a broader
practice situated in the geo-historic-political and cultural context, it
contributes to changing the disciplinary meanings of CSR.

Customary bases of self-identification

All these self-identifications are to varying degrees informed by
cultural notions of responsibility and native categories of *conducting* business. I identify three such notions at work in these self-
identifications namely; obligation or duty, person-business as an
undifferentiated unity, and public/society as spatio-temporally
located communities.

Obligation or duty: Indian society is held together by the idea of
obligations or duties of different groups and communities towards
each other. As Mookerji (1919:b1) says, 'We owe largely to her

(India) elaborate system of local [decentralised] government the preservation of the integrity, independence, and individuality of Hindu culture, despite the world shaking and catastrophic political movements to which that culture was frequently exposed in the course of her history.' The word *Hindu* in the above quote should be read to mean India, following the usual practice during colonial period of referring to India as Hindu or Hindustan and not as Hindu religion. This decentralised system of governance through mutual obligations enabled Indian society to survive countless revolutions and invasions.

This social structure implied that political authority too was restrained. 'Political rulers could not alter the rules of this social consensus of individual and community obligations, but were expected to uphold and administer its "immutable" norms, and crucially, were themselves subject to its segmentally relevant rules' (Kaviraj, 2009). Consequently, in this social world, the power of political rulers was limited to 'executive' functions: i.e. to protect the social consensus, punish infringements and return it to its order of normalcy. In this sense, the political rulers did not have the 'legislative' authority to reconstitute this order, except in marginal ways. Thus governance and state here were not viewed as guarantors of unalienable natural rights but as enforcers of social consensus framed around obligations. The idea of modern sovereignty therefore did not apply to the power of the political authority in this society (Kaviraj, 2009).[2] The post-colonial state itself came into existence by usurping customary rights and displacing customary notions of governance. Even though the colonial way of organising social life through an authoritative state-centered politics, and a modern rights' enforcing nation-state continued into the post-colonial period (Chatterjee, 1998, 2011; Jammulamadaka and Murphy, forthcoming; Kaviraj, 2009) the moral legitimacy of the state still resided in customary notions of obligations for the well-being of people (Chatterjee, 1998, 2011; Jammulamadaka and Saha, forthcoming). Thus the state was still expected to provide for the well-being and welfare of this people, irrespective of the legal status of their citizenhood and legal validty of the people's claim. It assumed a moral significance. This moral dimension as Partha Chatterjee demonstrates is evident in Indian government's responses to legalisation of illegal settlements in slums. Thus, in essence, the social order continues to be characterised by obligations of different groups, including the state to uphold widely recognised social norms.

Therefore the cultural notion of a state or central authority that *overpowers every citizen and guarantees civil rights* to these citizens is alien to this society. Instead what drives it is a *sense of obligation*. Thus whether it was: Bombay Plan, building institutions, providing livelihoods through skills building, or distributing wealth through ESOPS in IT companies, or volunteering to help the underprivileged or providing advances and leave to workers – all were informed by a sense of obligation of being wealthy, of being the owner of the business. Even section 135 simply reminds this obligation in legislative terms. It is therefore interesting to note that India's CSR discourse has a legislative reference to 'obligation of wealth', whereas it does not speak with the same vigour about rights of workers, communities, environment etc., like the rights-centric discourses of UNGC and modern CSR. Even codes of conduct of Indian companies which engage in elaborate TBL reports generally do not carry a rights-centric language. Instead their language is informed by caring, duty and obligation-centric expressions. The generalised reluctance within businesses to engage with unions or communities, and attempts to undermine such engagement when mandated, are also manifestations of this broader antipathy towards the logic of rights. Instead, to the extent, MSMEs and some large businesses engage in voluntary practices towards supporting workers and/or communities they are informed by the discourse of *just obligation* that invokes the status of various actors. The matter of fact 'I have to' that we saw in the attitudes of MSME owners underscores this point. The recent criticism of Tata group chairman Cyrus Mistry's ouster from Tata Sons' board and the subsequent revelations around how Ratan Tata's ego may have 'placed many jobs at risk' also indicates this sense of obligations towards other stakeholders.[3]

This is not to say that all is well and grand within Indian business. In the absence of the countervailing power in the form of adverse reputations which materially affect status and business, expecting business to honour obligations has become much more problematic; and workers, communities and environment have become susceptible to business abuse. As stated previously, this is the messiness of the post-colonial condition, the borderland of responsibility.

Person-business as an undifferentiated unity: We have already seen that historically Indian society has generally managed itself by deploying a priori categories of social life such as economic, political, social or even public and private. Instead it is a wholistic human way of life and this embeds responsibility into everyday life of the businessman. Even though colonial law introduced distinctions of public–private and rendered business, informed by the German scholar Weber's distinctions about formal organisation, especially the family firm as a liminal entity that exists on the border of the modern public–private, 'the family firm defied the public/ private dichotomy in its very liminality as an institution that produced a public exchange of credit and goods based on marriage and kinship, and predicated marriage and kinship on the necessities of credit and trade' (Birla, 2009:52). The defiance of this Weberian distinction between the family and the business as an organisational entity has continued into the present times to varying degrees. Even so, business families continue to remain synonymous with the business organisation in India and this is independent of the stake held by the owners' family. Even the recent case of Ratan Tata taking over the Tata Sons board and debates about propriety surrounding this decision (even though it is said to be legally correct) suggest that Indian business continues to look at individual/family and the business as an undifferentiated entity which does not necessarily respond to market logics. The same consideration informs critiques of loan delinquents like Vijay Mallya. Interestingly even courts are interested in making Mallya repay even though a purely commercial law logic would keep Mallya's personal assets outside the scope of debtors' claims.

According to the logic of modern CSR, different businesses should lead to different forms of CSR activities that are consistent with the specific business. But, in India, even highly diversified business groups have very similar CSR practices. In a sense, these are not linked to the business strategy of the company. This appears to be the case because in India, all these diverse businesses are held together by a single owner family and it is the family's belief instead of business strategy that informs CSR practices in all the diverse businesses. Family businesses not only constitute a large part of Indian business, families still retain significant control over everyday business even in large globalising Indian companies. Even in listed companies, the extent of owner control is often not a direct function of ownership holding. Strong family control enables widely diversified groups to exist and manage risk. The non-weberian organisation that results from this arrangement retains a strong imprint of the owner on the business and the specific practices of responsibility.

Even though there have been cases of commercially oriented CSR for creating shared value, such practices constitute a smaller portion of the total portfolio of CSR activities cumulatively carried out in India over the last several decades. The absence of differentiation between the owner as an individual and business as an organisation in India is the reason why the link between business strategy and CSR strategy is tenuous in Indian companies. It is the owners' views on whether Indian society needs more education, or needs to make people more employable, or to redistribute more wealth, or to improve self-sufficiency in minerals etc. that informs the specific activities carried out by businesses. Businesses' CSR activities merely become the means for fulfilling these personal beliefs of owners. This also explains the frequent presence of family members on the boards of various company foundations and trusts. Owner's spiritual beliefs too find place in CSR activities since the business is seen as an extension of the owner's persona. Businesses pursuing CSR activities in the native villages/areas of owners is another manifestation of owner-business.

It is this undifferentiated view of business owner and business organisation which forms the foundation of 'obligation'. The undifferentiated view also sustains the persistence of personalised, negotiated systems of decision making and employee management in Indian business, whether large or small. The undifferentiated view also helps explain why in spite of being a peripheral business activity, top management (or owner family) is involved in making CSR decisions in India and how obligation forms a prominent feature of India's responsibility practices.

The undifferentiated view also explains the specific character of the foundation approach in India. As we have seen, these foundations have an extensive involvement of owner family and work closely with the business organisation, unlike the grant-making foundations of the West. In the West, owner beliefs have been put into action, by creating endowments from the personal wealth of business owners, such as the Bill and Melinda Gates' foundation, Rockefeller foundation and Ford foundation. These foundations work independently of the business organisation itself. This is not the usual case in India which has many company foundations. Even though foundations have also been established using personal wealth in India, such personal endowments still work closely with the business itself and at times also with the business foundation.

Public and society as spatio-temporally located communities:
We had earlier made a reference to the customary notion of *jati*
as a fuzzy identity that utilised references to caste, kinship, geography, occupation and other markers in a contingent manner in
the pre-colonial period. We also spoke about how colonial trust
law and other governmental operations treated this as a fixed and
enumerative hierarchical category and replaced it in the context
of philanthropy with the notion of an abstract *public* and a universal citizen who held rights guaranteed by the state. In spite of
this change, customary practice of catering to specific communities
continues to survive in the post-colonial condition if only in transformed and subterranean ways. As Partha Chatterjee says about
community in contemporary Indian society (1998:282), 'the most
significant feature of the survival strategies adopted in the last few
decades by thousands of marginal groups is the way in which the
imaginative power of a traditional structure of community, including its fuzziness and capacity to invent relations of kinship' has
been commandeered to operate in contemporary political realities
because the 'normative status of the virtuous citizen will remain
infinitely deferred' in these post-colonial societies. He suggests that
in contemporary India, communities are to be recognised not in
the nature of abstract public or rights holding citizens but 'as concrete selves necessarily acting within multiple networks of collective
obligations and solidarities to work out strategies of coping with,
resisting or using to their advantage'. Thus, in spite of the violence
of colonial governmental technologies and practices of administration such as enumeration and census on communities, the public
in India still exists as a spatio-temporally specifiable group with
contingent identity markers. These groupings exist with definite
political expectations and impacts on other constituents of society
including businesses and nation-state.

This view of public and society informs practices of responsibility in Indian business. The most direct manifestation of this is
evident in legislation's prescription that companies pursue activities not just anywhere but in areas of their operations. Thus public
and community development is specified as the geographic community surrounding the company's plant/office. In fact, companies
have pursued such geographic specification of community even
before legislation mandated this. It is evident in companies concen-
trating responsibility activities in certain areas – near their factory,
near their operations, places of origin of business owners and/or

employees etc. Such concentration becomes particularly significant when these activities are juxtaposed against a business foundation's charter or memorandum of association which frequently refer to all citizens of India in order to be eligible for tax deductions. This charter is defined by laws such as trust and society acts which are still anchored in the concept of an abstract public. Consequently, focus on specific communities becomes illicit according to charter.

CSR practices once again invoke specific notions of public in defining demographic groups as project beneficiaries. Thus CSR activities focus on women, or poor women, girl children, disabled, unemployed youth, drivers, farmers etc.

A spatio-temporally specifiable notion of community also informs community resistance to corporate irresponsibility. Protests against companies for pollution, use of land, water and other resources for industrial activity specifically highlight the local community. These protests seek action from the company to redress the wrong done to the particular geographic or occupational community. In such resistances, the overall contributions of the company to a general public/society do not matter. What matters is, the here and the now of the community in question. Thus even those companies which have won awards for responsibility like Tatas, Vedanta group, Hero Motors etc. face protests. It is the importance of the local community that sets up the paradox where companies win awards for responsibility but still face resistance and criticism for irresponsible practices. Whereas awards and recognitions for service to society take into account an abstract public/society, resistance and protest is spatio-temporally specific, it is a local community.

The concreteness of a community specificity is also central to the operation of reputations. Reputations exist with reference to specific communities not abstract public. Similarly obligations too exist in relation to specific communities not abstract public. Abstract public and citizens are held together by a notion of rights, not obligations. In specific communities, business owner/organisation reputations travel to varying degrees across communities creating access to resources and countervailing power within the system of undifferentiated person-business. This embeds the firm within the social obligations of the owner, towards various communities. Such an embedding is not very apparent in the case of large businesses because of their sheer size and their overt compliance to modern legal systems, and to the extent it does it would usually be as an invisible practice. But, it is clearly evident in practices of MSMEs where reputations of business owners with specific worker communities help them attract workers. They also impel owners to strive towards maintaining those reputations or risk losing support from workers. Even workplace relations, and personalised and negotiated employment and workplace practices are rooted in specifiable communities rather than abstract public and equality of all citizens. Thus workers who have been loyal, or connected through kinship or other networks have access to some privileges that other worker groups may not have.

These three notions of customary practice inform contemporary practice of responsibility in Indian businesses which exist in the liminal space between tradition and modernity. Whereas the traditional notion sees the firm as an extension of the owner and embeds the firm in the social obligations of the owner, towards different communities, modern CSR is firmly anchored in the legal existence of the firm and its separateness from the individual owner. In spite of all the references to a social contract of business, modern code-based CSR is based on the firm's disembeddedness and economistic employment relationship. The responsibility practices of contemporary Indian businesses reflect the constraints and possibilities of this liminal space.

Where to from here?

Before beginning to chart out a map for the future trajectories of responsibility in India it is important to reiterate a few things: (a) that the discussion so far is not to be read either as pessimism or as a nostalgic longing for a past; and (b) in invoking custom, it does not seek to treat custom as a fixed, rigid sedimented notion. Instead its invocation of the past is in the context of a search for an identity for Indian CSR; and its invocation of custom is as a living idea that materialises itself according to changing conditions. With this recapitulation, we can now venture into thinking about future trajectories of Indian CSR. Theoretically, there appear to be three possibilities – wholly Western modern CSR, wholly customary CSR and a melange of both.

One possible trajectory is constituted by a complete shift to the modern global notion of CSR, the wholly Western notion. Though theoretically possible, in practice this appears unlikely due to four reasons. First, within the West itself, there is a crisis of legitimacy for the capitalist model. This crisis implies that the attendant model of CSR itself might be open to change. Second, India has already made a shift from the Western model through its legislation, it is unlikely that it would go back to a Western model. Third, completely embracing Western model would mean an effacing of customary practices. This again is unlikely. Native American custom has survived over 500 years of colonial encounter, it is unlikely that Indian custom will efface itself in this shorter period. Fourth, India is gaining power in the global arena and it is unlikely that it will face the same degree of subordination it had previously, that could compel India to accept a Western notion.

The second theoretical possibility is of a wholly customary notion of CSR. This again appears to be practically infeasible for several reasons. Pursuing a wholly customary notion at this time would be equivalent to philosopher Neurath's challenge of rebuilding a ship while sailing in it in the open seas. A wholly customary notion would mean overhauling the legal-institutional infrastructure to align with customary notions. That is unlikely because this structure provides a reasonable degree of stability in the post-colonial condition. This structure also forms the basis of India's participation in the global order. Restoration of custom would also mean the post-colonial state working to make itself weak, another remote possibility (Jammulamadaka and Murphy, forthcoming).

Therefore, the third theoretical possibility of a melange of practices comprising customary and modern elements appears as a most likely trajectory for Indian CSR. This is because, not only is India at the receiving end of modern CSR but Indian business is also instrumentally using this and its underlying neoliberal philosophy to expand its global footprint. The melange will help the nation-state in opportunistically using custom and modern notions of CSR for national well-being. It also permits individual businesses to choose their version of CSR in a manner that is more appropriate to their personal and business strategy context. The melange also enables a reconstruction and repair of the sailing boat one step at a time, in bits and pieces, thereby gradually decolonising colonial institutional apparatus while retaining national control and order in a globalised world.

In order to accomplish this and for Indian business to be truly responsible, it cannot be a blind imitation of Western CSR. It also cannot be a blind imitation of a fixed custom of the past. Custom needs to be recreated to suit contemporary challenges and possibilities. Thus:

- CSR in India 'cannot be limited to an independent voluntary mechanism of market governance devoid of state' as has been the notion and practice in the West.
- It has to necessarily involve the State not only as an active cheer leader for CSR (as in the West) but as an active participant in the bargaining and negotiation processes between communities and businesses through enactment of legislations and establishment of institutions that empower different stakeholders, at times businesses like in the case of SEZ Act and at other times the communities like in Land Acquisition Act. These legislations and institutions undo the violence of colonisation.
- It is the effectiveness of administrative and monitoring systems and the willingness of the state to rise above electoral politics to pursue social justice that is at the crux of compelling businesses to pursue responsibility and not simply the presence of stringent statutes in the statute books.
- It is the existence of weak monitoring that makes India in spite of having a vibrant democracy, a strong state and a strong economy get treated on par with many other developing countries which have weaker institutions that are ineffective in governing businesses. Thus, developing better ways of monitoring including non-bureaucratic ways of involving communities in monitoring is essential to stem irresponsibilities.
- Introducing the section 135 clause alone may not lead to a change of image. Like the other statutes, Section 135 too has micro-detailing (curtailing business flexibility) and very sparse monitoring and enforcement machinery. As such, Section 135 is likely to be of limited effectiveness in helping communities. It could only add to another layer of bureaucratic oversight that could foster yet more corruption and politicking.
- If India needs business participation in addressing social concerns then it is imperative that the administrative and monitoring systems be strengthened.
- It will also be essential to provide space for NGO and MSME voices and rectify internal domination and subordination of these key actors in the Indian business and responsibility landscape.

- Prevailing customary practices of responsibility have to absolve from the yoke of illegitimacy to the extent possible so that countervailing power of workers and communities can be made effective. Ultimately it is this ability to have countervailing power and negotiate that even the Western world is seeking. As the leader of the American Federation of Labour-Congress of Industrial Organization (AFL-CIO) says about codes, '. . . they are not a perfect solution. . . . Nevertheless, the fact that they are negotiated, instead of unilaterally imposed by companies, . . . means organized labour has been able to use them. . . .'

  (AFL-CIO, 2015:6)

- CSR in India has to fashion for itself a discourse of indigenous managerial knowledge to overcome the epistemic violence of 'Western managerialism' (Jammulamadaka, 2016b). Such an indigenous discourse will address the geopolitics of knowledge and enable customary business practices to absolve themselves from the yoke of illegitimacy. By linking economics with politics and society and culture, by legitimising negotiation and flexibility and by empowering actors including managements, workers and communities, it will enable a mutual interdependence and sustain better bargaining power for stakeholders.

Notes

1 http://fortune.com/2015/01/25/india-the-next-superpower/
2 In his essay, Kaviraj (2009) also explains how it is erroneous to think of this as a structure limited singularly to Hindu religious organisation and read hegemony into it. He explains that these were widely shared understandings and that this society did not consider itself Hindu. Hindu appellation was a subsequent development.
3 http://business-standard.com/article/companies/ratan-tata-s-ego-caused-financial-mess-for-group-firms-cyrus-mistry-116112201556_1.html

References

Chapter I

The Companies Act 2013. www.mca.gov.in/MinistryV2/companiesact. html, Accessed 27 January 2016.

Companies Bill Passed. www.thehindu.com/business/Industry/companies-bill-passed/article5003777.ece, August 8, 2015, Accessed 27 January 2016.

Sachin Pilot Economic Times, PTI, September 10, 2013. http://articles. economictimes.indiatimes.com/2013-09-10/news/41937985_1_csr-activities-new-companies-act-corporate-affairs-minister-sachin, Accessed 28 January 2016.

Secretary-General Proposes Global Compact on Human Rights, Labour, Environment, in Address to World Economic Forum in Davos. www. un.org/press/en/1999/19990201.sgsm6881.html, Accessed 1 March 2016.

Times of India Business, PTI, September 1, 2013. http://timesofindia.india-times.com/business/india-business/CSR-should-bring-smile-to-people-not-profit-for-companies-Sachin-Pilot/articleshow/22204015.cms, Accessed 28 January 2016.

Chapter III

A Brief History of Transnational Corporations. www.globalpolicy.org/ empire/47068-a-brief-history-of-transnational-corporations.html, Accessed 3 March 2016.

Brum, E. The Curse of Asbestos. www.ibasecretariat.org/eb-curse-of-asbestos.php, Accessed 3 March 2016.

Ceres Homepage. www.ceres.org/conferences/joan-bavaria-award/joan-bavaria, Accessed 3 March 2016.

A Chronology of Income Tax since 1950s. http://indiatoday.intoday. in/story/A+chronology+of+Income+Tax+since+1950s/1/84070.html, Accessed 3 March 2016.

Exxon-Valdez and the Birth of Credit Default Swaps. General Review Study of Small & Medium Enterprise (sme) Clusters in India. www.unido.org/fileadmin/import/userfiles/russof/small.pdf, Accessed 8 March 2016.

50-Year Trend of Indian Personal Tax Rates. www.businesstoday.in/union-budget-2011-2012/budget-news/50-year-trend-of-indian-personal-tax-rates/story/13502.html, Accessed 8 March 2016.

Goswami, M. and Patel, B. (2015). Rapid Industrial Growth in Vapi Has Led to Unchecked Pollution, Impacting Local Fishing Communities, Destroying Livelihoods. http://counterview.org/2015/10/09/rapid-industrial-growth-in-vapi-has-led-to-unchecked-pollution-impacting-local-fishing-communities-destroying-livelihoods/, Accessed 9 December 2015.

GRI Homepage. www.globalreporting.org/information/about-gri/gri-history/Pages/GRI's%20history.aspx, Accessed 3 March 2016.

Haq, F. United Ctates: Texaco Racial Flap Continues Despite Settlement. MSMEs in India. www.dnb.co.in/Nashik2013/PDF/MSMEsInIndia.pdf, Accessed 8 March 2016.

MSMEs in India. www.dnb.co.in/Nashik2013/PDF/MSMEsInIndia.pdf, Accessed 8 March 2016.

Planning Commission (2011). Report of Panel of Experts on Reforms in Central Public Sector Enterprises (CPSEs). Government of India. planningcommission.gov.in/reports/genrep/rep_cpse1912.pdf, Accessed 10 December 2014.

Report of Panel of Experts on Reforms in Central Public Sector Enterprises (CPSEs), Planning Commission, Government of India, New Delhi.

Special Economic Zones, Government of India. www.sezindia.nic.in, Accessed 2 April 2015.

SRI Basics. www.ussif.org/sribasics, Accessed 3 March 2016.

Sub-Group on Flow of Private Sector Investments for MSME Sector. www.planningcommission.nic.in/aboutus/committee/wg_sub_pvtsec_MSME.pdf, Accessed 8 March 2016.

Swarns, R. L. Drug Makers Drop South Africa Suit over AIDS medicine.

Talbot, C. South African court case ends in climb down by drug corporations.

United Nations conference on trade and employment held at Havana, Cuba Final Act and Documents www.cabinda.net/havana_e.pdf, Accessed 21 November 2016.

www.ipsnews.net/1996/11/united-states-texaco-racial-flap-continues-despite-settlement/, Accessed 3 March 2016.

www.marketwatch.com/story/exxon-valdez-and-the-birth-of-credit-default-swaps-2010-05-033, Accessed 3 March 2016.

www.moneycontrol.com/stocks/marketinfo/netsales.php?optex=BSE&opt topic=&group=All&indcode=All, Accessed 8 March 2016.

www.nytimes.com/2001/04/20/world/drug-makers-drop-south-africa-suit-over-aids-medicine.html?pagewanted=all, Accessed 3 March 2016.

www.wsws.org/en/articles/2001/04/aids-a21.html, Accessed 3 March 2016.

Chapter V

The CRISIL CSR Year Book. www.crisil.com/pdf/corporate/The-CRISIL-CSR-yearbook-20Jan2016.pdf, Accessed 5 October 2016.

FICCI Corporate Social Responsibility Survey. http://ficci.in/Sedocument/20361/csr_survey_ficci.pdf, Accessed 5 October 2016.

Ganguly, D. Hundreds of Jobs Opening Up as Companies Sharpen CSR Intent. http://economictimes.indiatimes.com/jobs/hundreds-of-jobs-opening-up-as-companies-sharpen-csr-intent/articleshow/51819011.cms?utm_source=contentofinterest&utm_medium=text&utm_campaign=cppst, Accessed 5 October 2016.

https://factly.in, Accessed 5 October 2016.

Chapter VI

Anand, U. India has 31 lakh NGOs, more than double the number of schools. http://indianexpress.com/article/india/india-others/india-has-31-lakh-ngos-twice-the-number-of-schools-almost-twice-number-of-policemen/, Accessed 16 October 2016.

Blacklisting no solution, NGOs pitch for a reformed Capart. www.business-standard.com/article/economy-policy/blacklisting-no-solution-ngos-pitch-for-a-reformed-capart-107061901019_1.html, Accessed 16 October 2016.

Constitution of Rural Markets http://linengage.com/core/rurallandscape/15.htm, Accessed 16 October 2016.

Corporate NGO Partnerships Won't Work If They Are Simply a Badging Exercise. www.marketingweek.com/2016/09/13/corporate-ngo-partnerships-wont-work-if-they-are-simply-a-cash-based-badging-exercise/, Accessed 16 October 2016.

CSR Platform Goes Live on BSE; Projects Worth Rs 2,000 Crore Listed. http://timesofindia.indiatimes.com/business/india-business/CSR-platform-goes-live-on-BSE-projects-worth-Rs-2000-crore-listed/articleshow/50158997.cms, Accessed 15 November 2016.

Empanelment of NGOs National CSR Hub. www.ngoportal.org/funding-agencies-811-Emapanelment+of+NGOs+-+National+CSR+Hub+-+TISS+-2.html, Accessed 16 October 2016.

Govt's funding of hundred of crores to NGOs is a scam. www.achrweb.org/press/2013/IND01-2013.html, Accessed 16 October 2016.

Hindustan Unilever Website. www.hul.co.in/sustainable-living/case-studies/enhancing-livelihoods-through-project-shakti.html.

India Releases CSR Policy Rules for Companies Act, 2013. www.lexology.com/library/detail.aspx?g=c8fed18d-68e8-49ba-b3ee-acd1775a10d4, Accessed 20 March 2014.

India's Funds to NGOs Squandered Edited by: SuhasChakma, Director, Asian Centre for Human Rights Published by: Asian Centre for Human Rights C-3/441-C, Janakpuri, New Delhi 110058.

Masters of Rural Markets in Association with Accenture. www.accenture.
com/. . ./Accenture-Masters-of-Rural-Markets-Selling-Profitably. . .,
Accessed 16 October 2016.
Moitra, S. NGOs to Help Companies Undertake CSR Work. www.
dnaindia.com/money/report-ngos-to-help-companies-undertake-
csr-work-2070591.
The Uneasy Relationship between Corporates and NGOs. www.
livemint.com/Companies/6nAPxHAA0s8P0EhA3Mx1kL/The-
uneasy-relationship-between-corporates-and-NGOs.html, Accessed 15
November 2016.
www.bsesammaan.com/, Accessed 15 November 2016.

Chapter VII

Arora, S. How Indian NGOs Can Mobilise Funds through CSR: A Guide.
www.fundsforngos.org/developing-countries-2/india/how-indian-ngos-
can-mobilize-funds-through-csr-a-guide/, Accessed 15 November 2016.
Collective Impact: When Government, Corporates and NGOs Collaborate.
www.forbesindia.com/blog/the-good-company/collective-impact-when-
government-corporates-and-ngos-collaborate/, Accessed 15 November
2016.
The Uneasy Relationship between Corporates and NGOs. www.
livemint.com/Companies/6nAPxHAA0s8P0EhA3Mx1kL/The-
uneasy-relationship-between-corporates-and-NGOs.html, Accessed 15
November 2016.

Chapter VIII

Government removes last 20 items reserved for production by MSMEs.
www.thehindubusinessline.com/economy/policy/govt-removes-last-20-
items-reserved-for-production-by-msmes/article7099156.ece, Accessed
20 November 2016.
Jha, P. and Chakrabarty, A. Post-Fordism, Global Production Networks
and Implications for Labour Some Case Studies from National Capital
Region, India. isid.org.in/pdf/WP172.pdf, Accessed 15 November 2016.
Micro, Medium and Small Scale Industry. www.cii.in/Sectors.aspx?enc=pr
vePUj2bdMtgTmvPwvisYH+5EnGjyGXO9hLECvTuNuXK6QP3tp4gP
GuPr/xpT2f, Accessed 20 November 2016.
MSME Sector: Epitomising Vitality. www.makeinindia.com/article/-/v/
nurturing-a-manufacturing-culture.
MSMEs at a Glance 2016, Government of India. msme.gov.in/Write
ReadData/ebook/MSME_at_a_GLANCE_2016_Final.pdf, Accessed
20 November 2016.

Selco Homepage. www.selco-india.com/about_us.htmlwww.businesstoday. in/magazine/special/innovation-energy-selco-solar-lamps/story/186623. html, Accessed 20 November 2016.

Singh, B. Kailash Satyarthi Pulled the Rug from under Child Labour Employers. http://articles.economictimes.indiatimes.com/2014-10-11/ news/54899660_1_child-labour-carpet-industry-carpet-makers, Accessed 20 November 2016.

Sports Goods Federation of India Homepage. www.sgfi.org/, Accessed 20 November 2016.

Venkateswarlu, D., Ramakrishna, R.V.S.S., Moid, M.A. Child Labour in Carpet Industry in India: Recent Developments. ilrf.org/sites/default/.../ child%20labor%20in%20carpet%20industry%20122706.pdf, Accessed 20 November 2016.

Chapter IX

Nadhe, S. S. and Chatterjee, D. Ratan Tata's Ego Caused Financial Mess for Group Firms: Cyrus Mistry. http://business-standard.com/article/ companies/ratan-tata-s-ego-caused-financial-mess-for-group-firms-cyrus-mistry-116112201556_1.html, Accessed 25 November 2016.

Sanghoee, S. India: The Next Superpower? http://fortune.com/2015/01/25/ india-the-next-superpower/, Accessed 25 November 2016.

Other references

AFL-CIO (2015). *Responsibility Outsourced: Social Audits, Workplace Certification and Twenty Years of Failure to Protect Worker Rights*, AFL-CIO.

Akbar, M. (2008). "Do the Governance, Strategic and Organizational Practices Differ in Indian Family and Professionally Managed Firms". *Vision: The Journal of Business Perspective*, July 2008, 12: 315–330.

Alam, M., and Subrahmanyam, S. (2007). *Indo-Persian Travels in the Age of Discoveries, 1400–1800*, Cambridge University Press, Cambridge.

Alamgir, F. (2014). "Business at the Cost of Life: Experience of the Apparel Workers of Bangladesh." Paper presented at the Academy of Management Annual Meeting, Philadelphia, 1–5 August.

Amaeshi, K. M., and Adi, B. (2007). "Reconstructing the Corporate Social Responsibility Construct in Utlish". *Business Ethics European Review*, 16: 3–18.

Anzaldúa, G. (1987). *Borderlands: La Frontera* (Vol. 3), Aunt Lute, San Francisco.

Arnold, E. C. (2012). "The Bombay Improvement Trust, Bombay Millowners and the Debate Over Housing Bombay Millworkers, 1896–1918". *Essays in Economic & Business History*, 30: 105–23.

Arora, B., and Puranik, R. (2004). "A Review of Corporate Social Responsibility in India". *Development*, 47: 93–100.

Awasthi, D., Pal, S., and Yagnik, J. (2010). "Small Producers and Labour Conditions in Auto Parts and Components Industry in North India" in Posthuma, A. and Nathan, D. (eds.) *Labour in Global Production Networks in India*. Oxford University Press, New Delhi, 272–299.

Badigannavar, V., and Kelly, J. (2012). "Do Labour Laws Protect Labour in India? Union Experiences of Workplace Employment Regulations in Maharashtra, India". *Industrial Law Journal*, 41(4): 439–470.

Bair, J. et al. (Eds.) (2014). *Workers' Rights and Labour Compliance in Global Supply Chains: Is a Social Label the Answer?* Routledge, New York.

Bajaj, R. (1970). *Social Role of Business*. Maharashtra Chamber of Commerce, Bombay.

Banerjee, S. B. (2008). "Corporate Social Responsibility: The Good, the Bad and the Ugly". *Critical Sociology*, 34: 51–79.

Banerjee, S. B. (2007). *Corporate Social Responsibility: The Good, the Bad, and the Ugly*, Edward Elgar, Cheltenham.

Bardhan, P. (2002). "The Political Economy of Reforms in India" in Mohan, R. (ed.) *Facets of the Indian Economy*, Oxford University Press, New Delhi, 123–135.

Barrientos, S., Kanchan, M., and Sood, A. (2010). "Decent Work in Global Production Networks: Challenges for Vulnerable Workers in the Indian Garment Sector" in Posthuma, A. and Nathan, D. (eds.) *Labour in Global Production Networks in India*. New Delhi: Oxford University Press. 127–145.

Barrientos, S., and Smith, S. (2007). "Do Workers Benefit From Ethical Trade? Assessing Codes of Labour Practice in Global Production Systems". *Third World Quarterly*, 28(4): 713–729.

Baxi, U. (1995). "Unorganized Labour? Unorganized Law?" in *Labour Law, Work and Development, Essays in Honour of PG Krishnan*, Westvill Publishing house, New Delhi, 3–19.

Bayly, C.A. (1983). *Rulers, Townsmen and Bazaars: North Indian Society in the Age of British Expansion, 1770–1870*, Cambridge University Press, Cambridge.

Bhattacharya, A. (2006). "Role of Government" in Dewan, S. M. (ed.) *Corporate Governance in Public Sector Enterprises*, Dorling Kindersley, New Delhi, 39–60.

Birla, R. (2009). *Stages of Capital: Law, Culture, and Market Governance in Late Colonial India*, Duke University Press, Durham.

Blowfield, M. (2005). "Corporate Social Responsibility: Reinventing the Meaning of Development?" *International Affairs*, 81: 515–524.

BMOA (1914). *Annual Report*, Claridge, Bombay.

BMOA (1924). *Annual Report*, Claridge, Bombay.

BMOA (1926). *Annual Report*, Claridge, Bombay.
BMOA (1928). *Annual Report*, Claridge, Bombay.
Bondy, K. et al. (2012). "An Institution of Corporate Social Responsibility (CSR) in Multi-National Corporations (MNCs): Form and Implications". *Journal of Business Ethics*, 111(2): 281–299.
Bowen, H. (1953). *Social Responsibilities of the Businessman*, Harper, New York.
Brejning, J. (2012). *Corporate Social Responsibility and the Welfare State: The Historical and Contemporary Role of CSR in the Mixed Economy of Welfare*, Ashgate Publishing, Surrey.
Budhiraja, S., Piramal, G., and Ghoshal, S. (2002). "Bajaj Auto Limited: Transformation of a Giant" in Ghoshal, S., Piramal, G. and Budhiraja, S. (eds.) *World Class in India*, Penguin, New Delhi, 3–32.
Carroll, A. B. (1979). "A Three-Dimensional Conceptual Model of Corporate Performance". *Academy of Management Review* 4(4): 497–505.
Carroll, B. (2008). "A History of Corporate Social Responsibility: Concepts and Practices" in Crane, A., McWilliams, A. Matten, D. Moon, J. and Siegel, D. S. (eds.) *The Oxford Handbook of Corporate Social Responsibility*, Oxford University Press, Oxford, New York, 19–46.
Chahal, M. (2016). "Corporate-NGO Partnerships Won't Work if They Are Simply a Badging Exercise". *Marketing Week*.
Chahoud, T. (n.d.). *Shaping Corporate Social Responsibility (CSR) in India – Does the Global Compact Matter?* www.die-gdi.de/CMS. . ./download%20document%20(127%20KB).pdf, Accessed 1 March 2012.
Chakrabarty, D. (1983). "On Deifying and Defying Authority: Managers and Workers in the Jute Mills of Bengal, Circa 1890–1940". *Past and Present*, 100(1): 124–146.
Chakrabarty, D. (1992). "Postcoloniality and the Artifice of History: Who Speaks for 'Indian' Pasts?". *Representations*, (37, special issue): 1–26.
Chakrabarty, K., Saha, B., and Jammulamadaka, N. (forthcoming). "Where Silence Speaks: Insights from Third World NGOs". *Critical Perspectives on International Business*, 13(1): 38–53.
Chandavarkar, R. (1991). "Workers' Resistance and the Rationalisation of Work in Bombay between the Wars" in Haynes, D. and Prakash, G. (eds.) *Contesting Power: Resistance and Everyday Social Relations in South Asia*, Oxford University Press, New Delhi, 109–144.
Chandavarkar, R. (1994). *The Origins of Industrial Capitalism in India*, Cambridge University Press, Cambridge.
Chandavarkar, R. (2008). "The Decline and Fall of the Jobber System in the Bombay Cotton Textile Industry, 1870–1955". *Modern Asian Studies*, 42: 117–210.
Chapple, W., and Moon, J. (2005). "Corporate Social Responsibility (CSR) in Asia: A Seven-Country Study of CSR Web Site Reporting". *Business & Society*, 44: 415–441.

Chatterjee, P. (1998). "Community in the East". *Economic and Political Weekly*, 33(6): 277–282.

Chatterjee, P. (2011). *Lineages of Political Society: Studies in Postcolonial Democracy*, Columbia University Press, New York.

Chaudhuri, K. K., and Barman, T. K. (1981). "Personnel Management Practices in Indian Family Business: A Case Study". *Economic and Political Weekly*, M117–M120.

Chopra, S., and Sachdeva, S. K. (2014). "Analysis of FDI Inflows and Outflows in India". *Journal of Advanced Management Science*, 2(4): 326–332.

Coomaraswamy, A. K. (1909). *The Indian Craftsman*, Probsthain & Company.

Crane, A., McWilliams, A., Matten, D., Moon, J. and Siegel, D. S. (2008). "The Corporate Social Responsibility Agenda" in Crane, A., McWilliams, A. Matten, D. Moon, J. and Siegel, D. S. (eds.) The Oxford Handbook of Corporate Social Responsibility, Oxford University Press, Oxford, New York.

Damodaran, S. (2010). "Upgradation or Flexible Casualization? Exploring the Dynamics of Value Chain Incorporation in the Indian Leather Industry" in Posthuma, A. and Nathan, D. (eds.) *Labour in Global Production Networks in India*, Oxford University Press, New Delhi, 231–250.

Damodaran, V. (2006). "Indigenous Forests: Rights, Discourses, and Resistance in Chotanagpur, 1860–2002" in Cederlof, G. and Sivaramakrishnan, K. (eds.) *Ecological Nationalisms: Nature, Livelihoods and Identities in South Asia*, Permanent Black, Ranikhet, 115–150.

Das Gupta, U. (2001). "The World of the Indian Ocean Merchant, 1500–1800" *Collected Essays of Aashin Das Gupta*, Oxford University Press, New Delhi.

Davala, S. (1995). *Labour Strategies in Multinational Corporations in India*, Friedrich Ebert Stiftung, New Delhi.

De Bakker, F. G. A. (2005). "A Bibliometric Analysis of 30 Years of Research and Theory on Corporate Social Responsibility and Corporate Social Performance". *Business & Society*, 44: 283–317.

De Haan, A. (1999). "The Badli System in Industrial Labour Recruitment: Managers' and Workers' Strategies in Calcutta's Jute Industry" in Parry, J.P., Breman, J. and Kapadia, K. (eds.) *The Worlds of Indian Labour*, Sage, New Delhi, 171–202.

De Neve, G. (2009). "Power, Inequality and Corporate Social Responsibility: The Politics of Ethical Compliance in the South Indian Garment Industry". *Economic and Political Weekly*, 44(22): 63–71.

De Neve, G. (2012). "Fordism, Flexible Specialization and CSR: How Indian Garment Workers Critique Neoliberal Labour Regimes". *Ethnography*, 15(2): 184–207.

Department of Public Enterprise (2010). Guidelines on Corporate Social Responsibility for Central Public Sector Enterprises. March 2010 Ministry of Heavy Industries and Public Enterprises Government of India.

Dewan, S. M. (2006b). "Introduction" in Dewan, S.M. (ed.) *Corporate Governance in Public Sector Enterprises*, Dorling Kindersley, New Delhi, xvi–xxi.

Dharampal (1971). *Civil Disobedience and Indian Tradition: With Some Early Nineteenth Century Documents*, Sarva Seva Sangh Prakashan, Varanasi.

Dobers, P., and Halme, M. (2009). "Editorial: Corporate Social Responsibility and Developing Countries". *Corporate Social Responsibility and Environmental Management*, 249: 237–249.

The Economist (1993). www.economist.com/node/3555212, Accessed 10 January 2016.

EDI (n.d.). *Diagnostic Study Report on Implementing BDS in the Kolkata Leather Cluster*. Entrepreneurship Development Institute of India, Gandhinagar.

Fagernäs, S. (2010). "Labor Law, Judicial Efficiency, and Informal Employment in India". *Journal of Empirical Legal Studies*, 7(2): 282–321.

Fleming, P., Roberts, J., and Garsten, C. (2013). "In Search of Corporate Social Responsibility: Introduction to Special Issue". *Organization*, 20: 337–348.

Friedman, M. (1962). *Capitalism and Freedom*, University of Chicago Press, Chicago.

Frynas, J. G. (2006). "Corporate Social Responsibility in Emerging Economies: Introduction". *Journal of Corporate Citizenship*, 24: 16–19.

Garriga, E., and Mele, D. (2004). "Corporate Social Responsibility Theories: Mapping the Territory." *Journal of Business Ethics*, 53: 51–71.

George, H. (1879). *Progress and Poverty*, Henry George School of Social Science, New York.

Ghose, S. (2003). "Alternate Dispute Settlement Mechanisms in India: A Study of Industrial Adjudication" in Sivanathan, A. and Venkata Ratnam, C.S. (eds.) *Prevention and Settlement of Disputes in India*, http://staging.ilo.org/public/libdoc/ilo/2000/100B09_349_engl.pdf

Ghoshal, S., Piramal, G. and Budhiraja, S. (Eds.) (2002). *World Class in India*, Penguin, New Delhi.

Ghoshal, S., and Ramachandran, J. (2002). "Reliance Industries Limited: Growth as a Way of Life" in Ghoshal, S., Piramal, G. and Budhiraja, S. (eds.) *World Class in India*, Penguin, New Delhi, 191–233.

Ghoshal, U. N. (1930). *The Agrarian System in Ancient India*, University of Calcutta, Calcutta.

GoI (2009). *Corporate Social Responsibility Voluntary Guidelines*, Ministry of Corporate Affairs, New Delhi.

GoI (2010). *Guidelines on Corporate Social Responsibility for Central Public Sector Enterprises*, Department of Public Enterprises, New Delhi.

GoI (2011). *National Voluntary Guidelines on Social, Environmental and Economic Responsibilities of Business*, Ministry of Corporate Affairs, New Delhi.

GoI (2013). *Guidelines on Corporate Social Responsibility and Sustainability for Central Public Sector Enterprises*, Ministry of Corporate Affairs, New Delhi.

Grant Thornton India (2010). *Vision 2020: Implications for MSMEs*. www.wcgt.in/html/assets/MSMEVision2020.pdf, Accessed 1 March 2012.

Greensmith, J. (2002). *Trends in Fundraising and Giving by International NGOs*, www.globalpolicy.org/component/content/article/176/31462.html, Accessed 4 September 2014.

Greer, J., and Singh, K. (2000). *A Brief History of Transnational Corporations*. www.globalpolicy.org/empire/47068-a-brief-history-of-transnational-corporations.html, Accessed 7 June 2015.

Guha, R. (1986). *Forestry and Social Movements in Uttarakhand*. Unpublished PhD thesis, Indian Institute of Management Calcutta.

Gupta, S. (2007). "Samaj, Jati and Desh Reflections on Nationhood in Late Colonial Bengal". *Studies in History*, 23(2): 177–203.

Gupta, S. (2009). *Sick MSMEs Increase Marginally, Says 4th MSME Census*. www.smetimes.in/smetimes/news/top-stories/2009/Sep/01/sick-msmes-increase-marginally-says-4th-msme-census60059.html, Accessed 4 March 2012.

Gupta, S., and Khanna, D. P. (2011). "Corporate Social Responsibility: An Analysis in SMEs at Faridabad Region". *International Journal of Strategic Corporate Social Responsibility Initiatives of MSME: A Study of Selected Multidisciplinary Research*, 1(8): 261–278.

Gupta, S., Sukhmani and Kalra, N. (2012). "Impact of Corporate Social Responsibility on SMEs in India". *Asia-Pacific Journal of Management Research and Innovation*, 8(2): 133–143.

Guttman, H. G. (1977). *Work, Culture and Society in Industrializing America: Essays in American Working-Class and Social History*, B. Blackwell.

Hall, P.D. (1987). "A Historical Overview of the Private Nonprofit Sector" in Powell, W. (ed.) *The Nonprofit Sector Research Handbook*, Yale University Press, New Haven, CT, 3–26.

Hamdani, K., and Ruffing, L. (2015). *United Nations Centre on Transnational Corporations: Corporate Conduct and the Public Interest*, Routledge.

Hanlon, G. (2008). "Rethinking Corporate Social Responsibility and the Role of the Firm-On the Denial of Politics" in Crane, A., McWilliams, A., Matten, D., Moon, J. and Siegel, D. S. (eds.) *The Oxford Handbook of Corporate Social Responsibility*, Oxford University Press, New York, 156–172.

Harriss, J. (2003). "'Widening the Radius of Trust': Ethnographic Explorations of Trust and Indian Business". *Journal of the Royal Anthropological Institute*, 9(4): 755–773.

Haynes, D. E. (1987). "From Tribute to Philanthropy: The Politics of Gift Giving in a Western Indian City". *The Journal of Asian Studies*, 46(2): 339–360.

Haynes, K., Murray, A., and Dillard, J. (2012). *Corporate Social Responsibility: A Research Handbook*, Routledge.

Hazari, R.K. (1966). *The Structure of the Corporate Private Sector: A Study of Concentration, Ownership and Control*, Asia Publishing House, Bombay.

Hirway, I. (2010). "Labour Market Adjustment and Female Workers: Global Production and Expiry of Quotas in India's Textile and Garments Industry" in Posthuma, A. and Nathan, D. (eds.) *Labour in Global Production Networks in India*, Oxford University Press, New Delhi, 166–189.

Hoen, E., Berger, J., Calmy, A., and Moon, S. (2011). "Driving a Decade of Change: HIV/AIDS, Patents and Access to Medicines for All". *Journal of International AIDS Society*, 14: 15.

Hu, X. (2006). *Corporate Codes of Conduct and Labour Related Corporate Social Responsibility: Analysing the Self-Regulatory Mechanisms of Multinational Enterprises and Their Impacts to Developing Countries*. The Japan Institute for Labour Policy.

Human Rights Watch (2012). www.hrw.org/report/2012/06/14/out-control/mining-regulatory-failure-and-human-rights-india.

IIM Lucknow (2010). *Evaluation of Central Pollution Control Board (CPCB) Submitted to Ministry of Environment and Forest Government of India*, Indian Institute of Management Lucknow, Lucknow.

Interim Commission for the International Trade Organization (1948). *Final Act and Related Documents*, Havana, www.Cabinda.Net/Havana_E.Pdf.

Jamali, D., Sidani, Y., and El-Asmar, K. (2009). "A Three Country Comparative Analysis of Managerial CSR Perspectives: Insights from Lebanon, Syria and Jordan". *Journal of Business Ethics*, 85: 173–192.

Jammulamadaka, N. (2007). *Towards a Model of the Formation of NGOs in a Third World Context: A Case of Andhra Pradesh*.Unpublished PhD thesis, Indian Institute of Technology Kanpur, Kanpur.

Jammulamadaka, N. (2009). "Do NGOs Differ? How, with What Consequences?". *Vikalpa*, 34(4): 9–24.

Jammulamadaka, N. (2013a). "The Responsibility of Corporate Social Responsibility in SMEs". *International Journal of Organizational Analysis*, 21(3): 385–395.

Jammulamadaka, N. (2013b). "Roundtable on Business, Governance and Society". *Decision*, 21(4): 143–155.

Jammulamadaka, N. (2015a). "Responsibility for the Third World Factory: Limits of Eurocentric CSR and Making Room for the State". *Decision*, 42(1): 71–82.

Jammulamadaka, N. (2015b). "Exploration in Responsible Business Practice in Colonial India: Case of Bombay Textile Mills". Paper presented at the Annual Meeting of the Academy of Management Vancouver.

Jammulamadaka, N. (2015c). "Partner Search Process in Business-NGO Collaborations: A Developing Country Nonprofit Perspective." Paper presented at the Annual Meeting of the Academy of Management Vancouver.

Jammulamadaka, N. (2016a). "Bombay Textile Mills: Exploring CSR Roots in Colonial India". *Journal of Management History*, 22(4): 450–472.

Jammulamadaka, N. (2016b). "A Post-Colonial Critique of Management Education Scene in India" in Thakur, M. and Babu, R. (eds.) *Management Education in India: Trends and Pathways*, Springer, New Delhi, 23–42.

Jammulamadaka, N. (2016c). "Microfinance: A Neoliberal Instrument or a Site of 'the Other's' Resistance and Contest" in Prasad, A. et. al. (eds.). *The Routledge Companion to Critical Management Studies*, Routledge, Oxford.

Jammulamadaka, N. (2017). "There Now . . . Gone Now . . . Sustainability in CSR Regulation in India" in Shaw, A. and Sarkar, R. (eds.) *Essays in Sustainability and Management*, Springer.

Jammulamadaka, N., and Bhattacharjee, S. (2013). "Of Gods and Demons: The Sacred Hills of Niyamgiri and Vedanta Alumina Limited" in Diochon, P. F., Raufflet, E. and Mills, A. (eds.) *Dark Side 2: Critical Cases on the Downside of Business*, Greenleaf Publishing.

Jammulamadaka, N., and Derry, R. (2013). "Beyond US and Eurocentric Models of CSR: India as a Locus of Enunciation". Academy of Management Annual Meeting, Orlando, Florida.

Jammulamadaka, N., and Jaiswall, M. (2012). "Corporate Governance in State Owned Enterprises: Can Apples be Used to Assess Oranges". International Finance Conference, December, IIM, Calcutta.

Jammulamadaka, N., and Kollegal, M. (2009). "CSR Practice in India: Some Suggestions for Empirical Investigation". *VNSGU Journal of Management and Administration*, 1(1).

Jammulamadaka, N., and Murphy, J. (forthcoming). "Governing the Post-Colonial" in Murphy, J. and Jammulamadaka, N. (eds.) *Governance, Resistance and the Post-Colonial State: Implications for Management*, Routledge, Singapore.

Jammulamadaka, N., and Saha, B. (2016). "What does critical mean in a post-colony elite business school?" paper presented at the Academy of Management Annual Meeting, Los Angeles.

Jammulamadaka, N., and Saha, B. (forthcoming). "Theorising The State (Or Its Absence?) in Anti-Corporate Protest: Insights from Post-Colonial India" in Murphy, J. and Jammulamadaka, N. (eds.) *Governance,*

Resistance and the Post-Colonial State: Implications for Management, Routledge, Singapore.

Jenkins, H. (2004). "A Critique of Conventional CSR Theory: An SME Perspective". *Journal of General Management*, 29: 37–57.

Jenkins, R. (2005). "Globalization, Corporate Social Responsibility and Poverty". *International Affairs*, 81: 525–540.

Jenkins, H. (2006). "Small Business Champions for Corporate Social Responsibility". *Journal of Business Ethics*, 67: 241–256.

Jenkins, H. M. (2009). "A 'Business Opportunity' Model of Corporate Social Responsibility for Small-and Medium-Sized Enterprises". *Business Ethics: A European Review*, 18: 21–36.

Jha, P., and Chakraborty, A. (2014). *Post-Fordism, Global Production Networks and Implications for Labour: Some Case Studies from National Capital Region, India*, Institute for Studies in Industrial Development, New Delhi.

Jones, M. T. (1999). "The Institutional Determinants of Social Responsibility". *Journal of Business Ethics*, 20: 163–179.

Joshi, A. (1975). *Lala Shri Ram: A Study in Entrepreneurship and Industrial Management*, Orient Longman, New Delhi.

Kalra, V.S. (2000). *From Textile Mills to Taxi Ranks: Experiences of Migration, Labour, and Social Change*, Ashgate, Burlington.

Kar, S. K., and Samantarai, M. (2011). "Narrative Research on 'Bothra': An Indian Family Firm". *Society and Business Review*, 6(2): 131–148.

Karnani, A. (2013). "Mandatory CSR in India: A Bad Proposal". Stanford Social Innovation Review, May.

Kaur, R. (2012). "Nation's Two Bodies: Rethinking the Idea of 'New' India and its Other". *Third World Quarterly*, 33(4): 603–621.

Kaviraj, S. (2005). "An Outline of a Revisionist Theory of Modernity". *Archives of European Sociology*, 46(3): 497–526.

Kaviraj, S. (2009). "The Post-colonial State: The Special Case of India" in *Critical Encounters: A Forum of Critical Thought from the Global South*.

Kennedy, V. D. (1958). "The Conceptual and Legislative Framework of Labor Relations in India". *Industrial and Labor Relations Review*, 11(4): 487–505.

Kennedy, V. D. (1965). "The Sources and Evolution of Indian Labour Relations Policy". *Indian Journal of Industrial Relations*, 1(1): 15–40.

Khan, F.R. Westwood, R. and Boje, D. M. (2010). "'I Feel Like a Foreign Agent': NGOs and Corporate Social Responsibility Interventions into Third World Child Labour". *Human Relations*, 63(9): 1417–1438.

Khanolkar, G.D. (1969). *Walchand Hirachand: Man, His Times and Achievements*, Walchand and Co. Pvt. Ltd., Bombay.

Kharas, H. (2007). *Trends and Issues in Development Aid*. Working Paper 1, Brookings Institution.

Koch, D. J., Dreher, A., Nunnenkamp, P. and Thiele, R. (2009). "Keeping a Low Profile: What Determines the Allocation of Aid by Non-Governmental Organizations?". *World Development*, 37(5): 902–918.

Kolk, A., and Van Tulder, R. (2002). *International Codes of Conduct: Trends, Sectors, Issues and Effectiveness*, Department of Business-Society Management, Erasmus University, Rotterdam.

Kudaisya, M. (2014). "The Promise of Partnership: Indian Business, the State, and the Bombay Plan of 1944". *Business History Review*, 88(1): 97–131.

Kudva, N. (2005). "Strong States, Strong NGOs" in Ray, R.and Katzenstein, M. (eds.) *Social Movements in India*, Oxford University Press, New Delhi, 233–266.

Kumar, R. (2004). *The State of CSR in India 2004: Acknowledging Progress, Prioritizing Action*, TERI, New Delhi.

Kumar, S., and Murty, M. N. (2011). "Water Pollution in India: An Economic Appraisal." *India Infrastructure Report 2011: Water: Policy and Performance for Sustainable Development*.

Kumar, T. (2004). *CSR in Industrial Areas/SME's: Activities, Policies and Strategies in Delhi India*, Business Community Foundation Publication, New Delhi.

Kydd, J.C. (1920). *History of Factory Legislation in India*, University of Calcutta, Calcutta.

Lala, R. M. (2004). *The Creation of Wealth: A Tata Story*, IBH Publishing Company, Bombay.

L'etang, J. (1995). "Ethical Corporate Social Responsibility: A Framework for Managers". *Journal of Business Ethics*, 14(2): 125–132.

Lindgreen, A. et al. (2009). "Corporate Social Responsibility Practices in Developing and Transitional Countries: Botswana and Malawi." *Journal of Business Ethics*, 90(S3): 429–440.

Lockett, A., Moon, J., and Visser, W. (2006). "Corporate Social Responsibility in Management Research: Focus, Nature, Salience and Sources of Influence". *Journal of Management Studies*, 43: 115–136.

Logsdon, J. M., and Wood, D. J. (2005). "Global Business Citizenship and Voluntary Codes of Ethical Conduct". *Journal of Business Ethics*, 59: 55–67.

Lorenzen, D. (2000). 'Who invented Hinduism?', *Comaprative Studies in Society and History*, 41(4): 630–659.

Lund-Thomsen, P. (2005). "Corporate Accountability in South Africa: The Role of Community in Mobilizing in Environmental Governance". *International Affairs*, 81: 619–633.

Lund-Thomsen, P. (2008). "The Global Sourcing and Codes of Conduct Debate: Five Myths and Five Recommendations". *Development and Change*, 39(6): 1005–1018.

Lund-Thomsen, P., and Nadvi, K. (2009). *Global Value Chains, Local Clusters and Corporate Social Responsibility: A Comparative Assessment of Sports Goods Clusters in Sialkot, Pakistan and Jalandhar, India*, UNIDO, Vienna.

Lund-Thomsen, P., and Nadvi, K. (2010). "Global Value Chains, Local Collective Action and Corporate Social Responsibility: A Review of Empirical Evidence". *Business Strategy and the Environment*, 19: 1–13.

Maira, A. (2014). "Rethinking Labor Law Reforms". *Indian Journal of Industrial Relations*, 50(1): 24–33.

Majumdar, R. C. (1920). *Corporate Life in Ancient India*, Calcutta. Calcutta University Calcutta.

Mani, M. (2013). *Readymade Garments in India: Manufacturing Cheap Commodities in Global South for the Global North*, Rosa Luxemburg Stiftung South Asia.

Marano, V. Tashman, P. and Kostova, T. (2016). "Escaping the Iron Cage: Liabilities of Origin and CSR Reporting of Emerging Market Multinational Enterprises". *Journal of International Business Studies*. doi:10.1057/jibs.2016.17.

March, J., and Olsen, J. P. (1989). *Rediscovering Institutions: The Organizational Basis of Politics*, The Free Press.

Marens, R. (2004). "Wobbling on a One-Legged Stool: The Decline of American Pluralism and the Academic Treatment of Corporate Social Responsibility". *Journal of Academic Ethics*, 2: 63–87.

Marens, R. (2010). "Destroying the Village to Save It: Corporate Social Responsibility, Labor Relations, and the Rise and Fall of American Hegemony". *Organization*, 17(6): 743–766.

Marens, R. (2013). "What Comes around: The Early 20th Century American Roots of Legitimating Corporate Social Responsibility". *Organization*, 20(3): 454–476.

Markowitz, C. (2008). *Merchants, Traders, Entrepreneurs: Indian Business in the Colonial Era*, Palgrave Macmillan, Hampshire.

Martin, R.M. (1862). *The Progress and Present State of British India*, S. Low, London.

Matten, D., and Moon, J. (2008). "'Implicit' and 'Explicit' CSR: A Conceptual Framework for a Comparative Understanding of Corporate Social Responsibility". *Academy of Management Review*, 33: 404–424.

McBarnet, D. J., Voiculescu, A. and Campbell, T. (eds.) (2007). *The New Corporate Accountability: Corporate Social Responsibility and the Law*, Cambridge University Press, Cambridge.

McIvor, A. (1996). *Organised Capital: Employers' Organizations and Industrial Relations in Northern England, 1880–1939*, Cambridge University Press, Cambridge.

Mignolo, W. D. (1995a). "Afterword: Human Understanding and (Latin) American Interests – The Politics and Sensibilities of Geocultural Locations". *Poetics Today*, 16: 171–214.

Mignolo, W.D. (1995b). *The Darker Side of the Renaissance: Literacy, Territoriality, and Colonization*, University of Michigan Press, Ann Arbor.

Mignolo, W.D. (2000). *Local Histories/Global Designs: Coloniality, Subaltern Knowledges andBorder Thinking*, Princeton University Press, Princeton, NJ.

Ministryof Corporate Affairs (2014). Notification on Section 135, dated February 27, 2015.

Mir, R. et al. (2008). "The Corporation and its Fragments: Corporate Citizenship and the Legacies of Imperialism" in Scherer, A. and Palazzo, G. (eds.) *The Handbook of Corporate Citizenship*, Edward Elgar, London, 819–852.

Mitchell, R., Petra, M. A. H. Y., and Gahan, P. (2014). "The Evolution of Labour Law in India: An Overview and Commentary on Regulatory Objectives and Development". *Asian Journal of Law and Society*, 1(2): 413–453.

Mitra, M. (2007). *It's Only Business*, Oxford University Press, New Delhi.

Mohan, A. (2001). "Corporate Citizenship: Perspectives from India". *Journal of Corporate Citizenship*, 2: 107–117.

Mookerji, R. (1919). *Local Government in Ancient India*, Clarendon Press, Oxford.

Moore, G., and Spence, L. (2006). "Editorial: Responsibility and Small Business". *Journal of Business Ethics*, 67: 219–226.

Morris, M.D. (1965). *The Emergence of an Industrial Labour Force in India: A Study of the BombayCotton Mills, 1854–1947*, University of California Press, Berkeley.

Morsing, M., and Perrini, F. (2009). "CSR in SMEs: Do SMEs Matter for the CSR Agenda?". *Business Ethics: A European Review*, 18(1): 1–6.

Mountz, A. (2009). "Border" in Gallaher, C., Dahlman, C. T., Gilmartin, M., Mountz, A. and Shirlow, P. (eds.) *Key Concepts in Political Geography*, Sage, 87–98.

Mukherjee, A.S., Paudwal, S., and Mehta, V.M. (2015). *Study on Corporate Foundations: An Emerging Development Paradigm?* Prakruthi, New Delhi.

Mukhia, H. (1981). "Was There Feudalism in Indian History?". *The Journal of Peasant Studies*, 8(3): 273–310.

Mukhia, H. (1985). "Peasant Production and Medieval Indian Society". *The Journal of PeasantStudies*, 12(2/3): 228–251.

Naidu, S., and Yuchtman, N. (2013). "Coercive Contract Enforcement: Law and the Labour Market in 19th Century Industrial Britain". *The American Economic Review*, 103(1): 107–144.

Nandy, A. (1983). *Intimate Enemy*, Oxford University Press, Oxford.

NASSCOM-BCG (2015). *Catalysing Change through Corporate Social Responsibility*, New Delhi.

Nielsen, M. E. (2005). "The Politics of Corporate Responsibility and Child Labour in the Bangladeshi Garment Industry". *International Affairs*, 81: 559–580.

Newell, P. (2005). "Citizenship, Accountability & Community: The Limits of the CSR Agenda". *International Affairs*, 81: 541–557.

Okoye, A. (2009). "Theorising Corporate Social Responsibility as an Essentially Contested Concept: Is a Definition Necessary?". *Journal of Business Ethics*, 89: 613–627.

O'Laughlin, B. (2008). "Governing Capital? Corporate Social Responsibility and the Limits of Regulation". *Development and Change*, 39(6): 945–957.

Oosterhout, J. H., and Heugens, P. P. M.A.R. (2008). "Much Ado about Nothing: A Conceptual Critique of Corporate Social Responsibility" in Crane, A. et al. (eds.) *The Oxford Handbook of Corporate Social Responsibility*, Oxford University Press, New York, 197–226.

Palazzo, G., and Scherer, A. G. (2006). "Corporate Legitimacy as Deliberation: A Communicative Framework". *Journal of Business Ethics*, 66: 71–88.

Pande, S. (2011). *An Overview of Corporate Governance Reforms in India*.http://ssrn.com/abstract=1958031, Accessed 29 June 2012.

Papola, T., Pais, J., and Sahu, P. (2007). *Labour Regulation in Indian Industry: Towards a Rationale and Equitable Framework*, Institute for studies in Industrial Development, New Delhi.

Perrow, C. (1991). "A Society of Organisations". *Theory and Society*, 20(6): 725–762.

Perrow, C. (2002). *Organizing America: Wealth, Power, and the Origins of Corporate Capitalism*, Princeton University Press, Princeton, NJ.

Pettit, P. (1996). "Freedom as Antipower". *Ethics*, 106(3): 576–604.

Pilkington, E. (2009). "Shell PaysOut $15.5m Over Saro-Wiwa killing". *The Guardian*, June 8 2009, www.theguardian.com/world/2009/jun/08/nigeria-usa, Accessed 20 November 2016.

Porter, M., and Kramer, M. (2006). "Strategy and Society: The Link between Competitive Advantage and Corporate Social Responsibility". *Harvard Business Review*, 84: 78–92.

Posthuma, A. (2010). "Beyond 'Regulatory Enclaves': Challenges and Opportunities to Promote Decent Work in Global Production Networks" in Posthuma, A. and Nathan, D. (eds.) *Labour in Global Production Networks in India*, Oxford University Press, New Delhi, 57–80.

Prahalad, C. K. (2006). *The Fortune at the Bottom of the Pyramid*, Pearson Education India.

Prakash, G. (1990). *Bonded Histories: Genealogies of Labour Servitude in Colonial India*, Cambridge University Press, Cambridge.

Prakash, G. (2011). *Mumbai Fables*, Princeton University Press, Princeton.

Prasad, A. (2003). "The Gaze of the Other: Postcolonial Theory and Organizational Analysis" in *Postcolonial Theory and Organizational Analysis: A Critical Engagement*, Palgrave Macmillan, 3–43.

Pratap, S. (2016). *Strategizing as Embodied and Materialized: Investigations into Shifts in Steel Distribution Practices in Post Liberalization India.* Unpublished PhD thesis, Indian Institute of Management, Calcutta.

Quazi, A., and O'Brien, D. (2000). "An Empirical Test of a Cross-National Model of Corporate Social Responsibility". *Journal of Business Ethics*, 25: 33–51.

Rajaram, T., and Das, A. (2008). "Water Pollution by Industrial Effluents in India: Discharge Scenarios and Case for Participatory Ecosystem Specific Local Regulation". *Futures*, 40(1): 56–69.

Ramanujam, K. S. (1993). *Glimpses of a Prince among Patriots*, Sundara Prachuralyam, Madras.

Ray, R. K. (1979). *Industrialization in India: Growth and Conflict in the Private Corporate Sector, 1914–47*, Oxford University Press, New Delhi.

Revenkar, A. V. (2004). *Corporate Social Responsibiilty in Small and Medium Scale Industries*, Business Community Foundation Publication, New Delhi.

Rudner, D.W. (1994). *Caste and Capitalism in Colonial India: The Nattukottai Chettiars*, University of California Press, Berkeley, CA.

Ruggie, J. (2008). "Promotion and Protection of All Human Rights, Civil, Political, Economic, Social and Cultural Rights, Including the Right to Development." United Nations Human Rights Council.

Russo. (1999). *Strengthening Indian SME Clusters: UNIDO's Experience.* UNIDO.

Russof. (2001). www.unido.org/fileadmin/import/userfiles/russof/small.pdf, Accessed 29 February 2012.

Sachdeva and Panfil. (2008). *CSR Perceptions and Activities of Small and Medium Enterprises (SMEs) in Seven Geographical Clusters*, UNIDO.

Saha, B., and Jammulamadaka, N. (2016). "Revealed Breakdowns in Pollution Control: Institutional Fractures and Elusive Dialogues." Observer Research Foundation, Kolkata, 23 April 2016.

Saini, D.S. (1997). "Labour Court Administration in India: In ILO, Labor Adjudication in India." International Labour Organisation – South Asian Advisory Team (ILO-SAAT), New Delhi.

Saini, D. S. (2014). "Indian Industrial Relations Law: Case for Reform". *Indian Journal of Industrial Relations*, 50(1): 118–133.

Sancheti, N. (1986). *Educational Dependency: An Indian Case Study in Comparative Perspective.* Unpublished Doctoral thesis, University of London, Institute of Education, http://eprints.ioe.ac.uk/7430/, Accessed 25 March 2015.

Sanchez, A. (2016). *Criminal Capital: Violence, Corruption and Class in Industrial India*, Routledge.

Scherer, A. G., and Palazzo, G. (2007). "Toward a Political Conception of Corporate Responsibility: Business and Society Seen From a Habermasian Perspective". *Academy of Management Review*, 32: 1096–1120.

Scherer, A. G., and Palazzo, G. (2008). "Globalization and Corporate Social Responsibility" in Crane, A. et al. (eds.) *The Oxford Handbook of Corporate Social Responsibility*, Oxford University Press, Oxford, New York, 413–431.

Sen, R. (2003). *Industrial Relations in India: Shifting Paradigms*, MacMillan India Ltd.

Sengupta, A. K., and Sett, P. K. (2000). "Industrial Relations Law, Employment Security and Collective Bargaining in India: Myths, Realities and Hopes". *Industrial Relations Journal*, 31(2): 144–153.

Shyam Sundar, K. R. (2014). "Institutional Framework of Industrial Relations in India: Still and Muddy Waters". *Indian Journal of Industrial Relations*, 50(2): 195–204.

Shyam Sundar, K. R., and Ratnam, V. C. S. (2007). "Labour Reforms in China and India: Reform Aggression (China) versus Reform Allergy (India)". *Indian Journal of Labour Economics*, 50(3): 497–512.

Sikka, P. (2011). "Accounting for Human Rights: The Challenge of Globalization and Foreign Investment Agreements". *Critical Perspectives on Accounting*, 22(8): 811–827.

Simeon, D. (1999). "Work and Resistance in the Jharia Coalfield" in Parry, P.J., Breman, J. and Kapadia, K. (eds.) *The Worlds of Indian Industrial Labour*, Sage, New Delhi, 43–75.

Singala, S. et al. (2011). "Special Economic Zones in India: Policies, Performance and Problems". *ASCI Journal of Management*, 40(2): 21–59.

Singh, V. (2013). *A Study of Environment Protection Act with Special Reference to State of Haryana*. Unpublished PhD thesis, Maharshi Dayanand University, Department of Law.

Smith et al. (2010). *Global Challenges in Responsible Business*, Columbia University Press, Cambridge.

Spivak, G. C. (1988). "Subaltern Studies: Deconstructing Historiography" in Guha, R. and Spivak, G. C. (eds.) *Selected Subaltern Studies*, Oxford University Press, New York, 3–32.

Subrahmanyam, S. (2005). *Explorations in Connected History Mughals and Franks*, Oxford University Press, Oxford.

Sundar, P. (2000). *Beyond Business: From Merchant Charity to Corporate Citizenship: IndianBusiness Philanthropy through the Ages*, Tata McGraw-Hill Publishing.

Sundar, P. (2013). *Business and Community: The Story of Corporate Social Responsibility in India*, Sage, New Delhi.

Taknet, D.K. (1996). *B M Birla: A Great Visionary*, Indus Books, New Delhi.

Tata, J.R.D. (1986). *Keynote*, Tata Press, Bombay.

Tewari, M. (2010). "Footloose Capital, Intermediation, and the Search for the High Road in Low Wage Industries" in Posthuma, A. and Nathan, D. (eds.) *Labour in Global Production Networks in India*, Oxford University Press, New Delhi, 146–165.

Tripathi, D. (1981). *The Dynamics of a Tradition: Kasturbhai Lalbhai and His Entrepreneurship*, Manohar, New Delhi.

Trivedi, R. C. (2014). "Regulation of Water Pollution – Limitation and Remedies". *NGT International Journal on Environment*, 1: 109–126.

UNIDO (n.d.). *General Review Study of Small and Medium Enterprise (SME) Clusters in India.* www.unido.org/fileadmin/import/userfiles/russof/small.pdf, Accessed 12 March 2012.

Upadhyaya, R.B. (1976). *Social Responsibility of Business and the Trusteeship Theory of Mahatma Gandhi*, Sterling Publishers, New Delhi.

Utting, P. (2008). "The Struggle for Corporate Accountability". *Development and Change*, 39(6): 959–975.

Venkateswarulu, D., Ramakrishna, R. V. S. S., and Moid, M.A., (n.d.). *Child Labour in Carpet Industry in India: Recent Developments, International Labour Rights Fund.* ilrf.org/sites/default/. . ./child%20labor%20in%20carpet%20industry%20120122706.pdf.

Visser, W. (2008). "Corporate Social Responsibility in Developing Countries" in Crane, A. et al. (eds.) *The Oxford Handbook of Corporate Social Responsibility*, Oxford University Press, New York, 473–502.

WCL (2004). *Corporate Social Responsibility and Codes of Conduct.* New Stakes or Old Debates.

Wolcott, S. (2008). "Strikes in Colonial India, 1921–1938". *Industrial and Labour Relations Review*, 61(4): 460–484.

Wolcott, S. and Clark, G. (1999), "Why nations fail: managerial decisions and performance in Indian cotton textiles, 1890–1938", *The Journal of Economic History*, 59(2): 397–423.

Wren, D. A. (2005). *The History of Management Thought.* John Wiley & Sons, New Jersey.

Yolland, Z. (1994). *Boxwallahs: The British in Cawnpore, 1857–1901*, M. Russell, Norwich.

Zerk, J. A. (2006). *Multinationals and Corporate Social Responsibility: Limitations and Opportunities in International Law*, Cambridge University Press, Cambridge.

Index

For Product Safety Concerns and Information please contact our EU
representative GPSR@taylorandfrancis.com
Taylor & Francis Verlag GmbH, Kaufingerstraße 24, 80331 München, Germany

www.ingramcontent.com/pod-product-compliance
Ingram Content Group UK Ltd.
Pitfield, Milton Keynes, MK11 3LW, UK
UKHW021633240425
457818UK00018BA/383